The Twenty-Seventh Child

The Twenty-Seventh Child

A Witness of History

HARPER GARRIS

ARCHWAY
PUBLISHING

Archway Publishing books may be ordered through booksellers or by contacting:

Archway Publishing
1663 Liberty Drive
Bloomington, IN 47403
www.archwaypublishing.com
1-(888)-242-5904

ISBN: 978-1-4808-0666-5 (sc)
ISBN: 978-1-4808-0667-2 (e)

Library of Congress Control Number: 2014905206

Printed in the United States of America

Archway Publishing rev. date: 3/24/2014

Chapter One

Many historians say the era of the Wild West begin in the late 1840s, and came to an end in the early to mid-1880s, although some would say the early 1900s.

Billy the Kid was born in Manhattan, New York City, in November 1859. Pat Garret shot and killed him in July, 1882.

Jesse James was born in 1847, and died in 1882. Daddy was thirteen years old when Robert Ford shot Jesse in the back while he was hanging a picture of his mother on the wall.

Daddy was twelve years old when Sheriff Pat Garret shot and killed Billy the Kid.

The Civil War ended and President Abraham Lincoln was assassinated in the year 1865. Harper Burnie Garris was born on April 14ᵗ 1869, four years after President Lincoln was assassinated.

The name Harper B. Garris is one that is not nearly as well known as the other names mentioned above.

Harper B. Garris was not an American president; he was not a Wild West cowboy, bank robber, or murderer. He was a simple farmer, trying to scratch out a living for his family on farms around Waxhaw, North Carolina.

Harper Burnie Garris was my Daddy.

Oh, how I wish I could have sat down with Daddy and had him tell me all the stories of how life was back in his younger days growing up.

Oh, I know many people were around those days, but I'm talking about my daddy, and how he would have told me. Keep in mind we're talking about the era of about 150 years ago, four years after the Civil War ended. Daddy was born four years after our most popular and well-known US president Abraham Lincoln was gunned down in the Ford Theatre in Washington, DC

I was too young, of course, to have known and understand what he was telling me; however, I do have many memories of my father. He was a poor man, the years I knew and remembered him, but he was a man of very much pride. I've been told that I was a lot like him in my day. My older brothers and sisters told of his very harsh discipline. I never was a witness to any of his actions in that area, with one exception.

The family sat down at the table for our evening meal. Daddy always sat at the end of the table, and to his left was a long bench. I was on the bench and the one sitting closest to Daddy. Beside me, to my left was Brodus. I do not remember what was on the table for our meal. Whatever it was, it was not to the liking of my brother, Brodus. Brodus surveyed the food on the table and remarked, "Is this all we have to eat?" Daddy always kept his walking cane handy and within reach. You know, one of those canes with the half circles on the end. He reached over me with that cane, placed it around Brodus's neck, and jerked Brodus across me. He pulled Brodus right up to his face and said,

"Don't you ever say anything, about what is on the table to eat again." Scared me half to death. I thought he was gonna hang Brodus right there at our kitchen table that evening with his walking cane.

Chapter Two

We were not to ask Mama for any new nails. So, we didn't.

Then one day when Mama went to look in the mailbox, Daddy came out to the old car shed and pulled a can off the shelf. The can was full of nails. He gave us five nails each, and said,

"Don't tell Molly I gave these to you." Man, that was something to have brand-new nails to hammer in-to them old boards. Of course, we thought Daddy was good to us.

I remember another incident about Daddy.

There was this middle- aged black man who lived up the road from us, a very good person, everyone would say. If you ever needed help with anything, get hold of Will Morrison. That was his name. I never will forget him. He was always there if you needed help.

Daddy and a couple of other neighbors and Will were working in our field. I believe they were pulling corn. Mama cooked up a big meal for dinner. They call it lunch nowadays. We always kept a pan on the back porch filled with water to wash up before meals. Will washed up first and went into the house and sat down at the table. Daddy came in the dining room a short time later, looked at Will, and said, "Will, Molly has a table fixed for you on the back porch."

Will got up from the table. I sure don't understand. If he was good enough to work in the hot sun all day with the rest of the men, why wasn't he good enough to sit down and eat a meal with the rest of the men? It was my very first memory of segregation. I always have and always will remember that. Seems like just yesterday.

Those were just a few personal memories that I have of Daddy that I wanted to share in the book.

I do realize that Daddy mellowed as he grew older, and for the most part, Daddy was pretty good to my brother Brodus and me. Some of my older siblings, of course, had many memories of Daddy that were more vivid than mine were. We will talk later about some of the stories my older brothers, and sisters had to tell about Daddy, and their younger years growing up at home.

Chapter Three

Well, let's go back to Germany in the 1700s. Actual dates are unknown. Two young brothers, by the names of John and Amos Garris, stowed away on a freighter and traveled to Ireland. A short time later, the brothers managed to stow away on another freighter en route to the United States from Ireland. This ship docked at the port in Norfolk, Virginia. Upon arriving in Virginia, Amos made his way south to the area of Charleston, South Carolina. He settled down with a wife and children there. Very little information was ever known about Amos after he and John separated.

John Garris settled in the area of Lancaster, South Carolina and Waxhaw, North Carolina. John married, and he and his wife gave birth to five children. The fourth child was a male with the name of Harper Burnie Garris. We never knew or had any knowledge of Grandpa or any of his other children, which will be explained as the story unfolds.

Very little information is known about Daddy's growing- up years around Waxhaw, North Carolina. Some of Daddy's older children, who knew something about his younger life, tell stories. When Daddy was not working on the family farm at home, Grandpa would hire him out to some of the other farmers in the area, to do work on their farms.

The records show that Daddy married Ella May Fincher in the year of 1889, exact date unknown. Their first child Dixon Gerome Garris, was born, on March 25, 1890. The family always referred to him as Rome.

I remember Rome very well. He was a photographer. Rome had his studio in Great Falls, South Carolina for many years. He was always at the family reunion every year, taking photos of all the folks who came to celebrate Daddy's birthday, and there were many. He would put the black cloth over his head and camera (just like you've seen in all those old movies) each time he took a photo.

Following is a list of Harper and Ella Belle Garris's children.

2- Archie Garris .... October 20 1891

3-Agnes Etta Garris .... September 28 1892

4- Effie Pearl Garris .... December 17 1893

5- Robert Garris... Aug 25 1895

6- Lilly Garris .... March 12 1897

7- Viola Garris... August 7 1898

8- Flora Garris ....June 22 1900

9- Inez Garris...Nov. 27 1901

10- Marion Garris .... May 11 1903

11- Willie Garris .... Dec. 22 1904

12- Infant born and died ....June 30 1907

13- Herbert Garris ....June 8 1908

14- Lois Garris...Jan 10 1910

15- Burk Garris...June 2 1911

16- Ruby Garris.. May 19 1913

17-Infant born and died ....June 29 1914

During the time prior to 1914, Daddy managed to acquire a large plantation with many acres and, a large home that, he needed for his large family. The main crop grown in the fields of the plantation was cotton, acres and acres of cotton.

As fate would have it, the good times didn't last forever. Devastation came, with the loss of his wife, Ella Belle, in 1917. The next couple of years remained rather calm and not very eventful.

A few miles from the plantation, lived a family by the name of Ghent. Mack and Mary Ghent lived there along with their ten children. Daddy became interested in their daughter Molly, although the difference in their ages was thirty-three years. Molly was not interested in Harper, but Harper kept coming to see her. Molly's Mama and Daddy kept encouraging Molly to see him. Knowing Harper lived on that big plantation, and they assumed he was wealthy.

As things turned out, Molly's parents had a say about whom she would marry, (that's the way things were back then), and they said she would marry Harper!

Harper Bernie Garris was married to Molly Geneva Ghent on December 13, 1919. Molly was seventeen years old at the time. Harper was fifty years old.

So went the years of planting cotton and picking cotton, milking cows, raising hogs, working the garden, canning food for the long winters, and the older children growing up, getting married, and leaving home.

Here came the beginning of the bad times that would go on for years and years.

The boll weevil came, and the cotton crops left, many farmers lost everything they worked for. Our family was no exception. Daddy lost the plantation to the boll weevil, drought, and economy. The depression was coming on.

When all of this was going on, Mama and Daddy were having more children, ten more to be exact. The population in our family grew.

THE NEXT TEN

18- Henry Boyd Garris .... March 26 1922

19- Paul Garris .... March 1 1923

20- Nola Garris .... Feb 16 1924

21- Mack N. Garris.................................... Sept 2 1925

22- Annie P. Garris .... Dec 18 1927

23- Cecil Garris .... June 5 1929

24- Dallas Garris .... July 30 1931

25- Clara "Callie" Garris .... June 4 1933

26- Brodus H. Garris................................. June 23 1937

27- Harper B. Garris .... April 19 1939

Did you notice? When I was born, my oldest half-brother was forty nine years old. They say it was a big day around our house. There were newspaper people there to interview Daddy. Daddy was seventy years old. A reporter from a nationwide newspaper, 'The Grit', was at our home. Daddy jumped over the mule, just to show-off a little bit. They took a picture of me, sitting on Daddy's lap.

Harper and oldest half brother Jerome

Chapter Four

The very first of my memories, I think I was about two and a half to three years old.

I am setting on this cotton sheet, at the edge of the cotton field. Mama and the others will be coming soon, to empty their cotton sacks. They do that when they fill their sacks with the cotton they pick. They bring their full sacks of cotton, and empty them on the sheet where I am sitting. Each member of the family has their own sheet, that they empty their sacks on.

I must be at least three years old. How are you supposed to know how old you are, when your first memories come into your mind?

Brodus was with me.

Mama probably told him to look after me while she and the rest of the family were picking cotton. He was looking after me alright. Aggravating the pure daylights out of me. He had my rubber baby doll, and teasing me with it. He acted like he was going to give it to me, then he would jerk it away. He was throwing it up in the air and trying to catch it, he never did catch it.

He threw the baby doll so high in the air, and when it came back down, it hit a rock and busted, there was a big hole around it's head. That hurt my feelings very much, and made me mad. I began to cry. Then I saw Mama coming, and she saw me crying. I told Mama that Brodus broke my baby doll. She found a switch and gave Brodus a whipping. Yeah, he is crying now, not so big is he?

The rest of the family is coming now to empty their cotton sacks on the sheets. I guess it is time to quit for the day. They began tying up their sheets.

They pick up a corner of the sheet and pull it across to the other far corner and tie it to that corner, and do the same thing to the other two corners of the sheet.

Here comes Mr. Stringfellow with the wagon and horses, to weigh the cotton and haul it to the barn.

"Hey folks," he said, "Ya'll must be done for the day." After weighing all the sheets, all the boys pitched in and loaded it all on the wagon. Mama picked me up and was holding me. Mr. Stringfellow walked over to us and said to me, "Do you want to ride with me on the wagon to the barn?"

Man, just look at me, I am the king now.

Dallas told me about the time when sister Effie and cousin Lee Ella came to visit us for a couple of days. Mama was doing some sewing. She sent Dallas, Cally, and Lee Ella to the store to get a pattern for a dress she wanted to make. On the way home the girls didn't hurry. As young girls, they just played around running up and down the embankments on either side of the road.

Daddy was working in the garden by the road, as they returned back home.

Daddy asked, "What took you girls so long to go to the store and back? Come here," He hit each one of us a couple times with the hoe handle. Daddy said, "Next time you are told to go to the store, you will not take so long."

I've heard my older brothers and sisters talk about how Daddy would discipline them if he thought they did something wrong, he would use the first thing he could get his hands on to hit them. I never saw much of that, I guess we were too young, and Daddy was too old to punish Brodus and me, like he did the older children.

Mama said she was never afraid of Daddy, but she always did what Daddy told her to do; that's what I've heard the older children say.

If Daddy was talking to another person, and one of his children would walk up to him and attempt to ask a question, Daddy would knock you backwards. Don't ever interrupt Daddy!

If one of his tools was missing and he could not find it, he would take a razor strap or his buggy whip and whip every one of the kids.

There was the time at the end of one long day at the end of the cotton field, everyone had tied up their cotton sheet, and was waiting for Daddy to weigh the sheets to see how much cotton each one picked that day.

Daddy had gone to town that morning and did not pick cotton before noon. Well, he weighed Boyd's cotton sheet, set it down and said, "Well, you didn't pick very much," he weighed Annie's sheet, and said, "You didn't either." He told Cally, "You didn't do anything today." After he weighed all the sheets, and telling them they didn't do any work that day, he hooked the scales to his sheet and weighed it. Mack leaned over and looked at the scale and told Daddy, "Well, you sure as hell didn't do anything today either." Daddy pulled a cotton stalk out of the ground and beat the living daylights out of him.

Mack, by far was the most daring of all Daddy's children, I guess he had so many whippings from Daddy, that he just really didn't care.

Daddy was somehow able to gather up enough money for a down payment on a 39 acre farm outside of Lincolnton, North Carolina.

Going north out of Lincolnton on Highway 321, go about seven miles, the road goes down a long hill, and at the bottom of that hill the road goes up another very long hill. Do not go up the hill. At the bottom of the hill there is an unmarked dirt road, that turns to the right. Turn right on that road, go about one half a mile and the road goes through a "branch" as we always called it. Many people would call it a creek, especially northerners. It was about forty feet across, and could get very deep after a heavy rain.

As you travel on east for a little ways, you go around a few curves, go past a house on your left, and begin to climb up a long, steep, hill, all red clay and very slippery after a rain. As the road levels off you will go past a large, electric wire tower. Roughly, another 500 feet and you can pull into our horseshoe driveway, that goes very close to our front porch, and park anywhere you please. If you were to drive past our house, and up the hill, you would pass a real big tree on your left. We used that tree for a landmark. Continuing on up the road, the next house on the left was the home of Walter Cantrell and his wife, Marie. Further on up the road you will come to the home of Bart McMurry, and the next house, is the home of Grandma McMurry.

The big house you see just up the road is the home of A,Y. McMurry, his wife Macy and their children, Jim, Ruth, Paul, and Martha. Mr.

McMurry has a very big farm, and he also owns the Smith-Douglas fertilizer company store in Lincolnton.

Please allow me to give you a tour of the house that we live in.

There were two front doors in our house. As you go in the door to the right, that is Mama and Daddy's bedroom. That door is never used to enter or exit. However, if you did go thru that room and in to the next room, it is sometimes a bedroom, other times a setting room, because there is a fireplace in there. We can have a fire in the fireplace in the winter time. It's a good place for Mama's sewing machine. Going on through that room, you will enter the kitchen. Once in the kitchen, you will see Mama's wood burning cook stove, where she cooks the best meals any person could eat. Not to mention the coconut cake that she makes using the coconut from a real coconut, and after the cake layers are baked, she pours the coconut water over the cake layers, ummmm, so good. Oh yes, and the ice box is in there.

When the man comes to deliver ice at least twice a week, Brodus and I would run out to the truck and ask, "Hey ice man, can we have a piece of ice?" and he would give each of us a little piece.

And of course you will see a table by the wall, where she puts all the meals together. We have no electricity or running water. There are a couple cabinets where Mama keeps the dishes and silverware, and stuff like that.

As you go through the back door, there is a small covered porch with a table, where the water bucket sits with a tin dipper, where we get a drink. Everyone drinks out of that bucket, using the same dipper. There is a pan where we wash our hands before every meal. If you go out the back door, you will see the water well, that is about ten feet from the back steps. There are times that the well will run dry for a while. When that happens, we take the milk, butter, and things that need to be kept cool, to a natural cold water spring. The spring is back around the barn, and through the woods for a ways, until you come to the spring.

Back in to the kitchen, the next room to the west is our dining room. There you see the big long table where we eat our meals. In the center of the dining room, there is a hole in the floor. When the girls scour the floor, the water can run out through that hole. Mama insisted on cleanliness, she would say even poor people can be clean. If the family was setting around the table, you would see Daddy's back, to his left on the bench would be me, Brodus, Cally And Dallas, at the end of the bench. At the other end of the table, facing Daddy is Boyd. He, of course is the oldest child, and he is important, well, he thought he was. Mack was to his left, then there is Annie, Cecile and Mama to the right of Daddy.

We do not have indoor plumbing, as a matter of fact, we do not have an outhouse, but we do have a lot of woods to go to.

On thru that room, and thru the next room, the middle room is a bedroom where I sleep with Cally.

She is not easy to sleep with. When we go to bed, every night she would tell me, "Don't breathe so loud, be still or I will tell Mama." That makes me so mad! We can lay there in bed, and look up through the cracks in the roof, and sometimes see the stars. The rain would always wake us up when it would leak through the holes. We had to get the buckets and pans to put under the leaks.

The next room is either a bedroom or a sitting room, depending on the season. There is a fireplace where we can build a fire.

Cally told me later that when they first saw the house, she and Dallas went out in the woods and cried.

Behind the barn there was a big lean-to where there was a lot of hay piled up against the back of the barn under the lean-to. It was obvious that it had been there a very long time. Daddy and the girls went down there one day to clean the hay out from under the lean-to. As they threw the hay out from under there with pitch forks, they found a bed of coral snakes. Daddy is scared to death of snakes, the snakes were all over the place.

Daddy hollered, "Watch out, get back, get them boys away from here. What are they doing here anyhow?" He got a hoe and killed all of the snakes, he thought! As they continued to work they found another bed of snakes, more than the first. Daddy brought the biggest snake he killed to the back yard and measured it, and it was almost five foot long.

Oh yes, I heard people, even our family, talk about how poor we were, but I did not know what that word meant. I always had plenty to eat, I was never hungry. There is always biscuits .

One of the best times that I ever had was when the family loaded up our corn, and we went to a corn shucking. Maybe some of you have never been to a corn shucking. It is when the area farmers bring their corn to a farmer's home, and unload the corn in their own pile in the barn yard. The women prepare food and bring it to the farm. After everyone shucks corn for a while, the women bring all the food out and place it on a very long table, and everyone eats. There is more food than everyone can possibly consume.

When the meal was over, everyone began shucking corn again, and they continue until every pile of corn has been shucked. In the meantime there are a lot of kids like me. We are having a big time playing around in the high piles of corn shucks.

After hours of playing, most of us began to lay down on some piles of corn shucks and go to sleep, we got so tired!

Most of the seventeen children from Daddy's first wife, seemed rather distant to the ten children born of my mother, I said, most of them. Some of them seemed very caring about us.

We felt that most of our half brothers and sisters did not want Daddy to remarry after his first wife, Ella May passed away. But he did. The fact that we were born, was not any decision of ours at all, although some of them would have us believe it was our fault.

The fact of the matter was, when certain members of the original family would come to visit us, we did not want to see them any more than they wanted to see us, although we knew they came to visit with Daddy, and not us, and that was well understood.

And of course there were half brothers and sisters that we dearly loved, who came to visit us and we would be so happy to see them. They made us feel like they truly cared about us. For us, that was some of the few good times in our lives, when times were bad.

I will attempt to tell what I know about the members of all my brothers and sisters, all twenty seven.

I already talked about Jerome and his photography career.

And there was Archie, I never knew anything about Archie, maybe he did not live very long, I don't know. I don't remember ever hearing any one talk about him. I do know he was the second child born to Daddy, and Ella Belle. His birth is documented in the records of Lancaster County, South Carolina.

And then, there was sister Agnes, married to Burl Belk. They did not have any children. I know them very well. They live in Pineville, North Carolina, just south of Charlotte, out in the country. Their home is very interesting to say the least. One part of their house is like any other house, living room, bedroom, closet, and so on. Then you stepped down into the kitchen, that part of the house is a tent, dirt floor and all. Kinda like stepping out of 1946 right back into 1720.

They own a few acres, in which were large pastures, with many cows. The cows graze on what grass is growing in the pasture, and the wild onions that grow there also. They milked the cows, drank the milk, and Agnes churned and made butter, lots of butter. She had some butter molds, with different designs. They were really neat. And yes, she offered her butter for sale. Believe it or not, many people bought butter from her. Wild onion flavored butter. That entire home and outside the home smelled like wild onions. I guess you would just have to be there, on second thought, maybe not.

As I said earlier, they do not have any children of their own. My half-brother Marion, and his wife had three children. Their marriage ended when their children were very young. Agnes took their children to raise. I guess that worked out very well. Agnes and Marion were very close as brother and sister.

Agnes and Burl would come and visit us, maybe a couple times a year, when they could get someone to bring them. I do not remember that they ever owned a car.

I want to attempt to tell you a little story about Burl, it happened every time we all set down at the table for a meal. After the prayer was said, Burl would somehow be the first one to start telling one of his stories. Maybe you've had a family guest that you will be reminded of as you read this.

Remember, when someone is talking, you had better not interrupt, even if it is Burl Belk.

Just try to imagine the scene, if you can.

"Well, Mr. Garris," he would say, then take a bite of chicken, and chew, and chew, and chew, seemed like for minutes, then take a drink of ice tea, slosh it around in his mouth for a bit and swallow. And continue, "Me and Charlie got the mules," take a bite of mashed potatoes, and chew, and chew, "And uh, we uh, hooked them up," another bite of chicken, chew, chew, chew. "This sure is good fried chicken Molly." This would go on for the entire meal. He almost drove me crazy, and I'm sure the others at the table felt the same as I did.

Here is a story that was told in later years about Agnes and Mack.

We received a letter from Agnes, telling us that she was coming to visit us, telling us the time to pick her up at the train station. Well, about two days before she was to arrive, it began to rain, and it did pour, so much that the branch, (as we called it) some called it the creek, began to rise. The only way to get to the highway was to drive through the branch. We did have an old car, I believe it was a 1936 Plymouth. Mack went to the train station to meet Agnes. He was able to get through the branch, without any trouble. He arrived at the station, Agnes was standing outside, he went over and greeted Agnes, "Well, hello Agnes, how are you?"

"Oh just fine Mack, little tired from the ride but glad to be here."

Mack said, "Let me put your luggage in the car and we'll head to the house."

"How's Burl and the family down your way?" Mack asked.

"Oh, everyone is fine as far as I know. Burl is taking care of the place. Got to keep them cows milked, ya know."

By now the rain had stopped, but the water was still high in the branch.

Mack remarked, "Well, the branch is still pretty high, but I was able to drive through it when I came to town."

"Oh Mack, you are not going to try to drive through that branch are you?" Agnes said.

Mack replied, "Well, how else are we gonna get up to the house?"

The car is rolling forward,

"Oh Mack, you are crazy! You are gonna drown us, stop, stop!" Agnes hollered.

"Oh, we will make it, I'll be real careful."

Into the branch they went, and the engine in that old car went sputter, sputter, knock, chug, chug. Mack looked over at Agnes, "Damn, we didn't make it!"

"I knew we wouldn't make it, I told you, you are crazy!" Agnes said. "What do you think we are gonna do now?"

"O.K." Mack said, "Just calm down, pick your feet up, and don't get wet. I am gonna walk up to the house and get Toby, he will pull us right out of here."

"Who is Toby?" Agnes asked.

Mack replied, "Our mule!"

"Ain't no mule gonna pull this car out of this river."

"Yes he will, he has pulled cars out of here before," Mack said.

"And I guess you expect me to sit here in the middle of this creek, all by myself, until you get back with that mule that you say will pull this car out of here."

"Well, I sure don't think anyone is gonna walk out here in the middle of this branch to bother you! I'll be back as fast as I can," Mack said.

Mack kind of chuckled to himself as he opened the car door, and got out, walking on across the branch. He could hear Agnes hollering, "You hurry back here now, you hear, do you hear me?"

Agnes was a large woman, we used to say as big around as she was tall. She was a very short lady, generally good humored.

Mack returned home to the barn to get Toby, and harness him. Mama saw Mack at the barn and walked out to find out what was going on.

"Mack," Mama said, "What happened?" "Where's the car?" "Where is Agnes?" "What's..."

Mack interrupted, "Everything is ok. The car stalled out in the branch, Agnes is in the car, and I came to get Toby to pull the car out."

"You were gone so long and I saw you out here, I just wanted to find out what was going on!"

"Well, like I said, everything is ok, I'll go down and pull the car out of the branch, and I'll be back soon with Agnes."

As Mack made his way back to the branch with Toby, he could hear the car horn blow in intervals like beep.... beep,...beep. Mack began to wonder, now what's going on? Is Agnes in trouble or what?

Upon arriving back to the branch, the car was still setting in the branch. Agnes remained in the car, mad as a wet hen, the horn was still blowing. After surveying the scene, Mack just had to bust out laughing, just couldn't help himself.

"Mack," Agnes said, "Would you contain yourself long enough to hook that stupid mule to this car, and pull me out of this branch!"

Half laughing, Mack said, "Tell me the mule is not stupid, and I will get you out of there."

"O.K., the mule is not stupid, now get me out of here."

"Alright, alright," he said, as he began to back Toby down into the branch. After hooking Toby to the front bumper of the car, Mack walked to the rear of the car to push.

"Getup, getup Toby, come on, you can do it," Toby bearing down, Mack pushing with all his strength, the car began to roll forward, "Getup Toby." That old car rolled out on the other side of the branch.

Mack was standing there out of breath.

Agnes says, "Well it's about time."

"Well now, if you don't be nice I can push that car right back into the branch."

The horn had quit blowing, Mack raised the hood of the car, and discovered the small waves were just high enough under the hood, to cause two wires to touch, and make the horn blow.

Mack removed the distributer cap, and dried it off, as well as the sparkplug wires, then put it all back together. He took Toby out in the woods and tied him to a tree. Then Mack returned to the car, got in, pushed the starter, she started right up, thank God.

After taking Agnes on to the house, he returned to the branch and got Toby and returned home.

Agnes was not happy, and I'm sure it took a long time for her to get over that, although Mack said that was the funniest thing he ever saw, seeing Agnes setting there in that car when he returned to the branch with Toby.

Effie was a half-sister I remember very well, she was such a sweet lady. She was married to a gentleman who we called Mr. Thomas. That is the name that we were taught to call him. Actually, he was my brother-in-law, I never knew what his first name was. He was always nice to us when our families would get together. They had two daughters, Lee Ella, And Betty Lou. They were about the ages of my sisters, Dallas and Cally. They would visit us from time to time. They always lived in and around Bessemer City, North Carolina.

I never knew Robert Garris, he passed away at the age of twelve. I do not remember hearing the other family members talking about Robert.

And Lilly, Daddy's sixth child, She passed away at the age of six.

I do not know the circumstances or the reason for her death. There are a lot of unanswered questions in my life about some of my half brothers and sisters. I guess I waited too long to think about writing a book about the family.

I remember Viola and her husband, Horace Rollins, our family visiting them in Charlotte. Viola and Flora were very close sisters. I thought they even looked like each other. They were very pretty ladies as I remember.

Flora married Baxter Plyler, and they lived in Charlotte also.

Sister Inez, as we referred to her, was married to Ben Watkins. We called her sister Inez, because Mama had a sister named Inez. I never knew a lot about Inez, but I became acquainted with her son Calvin, years later.

Marion was the tenth child. He was rather flamboyant, outgoing, more so than most of the family. I knew him well and I liked him very much. He made us kids feel like he honestly cared for us, unlike some of the other half brothers and sisters. I will have a lot more to say about Marion later.

Willie Garris is the eleventh child of Harper Garris. I liked what I knew about Willie. He did not visit us very often. He spent many of his years working in cotton mills. The last twenty years or so that Willie lived, he and another gentleman owned and operated a funeral home in Rock Hill, S.C.

(This incident happened after we moved to Shelby, North Carolina.) One day as I was returning home from school, I saw a hearse parked in front of our house. I was so scared, of course I was wondering what was happening. I was so afraid someone had passed away. I learned that it was Willie, he had delivered a body to Shelby, and stopped by to visit with us on his way back to Rock Hill.

Once, as I was traveling thru Rock Hill, I stopped by to visit him. He gave me an extensive tour of the funeral home, and took me out to dinner. I considered that some good quality time. It was the only "one on one" time that I got to spend with him.

Two years before he passed away, he suffered a heart attack in the drive way of the funeral home. Other workers at the funeral home rushed out to revive him and keep him living en route to the hospital. He did survive, although the doctors said that he was dead for a short time. He was really upset they revived him. He said that he was in heaven, and did not want to return.

The twelfth child was stillborn June 30, 1907.

Herbert Garris the 13th child was born June 8, 1908 and died August 12, 1909

Lois Garris was born January 10, 1910. I did not know very much about Lois, but what I did know about her I learned by going to the family reunion each year. And what I did learn, was that she did not care very much about me, and Mama's children.

She married an educated man, and he was successful in insurance sales in Columbia, South Carolina. There is nothing wrong with that. Education and success is great. But I had the feeling that she thought she was just a little bit better than anyone else. If there is any of her close family members who read this book, and could change my opinion of my sister Lois Lowery, I would welcome it.

Burk Garris, the fifteenth child was born June 2, 1911. He was one of my favorite half-brothers. I have a lot to talk about him and his family later on.

Ruby Garris, sixteenth child of Harper and Ella May Garris, born May 19, 1913 and died May 22, 1913

Seventeenth child, born and died on June 29, 1914

Following, are the children born to Harper B. Garris and Molly G. Garris.

Henry Boyd Garris was born March, 22 1926.

Boyd, (as we called him,) went to work in a cotton mill, where he met his wife Beulah, in Fort Mill, South Carolina. Beulah gave birth to a son, Jerry, in October, 1942.

Shortly after Jerry was born, Boyd was drafted into the Army. Boyd was very serious about life and I was kind of afraid of him, he never gave me any reason, I guess. I wasn't around him enough to get to know him. Boyd and his family relocated in 1958. He enrolled in the seminary in Graceville, Florida. There he became an ordained minister.

He pastored some churches in central Florida, before moving to Bristol, Virginia. There, he was invited to lead their Baptist Church. He worked to start some new Baptist churches in and around the Bristol area.

After a few years, he left Bristol and went to Clintwood, Virginia.

In Clintwood, he led the church until he retired in 1982. Shortly after his retirement, he was diagnosed with throat cancer, and passed away August 20, 1983.

Paul B. Garris was the nineteenth child. Born and died on March 1, 1923

Nolie Geneva Garris, born February 26, 1924 was the twentieth child born to Harper and Molly Garris.

Nolie was born with very dark skin, leading some people to suggest that maybe she was part Negro, or possibly Indian. After all, Mama's mother was half Cherokee Indian.

Members of the family refused to believe that she had any Negro blood in her at all, but I heard that Daddy could not be convinced otherwise.

Any member of the family would be quick to tell you that Daddy was not an affectionate person in any way, shape or form. For that matter, if there had been any infidelity in Mama's life, who could blame her.

When company came to visit, Daddy would send Nolie to another room until the guest would leave. He did not want people to see her.

My sister Annie was very close to Nolie, they played together and was always together growing up. I talked to Annie many times about Nolie. Annie said that Nolie was a very smart girl, and very popular in school.

The time came, when Daddy just could not stand having her in our house. He had someone come and get her, and take her to Agnes and Burl's for them to raise her.

On January 20, 1940 Nolie became very ill. She was taken to the hospital. She was diagnosed with strep throat. For two days, her condition did not improve, and she passed away on January 23, 1940.

There was a knock on our door, Mama went to the door. It was a neighbor who lived about a mile down the road, they had a telephone.

Mama said, "Well, hello there, come on in, I haven't seen you for a while."

The neighbor said, "I can't stay. I had a phone call a while ago, and I'm afraid there is bad news for your family."

"Oh my Lord," Mama said, "What is it?"

"Well, as you know I can't hear very well, especially on that darn phone, I do know the person who called said there was a death in your family."

"Oh my," Mama said, "who was it that died?"

"The best that I could hear, I'm pretty sure they said it was Viola. I'm so sorry to bring you the bad news, Molly."

Mama said, "I sure thank you for letting us know, I'm sure some of us will be going down there to the funeral."

Daddy and the children came in later that evening, and sat down around the table.

Mama said, "Mrs. Abernathy came this afternoon, she had a phone call, asking her to tell us there was a death in our family. I guess Viola has passed away."

"Viola is a half-sister to you children, some of us need to go and show our respect. With Harper and Brodus being as sick as they are, I am going to stay here and take care of them. I want the rest of you to take your Daddy and go to her funeral. Be sure and tell them why I couldn't come."

Two days later, after the funeral, when they all returned home, Mama got more bad news. Viola was not the one that passed away. It was Nolie.

Mama was so hurt. I have never seen her so upset. Mama cried for days.

And then, there was Mack. The twenty-first child was born Sept 2, 1925, what a deal. It was pretty well known by other members of the family, Mack was Mama's favorite child. Mack did not go to school very long, his reading and writing was very poor.

While he was in the Navy, he tried to write letters home to Mama, he couldn't spell most of the words he wanted to say, so he would try to draw pictures to explain. On leave from the Navy, he married a local girl named Maude Parker, from Shelby, North Carolina. You will read a lot more about Mack later on.

Annie Pauline Garris. The twenty-second child, was born December 18, 1927.

I don't remember when she lived at home. She worked on the farm, and went to school. In the eleventh grade, she quit school and married Jack Carter, at the age of sixteen, in 1942

She has said that she just couldn't wait to leave home, to get away from Daddy, she said he was so mean.

She was so tested by her God in Heaven, and I know she passed the entire test that was laid out before her. As I write this, January, 2014. Annie is living in a nursing home in North Manchester, Indiana. She will turn 87 years old later this year, and in pretty good health. She has been a very special sister in my life. You will read a lot more about Annie.

Cecile Garris was the twenty-third child, born June 5th 1929. I cared about Cecile very much, she was very pretty as a young girl.

I remember in the mid-forties before she left home, we had an old Buick, 1935 or 36. Cecile did all the driving. The gear shift would not stay in high gear. Either Brodus, or I would set in the middle of the front seat, to hold the gear shift in high, and we had many arguments about which one of us was going to get to do that.

I remember stopping at Dutch Dietch gas station to get gas. Mama had to get the ration stamps out of her purse, and it took her forever. Mama was always so slow.

During the war, and a while after, gas was rationed. If you owned a car, each car owner would get a certain amount of rationed gas stamps each month. Gas sales were controlled by the government, because of the war that was going on.

Dallas Garris, born July 30, 1931 was Daddy's twenty-fourth child. She married Max Helms and had three children, one graduated from the Seminary in Graceville, Florida.

The twenty fifth child, Clara Jean (Cally) Garris was born June 4, 1933

Cally claims she received more whippings from Daddy than any of the other children, I have no comment.

Brodus was the twenty sixth child. He was born June 23, 1937. Oh boy, we loved and fought, argued, and played together. Maybe we didn't like each other at times, but we sure did love each other. He worked hard his entire life, the last twenty years of his life was spent as an insurance salesman. He was a very devoted member of the Sanford, Florida Baptist church. He was a Sunday school teacher, and a deacon for many years. He was so loved by so many people.

Brodus battled colon cancer for a few years, enduring surgery and a lot of suffering. He passed away at the age of sixty nine, with cancer.

The twenty seventh child of Harper Burney Garris is, Harper Burney Garris, Jr. born April 19, 1939

Chapter Five

Growing up in Lincolnton, North Carolina, the winter weather is bad in January. We are using up a lot of the vegetables that Mama, and the girls canned last fall. Mama said she hopes they will last until late spring, although we have plenty of meat in the smokehouse, from a couple hogs we killed last fall.

My, time seems to go so slow when you are hoping spring will hurry and get here.

Mr. McMurry brought us a pickup load of wood to burn in Mama's cook stove, and fireplace. That was a blessing for us. The siblings didn't have to go out in the woods to cut down trees, and drag them to the house, and cut it up to burn. I imagine Toby likes that, because he doesn't have to drag the logs to the house.

Well, spring is showing signs of arriving. Dallas, Cecile, and Cally are beginning to think about plowing the fields, to get ready to plant the crops.

It has been a rough winter for Daddy, he has had several "spells". We call it a spell, when he passes out where ever he is, and Mama finds a way to get him back in the house, and in the bed. He has passed out several times through the winter. Mama keeps a camphor bottle close by. When Daddy has a spell, Mama gets the camphor, and puts it on a cloth, and holds it under his nose. Pretty soon he comes back around, and will stay in bed a few days, until he is feeling better.

Well, Dallas went to the barn, and got Toby, and she is out there harnessing him up, and is about to start plowing.

"Dallas, will it be okay if I just follow you down the rows?"

"Yes," she said, "But you had better stay out of the way."

I really like to walk behind the plow when someone is plowing. The dirt is soft, and feels cool to my bare feet. I followed her for a couple rows, and I just stood there watching her plow.

Pretty soon, you will find Brodus and me under the front porch playing with our "trucks" (a block of wood). We had miles, and miles of road under that porch. That is one of our favorite places to play.

Mama just walked out on the porch. "Ya'll come on and get ready for dinner," she hollers.

"What about Dallas?" I asked.

"She knows when it's time to come in for dinner."

Our meals are called breakfast, dinner, and supper.

Everyone is at the table.

Dallas says, "I'll tell you, when that plow hits a rock, and the plow handle flies up and hits me in the ribs, that sure does hurt. My ribs are so sore."

Mama said, "Can't you see the rocks ahead of time and not hit them?"

"If I could see them ahead of time, I still have to try to plow a straight row. Most of the rocks are under the ground and I can't see them."

Mama said, "Cecile will be plowing after dinner, and you can rest up for tomorrow."

It's the middle of April, another week and the fields will all be plowed. That's what I heard them say, and then they will began to plant the cotton and corn.

Mama has been working in the garden for the last couple of weeks, planting all the vegetables. Every year she plants okra, butterbeans, green beans, sweet corn, onions, tomatoes, potatoes, and strawberries.

First of May and all the crops are in the ground. I suppose the summer will be spent hoeing the weeds out of the crops, when they start to grow above ground.

Middle of July and Burk, Myrtle, and their three children, Billy, Bradley, and Juanita, came up from Florida to visit for a week. They come every year. We really like them very much. We have so much fun playing with their kids, dodge ball, giant step, soft ball, tag, hide and seek, or any game we can think of. We were playing tag a couple nights ago, and I stepped on a rusty piece of wire, about one inch long. It went all the way through my second toe, and was sticking out the top of it.

We went to the front porch where everyone was sitting. Billy said to Burk, "Daddy, Harper stepped on a piece of wire, and it went all the way through his toe."

"Come here Harper," Burk said, "Let me take a look at it."

So I asked him, "Can you pull that out?"

"I'll be right back," Burk said, "I'll get something out of my car."

Looks like he's got some pliers in his hands, I thought.

"Let's just see what we can do with these," Burk said. He clamped the pliers down on the piece of wire that came through the top of my toe.

"Are you gonna pull it all the way through my toe?" I asked. Everyone was standing around us, wanting to see how he was going to do this!

"We'll see, now take a deep breath," I did, and he pulled. "Oh, that hurts!" Yes, it sure does hurt, but not nearly as bad as it hurt when he poured kerosene on the top and bottom of where the wire came through. Felt like he cut my toe off. I didn't think I could stand the pain, but I did.

"Now," Burk said, "That will keep it from getting blood poisoning or infection."

Mama said, "O.K. kids, wash your feet and go to bed."

We got the foot tub, and all of us washed our feet. Bradley, Billy, Brodus and I went to bed, laying cross-ways on the bed. That's the way we slept when we had company. I liked that!

Next day, Burke asked Mama, "Molly, are you going to make us some of that homemade ice cream today?"

"Now Burke, you know I will."

Burk said, "I've been thinking about that ice cream ever since we left Florida. You know, as far as I'm concerned you make the best ice cream that I have ever put in my mouth. I'll run in to town, and get some ice, and the ingredients you will need to mix it up. Does anyone want to ride along?"

Mama said, "Well, I guess I could ride along with you. Can't do anything until you get back."

"Hop in!" Burke said.

Brodus said, "Mama always likes to go. She will go any time she gets a chance."

Burk bought enough stuff to make two churns of ice cream, just look at them crank those ice cream churns, it won't be long now.

After at least two big bowls of ice cream, Burke said, "I cannot eat another bite, this is absolutely worth the trip up here from Florida."

Summer is just flying by. All the family has been hoeing the weeds out of the cotton, for the last few weeks. Days seem to be getting shorter.

Guess they'll be picking cotton before long.

It's the day after Labor Day, and Brodus starts to school today. He has been saying that he is not going to start to school until I start.

Mama asked Brodus, "What do you want to take to eat for dinner?"

Brodus replies, "I'm not going to school!"

Mama said, "Yes you are, now what do you want me to fix for you?"

"I said, I'm not going to school!"

Mama fixed two biscuits, with butter and brown sugar in them, put them in a poke (that's what we call a brown paper bag).

"Come on," Mama said, "I will walk with you."

"No I'm not going."

"Do I have to get a switch?"

"I'm not going!" Brodus said.

Mama went outside, and got a switch from the peach tree, came back, got Brodus by the arm, and out the door they went, Brodus just bawling. He's pulling back, and Mama is pulling him, and switching him on the legs. They went out of sight, on past the power lines, Mama pulling and switching, Brodus bawling, and hollering, "I ain't going to school."

About two hours later, here comes Mama up the road, Brodus tagging along behind her. She told Daddy, "I practically had to drag him all the way to that school house, and whipped him half of the way. When we arrived there, I took him to his class room, and he just absolutely pitched a fit, hollering."

The teacher finally told me, just bring him back home. She said to talk to him this evening, and tell him what to expect here, and bring him back tomorrow. Maybe he will be able to stay with us."

When the girls returned home from school, Mama was telling them about taking Brodus to school.

Dallas asked Brodus, "What in the world is wrong with you

Brodus? Why don't you want to go to school? All kids go to school when they turn six years old."

"I'm not going to school until Harper goes to school," Brodus said.

Cally chimed in, "I'll bet you do. Don't you know, Brodus, if you don't go to school, they will come and get Mama and put her in jail. Is that what you want to happen?"

Brodus said, "I just know one thing. I am not going to school until Harper does!"

After supper was finished, and the kitchen was all cleaned up, Dallas told Brodus, "Come on in the living room so Cally and I can tell you some good things about going to school."

Brodus remarked, "Don't care what you tell me, I ain't going to school!"

"Why are you being this way, Brodus?"

"Why do I have to go to school, Harper don't have to go to school!"

"Yeah," Cally said, "you are two years older than he is. When he is six years old, he will start to school too."

"Would you listen to me for a little bit?" Dallas asked Brodus.

"Yes I will," Brodus said, "but I'm not going to school tomorrow."

"Well for one thing," Dallas said, "at school you will learn to count, like one, two, three, and all the way up to one hundred, and you will learn to spell words like cat, dog, horse, and you have a whole year to learn all of that. You don't have to learn that in a day, or week, or a month. The good part is, you will get at least two recesses every day."

"What's a recess?" Brodus asked.

"You can go out and play with the other kids for a while, every morning, and afternoon. Now don't you think that would be fun?" Dallas asked.

"I think so." Brodus said.

Dallas asked, "Are you going to school tomorrow?"

"No!" Brodus replied, emphatically.

"For a six year old, you are the most stubborn person I've ever seen. You had rather sit at home all day long doing nothing, than go to school and have fun. I'm sure Mama will have something to say about that!"

Mama did have something to say about that the next morning! She said "Brodus, I've got your lunch packed in this poke, and you are going to school, I'm tired of messing around with you, now come on, let's go."

"Mama, I don't want to start to school 'til Harper starts, I'll start when he does."

"No," Mama said, "you will start today," as she pulled the switch off the top of the ice box, getting Brodus by the arm, and out the door she went, down the road pulling him by the arm with one hand, and switching him with the other."

Two hours later, here comes Mama, walking into the drive way, yep, Brodus is right behind her.

She says to Daddy, "I just don't know what I'm gonna do with him. He was worse today than yesterday. I took him to the principal's office, and he told me to keep him home this year. We'll try again next year."

Daddy said, "I wish I felt better, I bet he would go to school, and stay there, or he would be wishing he had." And I'm betting he would too!

Chapter Six

I guess it's time to start picking the cotton, Mama is sewing up some cotton sacks.

Daddy said. "Ya'll get on out there in the morning and start picking." I guess everyone is dreading that!

It's a new day, not daylight yet. Everyone is up. Mama is fixing breakfast, Dallas went to milk the cow. I think Cally is slopping the hogs. Daddy is in the kitchen with Mama. Brodus went out to get some wood for the cook stove. Man, oh man, them biscuits baking in the oven smell so good.

After breakfast, everyone (including Brodus) is heading for the cotton field, except me and Daddy. Daddy is not able to pick cotton any more, and I guess I'm not big enough. It's kind of lonely here at the house with Daddy.

September is almost gone, a lot of cotton has been picked. About three weeks of picking left. I heard Mama say, when all of our cotton is picked, the family probably will go up and help the McMurry's finish picking their cotton.

It's the end of October. All the cotton has been picked. The cotton was taken to the cotton gin, and sold.

When Daddy is going to buy all of us new shoes, he gets some cardboard, and each one of us stand on the cardboard, and he traces around our foot with a pencil, to make sure he gets the right sizes.

When he gets paid for the cotton, he goes to the shoe store, and buys shoes for all of us kids to wear to school this winter. He brought new shoes home for everyone. My goodness, all the kids are so happy now.

Thanksgiving will be here before you know it.

There's a knock on the door. Mama went to answer it.

There are two men standing there.

"Hello" she said.

The men introduced themselves.

"Mam," one of them said. "Do you own this farm and the woods around here?"

"Yes I do," Mama replied.

"Well, as you probably know, since hunting season is in, we were wondering if you would allow us to hunt rabbits, and squirrels on your property?"

Mama said. "Yes, you are welcome to hunt on our property, as long as you are not shooting toward our house."

"Oh, don't you worry Mam," the man said, "I promise we will not do that."

Mama said, "O.K., ya'll be careful out there."

Mama came back in the house, mumbling something about, this is the time of the year when there will be a lot of that.

Dallas and Cally went to get Bessie, the cow. They had her tied out somewhere, where there was still some green grass for her to eat.

Here they come back, and Cally is riding Bessie, as usual, she always rides her, when they take her somewhere to tie her out to graze. Cally says, why walk when you can ride.

They come into the kitchen where Mama is cooking supper, and stand close to the cook stove. Dallas said, as she stood there shivering, "It sure is getting cold outside, ain't it Cally?"

"Yes, it sure is, I bet it's gonna freeze tonight," Cally said.

Mama said, "I wouldn't be surprised. It's that time of the year, you know." (We don't have a radio or even a thermometer to know how cold it is.)

Mama said, "Brodus, you and Harper carry in some wood for the fire place, in the front room."

"Dallas, when the boys get some wood in there, better go ahead and get a fire started.

"Cally, get the table set, supper will be ready soon." Mama said.

Mama helped Daddy to the table. He hasn't been feeling his best lately.

Mama said to Daddy, "It sure is cold outside. I was looking at the Almanac, and it says it's supposed to be a pretty bad winter."

Daddy said, "As long as we have food to eat, and wood to burn, we'll be alright."

"Oh yes," Mama said. "I forgot to tell ya'll, we got a letter from Effie, and she and Mr. Thomas are coming for Thanksgiving again this year. Mr. Thomas wants to do some hunting."

We are taught to call Effie's husband Mr. Thomas. I never knew why. He was our half brother-in-law, I never knew Mr. Thomas's first name. I guess it really doesn't matter.

Anyhow, we were always taught to call everyone who was an adult, Mr. or Mrs, Sir, and no Sir, Mam, and yes Mam, and that's what we did.

Effie and Mr. Thomas arrived yesterday, they drove up from Bessemer City, North Carolina Tuesday, and Mr. Thomas went hunting this morning. Here he comes, walking up by the barn. I ran down to meet him.

"How many did you get this morning?" I asked him.

"Not enough," he said. "We will need another three or four rabbits for Thanksgiving dinner. I'll go back early in the morning."

Mama and Effie have been cooking this morning and dinner is about ready.

Dallas came in to the kitchen and asked Effie about Lee Ella and Betty Lou (their girls). "How come they didn't come?"

Effie said, "They had plans to go to a show, (movie) this afternoon with their friends."

Dallas said, "Cally and I was hoping they would have come with ya'll."

Up early this morning, it's Thanksgiving Day. Mr. Thomas is not here.

"Where is Mr. Thomas?" I asked. "Does anyone know where Mr. Thomas is?"

Mama said, "Oh, he got up over an hour ago. He left before day light to go hunting."

I said. "It's awful cold to be out there in the woods."

Mama said "Don't worry about him, he'll be alright."

Mr. Thomas came back with three more rabbits. He had enough

time to clean them, and Mama fried them for dinner. I'm telling you, we had a wonderful Thanksgiving dinner.

Effie and Mr. Thomas left after dinner to head back home. They sure are good people. We like them an awful lot.

It won't be long until Christmas. No one seems to be very excited. The sisters told me and Brodus to not be asking for anything for Christmas, cause Mama and Daddy didn't have the money to buy anything. Cecile said. "It's hard enough on Mama and Daddy, that they can't buy any gifts for us, and it would hurt them even more if we were to ask for something."

When we got up Christmas morning, we found a poke for everyone, even for Mama and Daddy. Everyone had a poke with their names on it.

In each brown paper sack there was an orange, apple, tangerine, English walnuts, all kinds of nuts, chocolate drops, some hard candy, candy canes, and a chocolate Santa Claus, and we all knew it came with an awful lot of love. We had a wonderful Christmas morning.

All the children were saying "Thank you, Mama and Daddy." It was the best Christmas that I had ever had in my four years of life.

January sure is cold. We are using a lot of wood in the heater, and cook stove. But like Daddy said, we're o.k., as long as we have food to eat, and wood to burn. And we do. There is a lot of meat in the smoke house, we even have some cracklings, that Mama made last fall, when we butchered the hog. Someone else can eat the cracklings, I don't like them!

It is much too cold to do anything outside, except making sure the animals are fed and have water to drink.

We all set in a half circle around the fireplace, eating boiled, and parched peanuts. That's a real good snack on a cold night.

Mama said to the girls, "Tomorrow, we are gonna start cutting some pieces out of some old rags and dresses, maybe some flour sacks. We have to make a couple quilts yet this winter. We should have started earlier I guess."

This morning, Mama and the girls found some rags, and flour sacks, and began cutting out square pieces, to start making a quilt.

Mama said. "I think I will walk down to the mailbox, maybe we will hear from one of the boys today. Ya'll just keep cutting out those squares, I'll get back as soon as I can."

"No need to hurry, Mama." Cecile said, "Take your time."

About an hour later, Mama returned from getting the mail, as she walked in, she remarked, "Looks like you girls have been busy. We received a letter from Marion. Guess what? Gaither is coming up here the last of April, to plow and help with the crops this year."

"Are you kidding us? Dallas asked?

"No, I'm not kidding." Mama said, handing the letter to Dallas, "Here, read the letter."

"Oh my goodness, I can hardly believe it. Thank God! What a blessing that will be." Dallas said.

The girls are so happy.

"I know, plowing those fields last summer was awfully hard on the girls." Daddy said. "That kind of work is for a man."

Annie has been dating a man by the name of Jack Carter. He is a distant relative of the McMurry's. Mr. McMurry's Mother lived alone, a couple hundred yards down the road from Mr. McMurry.

Mama said to Annie, "Will you go up to Mrs. McMurry's and sit with her for a while? She hasn't been feeling very good lately, and as you know she's getting up in the years."

Annie replied, "Yes, I will. If Jack comes, will you tell him where I am? I would like to see him tonight."

"Yes, I will tell him" Mama said.

The next morning , I was in another room, but I heard their conversation.

Annie said to Mama, "Last night, up at Mrs. McMurry's, Jack and I were setting in the living room, and Mrs. McMurry was in bed in her bed room. She hollered at me and said, Annie, I've got to piss. Now she knows better than to talk like that. I was so embarrassed." Mama said, "Maybe she didn't know Jack was there, but then again, she probably didn't care. She is old and her mind is slipping."

Not very long after that, Jack and Annie ran off and got married. They moved up to Marion, North Carolina. Annie was fifteen years old, Some people said, she was too young to get married.

Annie said, "I just wanted to get away from Daddy. He was so mean."

A truck pulled in our driveway, and a car pulled in behind it. A man got out of the car.

"I'll just be whiskered," Daddy said, "it's Marion."

Mama stepped off the porch, walking across the yard, Mama said, "It's good to see you. What brings you around this part of the country?"

Marion said, "I just need to ask a favor of you."

"What is it?" Mama asked.

Marion said. "I got a job over here at the cotton mill, east of town, and I am wondering, if you would have a room for me to stay here for a while, at least 'til Gaither gets here."

Mama said. "Annie just got married and moved away. Sure, you can have her room."

Marion said "Well, these men in the truck, friends of mine, will help me get my stuff moved in. I sure do appreciate this."

This evening, as we all set around the fireplace, the flames from the fire are lighting the room, with the help of a kerosene lamp. Marion turned around and removed his dentures, turned back around, with the most crazy stupid funny faces we ever saw.

Everyone busted out laughing, "Did you like that?" he asked. He continued to make faces, 'til we had laughed, 'til we couldn't stand it any longer!

"That's enough for one night," he said, "gotta go to bed."

Winter just seems to drag on forever. Food is beginning to get a little scarce. Mama said she thinks some of our vegetables under the house are missing.

Mama said, "Now, who would be so low, as to take vegetables from under our house?"

Marion began to give Mama a little money each week, not much, but what he could afford, and it helped a lot.

Winter was taking a toll, but I didn't know it.

I heard Cecile say one day, to Dallas, "Do you think we will always be poor?"

"Looks like it," Dallas replied.

I had heard the word "poor", many times before, but I don't know what the word means. We always had plenty to eat. There was nothing as good as filling a glass up with some of Mama's warm cornbread that she had just baked, and pour some buttermilk in that cornbread, mix it up, and enjoy! If you have never had cornbread, and buttermilk, you don't know what you have been missing! That is not being poor! A rich man would love that!

And I'll tell you something else. For breakfast, put a slice of real butter on your plate, take some clear Karo syrup, or honey, and pour that over the butter, stir that up really good, and take a biscuit, break off a little piece of it, and sop up a little bit at a time, and eat it. That is better than banana pudding.

It's the first of April. Guess it won't be long until Gaither gets here. Then they can start getting the ground all plowed up and ready to plant.

Cecile said, "Thank God, I am sure thankful that the girls won't have to do the plowing this year."

Dallas said, "I'm glad it's warm enough to sit out here on the front porch. It probably would not be this warm if the sun wasn't shining."

"That's true," Mama said.

Marion went down to Monroe today, and got Gaither and brought him up here. Everyone was glad to see him. He is a good sized boy for seventeen years old.

Next morning early, Gaither was out in the barn, getting Toby all harnessed up, and ready to plow, and plow he did.

The first week in May, he had all the fields plowed and disked.

Gaither said, "The fields are ready to plant."

Mama said, "Mr. McMurry said he would bring our fertilizer, and cotton seeds tomorrow. That's Saturday, so just plan on getting started on the planting on Monday."

"O.K." Gaither said, "that sounds good to me."

This morning, Gaither was riding Toby up and down the road. I guess he likes Toby quite a bit.

Brodus said to Mama, "Can Harper and I go look for some muskadines?"

She said, "Yes, if you don't go too far away from the house."

"We won't," we told her. And off we go.

We didn't have to go far, and we found muskadines, and picked our small bucket full, and went back to the house.

"That didn't take long," Mama said.

We set down on the floor to eat a few. Brodus ate three or four, and he got choked on a hull.

I hollered, "Mama, Brodus is choking! Dallas, Cally, come in here!"

Dallas picked Brodus up and started hitting him on his back, they were doing everything, but he still could not breathe.

They even picked him up by his feet, held him upside down, and he was still trying to breathe.

Dallas said, "Looks like he is turning blue."

Pretty soon, Cally hit him on the back, then he coughed, and the hull flew out on the floor. Everyone breathed a sigh of relief. It scared all of us pretty bad.

We went through a real bad winter. Mama performed some miracles on that old wood burning cook stove throughout the winter. I always had plenty to eat, and I was warm.

Mama said. "Mr. McMurry is gonna stop here on his way back to work at noon, and I am going back to town with him, and get a few groceries."

Dallas said, "So, I guess it will be after dark, when you get home from town."

"I'll have to come home when Mr. McMurry comes. He will have to load our fertilizer, and cotton seeds on his pick-up, after he closes his store. That way we will have it for Gaither to start planting first thing Monday morning. So I am afraid it will be kinda late when we get home."

We are afraid to be home alone, after dark.

We had a good weekend, everyone went to church yesterday, except Daddy, and Gaither.

Gaither is out in the shed, getting the sled hooked up to Toby, to take the fertilizer and cotton seed out to the field. I guess he will began making the rows, and putting the fertilizer down today.

It's only the last of April, and the days are warming up pretty good. After the cold winter, guess we will have a hot summer.

Mama said, "Tell everybody supper is ready, everyone is here but Marion, he has not came home from work yet. He is usually home before now.... well, I'll be dog, he just pulled in the driveway."

Marion came in, sat down at the table, "Sorry I'm late," he said. "The place where I used to work in Monroe, called and asked if I would come back to work there. I told him I would. I went by a fellows' house that I worked with at the cotton mill, and asked him if he would be able to haul my stuff down to Monroe. I know he has a pretty good size truck. He said he would, but he couldn't until next Friday, so I guess I will be leaving you good people."

Brodus said, "Can I go with you, and ride in the big truck?"

Marion replied, "I don't know of a reason that you can't go." That will be up to Molly."

"Mama, Mama, can I go?" Brodus asked.

"As far as I know now," Mama said, "I suppose you can go with them."

Well, a week has passed, Marion's friends showed up with the truck, to move his stuff back down to Monroe.

Brodus is all hyped up, and ready to go, but there is a problem. There are three men to ride in the cab of the truck.

Brodus said to Mama,

"Guess I will have to ride in the back of the truck!"

Mama said, "Now Brodus, you cannot ride in the back of the truck down to Monroe."

Brodus said, "Last week you said you would let me go."

"Yes," Mama said, "But I did not know there would be three men riding in the cab of the truck."

Brodus is starting to cry, no, pitch a fit, oh he is so mad. Bawling and screaming, "You told me I could go, I wanna go." He is jumping up and down and hollering, "I want to go!"

Mama said, "Brodus, you know your Daddy is in the bed, sick, and you're acting like that, you better go outside. He does not want to hear you pitching a fit like that. He went outside and the next thing we heard from him, as loud as he could scream,

"G*& D %*$#, Son of a b#@%h." You could hear him from a mile away.

Out the door Mama went with a leather belt. It was the worst whipping I ever saw him get. He will be sore for days. I don't know where he ever heard words like that.

Gaither has been working his tail off for the last three or four weeks, guess he has the cotton and corn planted, with the help of Dallas and Cally. Mama has been planting vegetables in her garden.

We are beginning to have some pretty hot days now, unusual for the last of May.

One day the McMurry boys rode the horses down to an old dam, it is way back in the woods, there was no water in the dam to speak of. The concrete is still there. At the top of the dam was a narrow strip of concrete, maybe three feet wide. You could walk across there, and see the water below, or maybe go fishing back when there was water.

The boys decided to ride their horses across that narrow strip of concrete, but their sister Ruth didn't want to do that. The boys began to tease her about it,

"Oh come on Ruth, you can do it."

One of the boys said, "I will take the reins and lead the horse across, and one of us will be behind to make her go. Ruth kept telling them to leave her alone, but they wouldn't listen, they kept going. About half way across the dam, the horse reared up, and lost her footing, and fell off the deep side of the dam.

The story we heard was that they had to amputate Ruth's arm at the shoulder. I remember Ruth, she would visit us once in a while. She was friends with Dallas and Cally.

Well, here it is June. The girls are out in the fields hoeing the weeds out of the cotton, there are those who would say, one of the worst jobs on the farm. That hoe handle will rub blisters in your hands. No fun!

I tell you a story about what Mack did to get out of hoeing cotton. This happened before I could remember anything. This was told to me in later years, by Annie, my older sister.

Mack hoed to the end of the row before any of the others were in sight. At the edge of the field was woods, and that's where the water bucket and dipper set. He walked over to get a drink of water and saw some poison oak, that's when he got the idea! *If I had poison oak bad enough, maybe I wouldn't have to hoe cotton*, so he preceded to pull poison oak off the vine and rub it all over himself, on his arms, and face, he even dropped his pants and rubbed it between his legs, actually all over his body. Needless to say, he did get out of hoeing cotton. And he was very sick, his eyes swollen shut. Annie said he was absolutely miserable. He remarked that he had rather hoe the weeds out of cotton any day. That was a very bad idea no doubt!

It's a very hot July day. Mama, Brodus and I were on the front porch. Mama said, as she was looking up the road, "I wonder who that is, running down the road, whoever it is they sure are in a hurry." As he got closer, we could tell it was Albert McMurry, and he was hollering and bawling. Mama hollered at him as he went by our house,

"What's the matter, Albert, what's going on?"

Albert hollered back, "Jim just shot Paul in the head with a shotgun, I've got to hurry and go find some help."

It wasn't very long 'til we saw an ambulance, and a deputy coming up the road, then more police. My goodness, this is horrible, wonder what has happened that he shot Paul. I'm wondering if they were fighting. They did that often.

As it turned out, the boys were hoeing cotton, and they saw some rabbits in the field, and one of the boys went to the house and got the shotgun. In case they scared up another rabbit, they would shoot it. The boys began messing around with the shotgun, and Jim handed the gun to Paul, and Paul asked Jim if it was loaded. Jim said no, and grabbed the barrel of the gun, with Paul holding the other end, and put the end of the barrel to his ear, and told Paul to pull the trigger.

"Are you sure?" Paul asked,

"It's not loaded." Jim said, "Do you think I would have told you to pull the trigger, if I thought it was loaded?" as he put the gun back to his ear, "Pull the trigger!" he said.

Click, Paul pulled the trigger, "Sure was an interesting sound," Jim said.

"Let me hear it," Albert said.

Jim took the gun and put it up to Albert's ear, and pulled the trigger.

"Wow," Albert said, "that does sound different than any gun I ever heard, when pulling the trigger of an empty gun."

Paul said, "Okay, let me hear what it sounds like."

Jim put the gun barrel to Paul's ear and pulled the trigger. The gun fired.

The court ruled it was an accident, that the shell had become jammed in the barrel, the first two times the trigger was pulled.

Daddy's birthday reunion will be coming up soon, on August the eleventh.

Gaither has somehow been able to buy a saddle. Evenings and Saturdays he's been putting that saddle on Toby, and riding him around the farm.

When Gaither rode Toby around the farm, or used Toby to plow, when he brought Toby back to put him in the fence in front of the barn, he would turn off the road at the east entrance of the driveway. That driveway went all the way to the barn. There was a large Chinaberry bush on the left just as you would enter the driveway. (A chinaberry bush is hundreds of little trees about one inch thick, and about ten foot tall growing out of the ground, very close together, to form a big circle, approximately six foot across.) It looks like a real large bush. He would go straight on past the house to the barn.

Why am I telling you this, you may ask? Just keep reading and you will find out very soon.

It's Friday before the reunion, and Agnes, and Burk and Myrtle, and children arrived today. We are all looking forward to Sunday. Of course, Mama is spending most of her time cooking, and baking. Daddy is up and around, and we are thankful for that, although we know that he is not feeling very well. We know that all of us children will have to sleep on a pallet on the floor. Oh well, that will be fun. The old folks will have the beds to sleep on.

Saturday, the girls have to clean the house, and sweep the yard, in preparation for the big day Sunday. There are more of Daddy's older children expected to arrive today. When there are twenty seven children in a family, there are a lot of kids and grandkids expected to be here.

Tonight, everyone seems to be staying up late visiting, and just reminiscing about the past. It sure is interesting to listen to them talk about their memories of years ago.

Mama keeps telling us, "You kids go to sleep, you know tomorrow will be a long day."

Today is the day that we were so excited about yesterday. Yes, today is Sunday. So much excitement!

Many cars are coming up the road, and turning in our driveway. Wow, lots of folks that I don't even know. Every now and then Mama calls me in the house to tell some family members, "This is my baby," and I am so embarrassed, hardly a baby, I guess because I am her youngest child. I always looked like I was older than Brodus. I guess because he suffered so much illness.

A couple of years ago, Brodus complained of bugs crawling all over his body. He cried and cried, he just would not quit crying. Daddy whipped Brodus, and he just kept on crying. He cried day, and night, and Daddy whipped him several times. Mama removed all of his clothes, to show him there were no bugs on him, but he continued to cry, and kept saying there were bugs all over his body. Mama finally asked someone to take her, and Brodus to the doctor. They found out that Brodus had Rickets. The doctor gave Mama some medicine, and he recovered in time.

It's about mid-morning, lots of half-brothers, and their children, and many people were standing around on the front porch, and in the yard.

Someone said, "Look a yonder!" Way up the road, came someone on a horse, couldn't tell who it was, but he had that horse in the wind, kicking up dust as far as you could see on that 'ole dirt road.

"Well, just look at that!" someone said, "It's Gaither, riding Toby." I'm sure he was planning on riding on past the house, but Toby had other plans. Always, when he came up the road, he would turn in to that driveway. And that is what he attempted to do, but the problem was that he was going too fast to make the turn. Toby tried to turn off, but instead of making the sharp turn, he went right through the middle of the Chinaberry bush. Toby came out the other side, but Gaither did not. That little trip took him right off of Toby's back. In a few seconds Gaither came pushing himself through the bush, out the other side, slapping the dirt off his side and buttocks. Someone hollered, "Are you hurt, Gaither?" No answer! He took off, running around the house without a word. He is just too embarrassed! When everyone determined that he was not hurt, they began to laugh, it was quite a show!

As it turned out, Gaither went looking for Toby. Believe it or not, Toby was in the fence, in front of the barn, drinking water.

"Dinner is ready," someone announced. They started lining up to fill their plates, there is more food to eat than twice the amount of people could eat. I've never seen so much food in my life.

Rome's son, Toy is setting up his equipment to walk the tight wire. He did that last year, he puts on a good show. He will put a piece of plank, about three foot long, on the wire cross ways, and balance himself on that, and I remember several other tricks he did last year. He sure keeps the attention of everyone.

People are beginning to leave, and we sure hate to see them go, it has been so much fun the last few days, visiting with everyone, and having all the kids to play with.

Chapter Seven

Monday morning, the family is getting back to their usual chores. There's more hoeing to do, and the family is in the field doing it.

I had my fifth birthday back in April, no big deal, ain't no big celebration, maybe someone will say "happy birthday." And they did. I'm just thinking that Brodus is supposed to start school after Labor Day. I wonder if he will. He was supposed to start last year, and didn't. I have to wait another year to start.

Here it is Labor Day. Everyone is in the field picking cotton except Mama and Daddy and me. Mama is cooking dinner. Daddy is not feeling very well, and Mama is very worried about him.

School days are here, Mama is fixing a lunch for Brodus to take to school, she got some clothes out for Brodus to put on, he is getting dressed, and crying the whole time, telling Mama that he is not going to school.

"Come on Brodus, it's time to go."Mama said.

"I'm not gonna go to school 'til Harper goes." Brodus told Mama.

Mama said, "I will not go through this again this year, like we did a year ago. You might as well make up your mind, you are going to start school this year. And I mean it." Mama picked up the switch and got Brodus by the arm, out the door, and down the road, they went.

I am worried about staying home with Daddy. What would I do if he had another stroke? Perhaps I could run to the cotton field and get Dallas or Cally, that's all I know that I could do, I suppose.

It's been about an hour and a half that Mama and Brodus left to go to school. She should be back soon.

I am on the front porch and here comes Brodus walking up the road, Mama was not with him. I'm gonna go meet him and find out what's going on.

"Brodus, where is Mama?"

"I don't know, I thought she would be here."

"How did you get here so quick?" I asked.

"After Mama left the school," he said, "I went out the back door, and I came through the woods. I thought she would get home before I did."

"Boy, I'll bet she's gonna be mad when she gets here, and sees that you are here."

"I know she will be." Brodus said, "but I'm not going to start school 'til you start, and I've told her that. No matter what she says I will not go to school until you do!"

"Here she comes, and I think she's mad, she sees you."

Mama said. "Brodus, what are you doing back here? And how did you get here so fast? I'm not going to punish you now, but you will stay in school tomorrow, if I have to set there all day with you. I don't know what I will have do with you!"

Next morning, it's time again to go to school, same thing is happening, Mama and Brodus leave to go to school, and Brodus is throwing a fit, as they go walking down the road. Mama is switching his legs as they walk.

Mama said later when they arrived back home. "When we arrived at school, he bawled and screamed so loud, he was interrupting the entire school. We ended up in the principal's office."

"Mrs. Garris," the principal (Mr. Schufford) said, "What do you think we can do about this? He has already missed one year of school, I sure hate for him to miss another year, which will put him way behind."

Mama said she told Mr. Schufford that she could not continue to whip him to school every day, he is not gonna learn anything this way.

"You're right, Mrs. Garris." he said. "Just keep him at home another year. If he is waiting to start school when his brother starts, there should not be any problem next year."

"So," Mama said, "I brought him home."

It's the end of October. The cotton has been picked, and taken to the gin. It is pretty quiet around here now.

Gaither is in the woods, cutting down trees. When he gets a couple trees down and trimmed, he will come get Toby, and go back and hook him to one of the trees that he cut down, and Toby will pull it back to the wood pile. Dallas and Cally will put it on the saw horses, and cut them up with the cross cut saw. Brodus and I will set on the log as they saw it, to keep it still. I suppose we will be doing this for two or three days, to try to get enough wood cut up, and on the wood pile, as soon as we can. It could be a cold winter.

Cally and I will have to go down in the woods to find a stump, and cut pieces of splinters off to start fires, pine if we can find it, Pine splinters starts a fire quick. When we need more splinters, Dallas and Brodus will have to get them, we alternate getting the splinters.

It's November, 1944 and getting colder every day.

At the supper table tonight Mama said "I'm gonna tell you kids now, expect anything to happen with your Daddy. He seems to get worse every day, and I don't know how long he can live. I will see if I can get the doctor here tomorrow. He might be able to help him. I hope so. After supper, all of us just set around the fireplace, we ate some boiled peanuts and popcorn. It was quiet for the most part, no one had very much to say. Mama was reading the Bible as usual. I think Gaither is writing a letter. The rest of us just try to stay warm.

The doctor did come today, Mama said. "Brodus, you and Harper go to the kitchen and wait while the Doctor examines your Daddy."

After the doctor left, Mama didn't say anything to us about what the Doctor said.

At the supper table, this evening, Mama said,

"The doctor came today, he examined your Daddy, and the news wasn't good. He said there was nothing he could do, that his heart was very weak, and that he could have a stroke, or a heart attack any time, the only thing we could do was to make him as comfortable as we can."

Mama said, "Tomorrow, I will write a letter to some of the children, and let them know what the doctor told me."

The third week of November, some of the other children began coming to the house, visiting with Daddy. Agnes and Burl came, and a few days later Viola and Flora came, Effie and Mr. Thomas was here.

I'm five years old and I don't understand what all is going on, we usually never have this much company.

It's the first week of December. There are more, and more of Daddy's older children coming to visit with Daddy. Of course Annie is here, and Cecile.

Willie, Marion, Rome, and Burk are here. From what I hear, a couple of them are setting up in the room with Daddy every night. I guess Daddy must be pretty sick.

It was the morning of December ninth, my nephew, Calvin Watkins came out where Brodus and I were playing, and asked us, "Would you boys walk with me down to the pasture, and show me your cow? Grandma told me ya'll had a cow."

"Yeah," Brodus said, "I'll go ask Mama if we can go with you."

"No," he said, "Your Mama told me to tell ya'll to go with me, so she knows we are going."

Calvin opened the pasture gate and closed it after we passed through.

He asked, "Do you boys come down here in the pasture to play sometimes?"

"Oh no," Brodus said, "we have asked Mama but she says we are too little to be playing down here in the pasture."

Calvin replied, "I suppose she is right, you boys are pretty young."

We walked down to the fresh water spring. I told Calvin, "This is where we put our milk and butter when we don't have any ice in our ice box at home, this water is really cold."

We kept on walking through the woods, in a small clearing we were able to see Bessie out there grazing. Calvin asked, "Is that Molly's cow?"

"Mama says she belongs to all of us. Bessie gives us a lot of milk and butter."

Calvin said, "We had better head back toward the house, soon be time to eat dinner."

We arrived back to the house and sat down on the back of the wagon that was in the back yard.

Calvin asked in a soft voice, "Did either one of you boys ever see a person that has passed away?"

I asked, "What's passed away?"

Brodus said, "Oh Harper, that's when someone dies. Why did you ask us that question?"

Calvin asked, "Do you know why all the people have come here the last few days?"

Brodus said, "Well I know that Daddy has been pretty sick. I thought they had all come to visit with him."

Calvin said, "Yes they did, yes, he was very ill, and this morning your Daddy passed away. He is in Heaven now. That was the reason Molly wanted me to take you boys for a walk out in the woods. They had to call an ambulance to come and get your Daddy and take him to the funeral home, to prepare him for his funeral," Calvin said.

"Your Mama didn't want you boys to be here when they came to get your Daddy."

Brodus was crying a little bit, I didn't know exactly why. I guess I do not understand what all is happening.

I know we still have a lot of family at our house, talking about Daddy. I heard Mama say she would go to the funeral home in the morning with Willie and Burk to make plans for the funeral.

Mama did some cooking this evening for anyone who wanted to eat, a lot of the people left. I guess they were going home, the ones that lived within driving distance.

Mama said, "I know it's early, but Harper, you and Brodus better go ahead and go to bed. Tomorrow will be a long day."

I smell the biscuits in the oven, that smells so good, so I got out of the bed and went to the kitchen where Mama is cooking breakfast. Mama is wiping her tears on her apron.

"What's wrong Mama?" I asked.

"I don't think you would understand, son." Mama said," I don't think Mack or Boyd is gonna get to come home for your Daddy's funeral, and that makes me real sad."

"I'm sorry Mama, I am real sad also. Why can't they come home?"

Mama said, "They are a long, long way from here in service. You will understand it all when you get older."

It has been three days since Daddy died. They brought him back today in a casket. They put the casket over against the wall in the living room and opened it up.

Mama asked, "Would you boys like to go in the living room and see your Daddy in the casket?"

Yes, we went in to see Daddy I asked if he was sleeping?

Mama said, "No, he is not living now, he has passed away. He is dead but his soul is in Heaven."

And Brodus is crying again like he did the other day, I guess he understands more than I do.

Lots of my brothers and sisters are here now, several of my half-brothers are in the room visiting with each other, just talking about everything.

Burk said, "It's really too bad Mack and Boyd couldn't get a leave to come home for Father's funeral."

Rome said, "That's the military for ya. When they are in battle, they won't let anyone go anywhere, for any reason. Anyhow, Mack being in the Navy, he could be out in the middle of the ocean."

"Yeah, that's right," someone said.

The half-brothers have been setting up all night the last two nights with Daddy.

The funeral was held today. Daddy was buried at our Church, McKendree Methodist, located on highway 321 north of Lincolnton. Some of the family came back to the house after they left the church.

Cally said, "Agnes told Mama that she would take a couple of the kid's home with her, and raise them if she wanted her to."

Mama told her that her children would not be separated, and to not ask again.

Marion told Mama that he was gonna take Gaither back home with him, at least until next spring. He could come back and help with the plowing, and planting, if she wanted him to. Mama told him, she would let him know.

It won't be long, Christmas will be here. Everyone is looking forward to getting their poke, Christmas morning.

Bessie didn't come to the pasture gate this evening like she always does. Mama told Dallas and Cally to go out in the pasture and try to find her.

They were gone for a little while, and came back and told Mama, they think she got out of the pasture, that they saw a place where she probably got out.

Mama told them to walk down the road a little ways, and go into the woods on the other side of the road, that's where they found her the last time she got out.

They were gone for a little while and came back in the house, all out of breath, they had been running. Cally was crying, they were acting like they were scared half to death.

Mama asked them, "What in the world is the matter with ya'll?"

Dallas said, "We were walking through the woods, like you told us to do, looking for Bessie. We were singing some Christmas carols as we walked, and a gun shot rang out. I know I heard a bullet go right by my head. We were so scared, so we hurried up, and went back, and got on the road to hurry home. We saw Mr. Farmer in his front yard holding a gun. That scared us so bad, we started to run. Mr. Farmer hollered at us and asked if that was us out there in the woods. I said yes, we were looking for our cow. He said he thought we were them damn McMurry kids, and he didn't want them hanging around down there."

Mama said, if she could get a ride to town in the morning, she would go to the Sheriff's office, and tell them what happened.

There is a knock on the door, Mama opens the door. It's Mr. McMurry, "Hello Molly, how are you and your family getting along?" he asked.

She said, "We are getting along pretty well, I guess."

He replied, "Is there anything ya'll need, that I could do, or get, that would be of help to ya'll?"

Mama answered, "I don't know of anything, uh well, do you think you could let us have a couple gallons of kerosene, to help get the fire started in the stove in the mornings?"

"Of course, you can have all you need, just bring a five gallon can and fill it up. You know where the kerosene tank is I suppose?"

Mama said, "Oh, yes we do, and we really do appreciate it. Thank you very much!"

"If you need anything else, just let me know."

Mama said, "Cally, you and Harper take that five gallon can, and walk up to Mr. McMurry's, and get about a half of can full. Don't fill it up, because you would not be able to carry it."

This has been a real rough winter for us so far. It's been very cold, and it's a long time until spring. I've heard the others talk about our family being very poor. I don't know about being poor, I've had plenty to eat, and the house is warm. I know Mama don't have very much money, but I think we are getting by.

It's three days before Christmas, Boyd came last night, what a surprise! He said he got a short leave from the Army, he sure is glad to be back in the states, and we were sure glad to see him. So thankful he was not injured.

He gave Brodus and me, each a pack of Spearmint chewing gum. We have never had a full pack of gum in our lives.

Boyd was married before he was drafted into the Army. He was married to a girl by the name of Beulah Stallings. He left last night to go to Rock Hill, South Carolina to surprise her.

Dallas and Cally went out in the woods and cut down a small tree to use as our Christmas tree. To decorate it, they used popcorn, and some ribbons they had found, and they put some twigs of holly on the tree. I think it is real pretty.

Santa is not bringing anything for any of us this Christmas, but I think we will get our poke again, that will make us happy.

January, 1945, Christmas has come and gone, it's cold outside but we are warm.

Annie and Jack moved to Norfolk, Virginia. They heard there was work up there, and I guess Jack got a job driving a taxi, Dallas said.

"We received a letter from Annie today," Mama said. She gave the letter to Dallas to read to us.

" Annie gave birth to a baby girl," Dallas said.

"What did she name her?" Cally asked.

"Says here in the letter, she named her Geneva."

"That is my middle name you know." Mama said.

"Well for goodness sake," Cally said, "That sure is nice of her to do that. I can hardly wait to see the baby."

There is not very much going on around here now a days.

Brodus has been sick several times this winter. He is not as big as I am, I heard someone say, because he has been sick so much. He has really bad ear aches, tooth aches, sore throat, and in general, bad health.

Mama has been sewing a lot this winter, I believe she is making Dallas, and Cally some new dresses.

Mr. Farmer's trial will began February first, I heard Mama say, "I guess you kids know that?"

Dallas said, "Yes, I know, that's all I have been thinking about. Mr. Farmer should not have been shooting at us."

Mama said, "Don't be nervous about it, when you're on the witness stand, just tell the truth, as you remember what happened that day. I'm sure Cally is just as nervous as you are. I'll be there in the court room too."

"Harper, you and Brodus go out and get some wood for the stove. I guess I'd better get some supper started."

We got the wood in by the stove.

Mama asked if we had enough kerosene to get the fire started in the stove, and heaters, the next few days.

Cally said, "I don't think we have any kerosene left at all."

Mama said, "Get the bucket, and go on up to Mr. McMurry's, and get a few gallons."

Here we go, up to Mr. McMurry's again, to get the kerosene.

Cally pumped the kerosene in the can, and we started to leave to go home. Well here comes A.Y. (that's what most people called him. We better not call him that if any grownups were around.) He came stomping out here where we are. Generally speaking, he was not one to swear in the usual way, although he did have his words.

He said, "By hail, do you people expect me to take care of everybody in the neighborhood! Gimme, gimme, gimme, that's all I hear any more. Dat dummet, this stuff is expensive, and by hail, it's gonna have to stop, and I mean it!"

Cally began to cry, she set the bucket down, and she said, "Come on Harper, let's go home."

As we walked in the house, Mama asked, "Well, where is the kerosene can?"

Cally says, "We pumped some kerosene in the can, and started to......"

Knock, knock; we heard on the front door.

Mama went to answer the door, opened it and there stood Mr. McMurry.

"Mrs. Garris," he said, "your kids came up to get some kerosene, and I saw them out there. I don't know what got in to me. I pitched a fit, and I am ashamed of myself. There has been so many people coming by, and getting this and that, and I guess I just lost my temper. I want to apologize to you and the kids. You folks are welcome to anything I have, and oh, I set your kerosene on the porch here."

Mama replied, "O.k., thank you so very much, we really appreciate it. I'll tell the kids."

Dallas and Cally had an appointment with the prosecutor this morning, to talk about the trial of Mr. Farmer. It begins tomorrow. They sure have been dreading it.

Mama, Dallas, and Cally went to the court house this morning, Mr. Farmers trial began today.

Cecile is in bed sleeping, she worked the night shift last night. We are supposed to be quiet, and not wake her up. We wonder when Mama and the girls will be home. We are o.k., we know where the peanut butter and the biscuits are!

The trial only lasted four days, they had done a background check on Mr. Farmer, and found that he was on probation when the incident happened back in December. Mama said that he will have to go back to prison. The family is sure glad that it's all over.

Mr. McMurry comes home for dinner every Saturday. Mama said she was going back to town with him today, to do some shopping. We sure don't like for Mama to be gone all afternoon on Saturdays. She usually doesn't get back home until after dark. Cally and Dallas is here, but it is still a little scary when Mama is gone after dark.

I'm just sitting here thinking about April the nineteenth, that is my birthday. I will be six years old. I will start to school in September, kind of looking forward to that. I am wondering if Brodus will start to school when I do, he said he would. I guess we will see then.

Jack, Annie's husband had an old model A Ford. I remember a while back when they lived in Marion, North Carolina, they took me and Brodus with them to Marion. We had to go over the mountain, and Jack had to stop and put water in the radiator a couple of times, going up the mountain, when the radiator steamed over.

This has been a very bad winter for the family. Not a lot of food, but Mama performed miracles in that kitchen, she could make a meal out of nothing. We had biscuits three times a day. There is nothing better than that for breakfast, well, maybe I could mix honey in butter. That is very good also.

It's springtime 1945; it's different now that Daddy is not here.

We did hear that Gaither was coming up again this year, to help with the planting.

Well, this year is starting out bad. Mama got word that Jack Carter, Annie's husband was killed in an automobile accident in Norfolk, VA while he was driving his taxi.

Mama said they were gonna bring his body back to Marion N.C. for the funeral, and burying. That is where his parents live. Then I guess Annie and Neva are gonna come back here to live.

Three weeks after the funeral, Annie and Neva arrived back home here. Annie is sure having a hard time over the death of Jack, which is expected. She keeps saying over and over, "He was just too young to die. What will I ever do now? I did not want to come back here and be a burden on y'all."

Mama is trying to console her the best way she knows how.

Mama told her, "It will take time, God has a plan for everyone, just trust in him. Healing takes time, and you will have plenty of time. Try to think about the beautiful daughter he gave you. Concentrate on taking care of her."

Well, time moves on, it's impossible to stop time, and you cannot reverse time. There is no going back. I cannot imagine what kind of shape this world would be in, if people could regulate time. Time can usually erase a lot of memories, such as death, divorce, maybe a cheating spouse, or maybe if a longtime boyfriend, or girlfriend, say they have to breakup.

In the case of my dear sister Annie, time did move on, and she began to realize that she could not set around, and drown in her misery. She began to take advantage of time.

Annie was talking with Mama.

"Mama," Annie said, "There were some neighbors living beside of us, in the trailer park, where we lived in Norfolk, VA. There were three men living there. One of the men was named Bill Bumgardner. He was very friendly, and nice to me, although he never made a pass at me. I liked him very much. I just want to ask you if you think it would be alright, if I wrote a letter to him. Has it been long enough since Jack got killed, for me to be talking like this?"

Mama replied, "I don't see any reason why you shouldn't write to him."

Annie said, "I'm gonna write to him, and see if he will write back."

Annie did write to Bill, and received the letter back, and on the letter was stamped "return to sender".

So Annie wrote a letter to the people that lived on the other side of them, and asked them if they knew where the Bumgardner's moved to.

In a little over a week, she received a letter back from them, not only telling her they moved to Indiana, but sent Bill's address to her.

Using that address, she wrote to Bill, and received a letter back from him, and Annie was a happy girl.

In the meantime, Brodus, and I had gone out all around the house, and the edge of the field, and carried some rocks back. We lined them up in the shape of a house, and we called it our playhouse, living room, kitchen, bed room and dining room. We are very proud of our house. Yes I know, we did have an imagination.

Alas, there was Neva to contend with. She is four years younger than me, just a toddler.

Oh no, Mama is bringing Neva out here, She says, "Brodus, you and Harper let Neva play with ya'll a while."

She is a problem for us. She keeps picking up the rocks, and throwing them, or taking them somewhere else, made us so mad. She just doesn't know how to play. After all, she is too young to play with us big boys. I will soon be six years old, ya know.

Of course, you know Neva is spoiled rotten. She gets all the attention around here, if it's not her, its Brodus, and I come in last. Oh well, that's the way it's always been. I can handle it.

Someone bought Neva a cute little white rabbit, about two months ago. We put him in a cage out close to the garden, by the corn field. He somehow manages to get out of the cage sometimes. Brodus and I have to go look for him. He never goes very far, either in to the garden or cornfield.

Annie and Bill are writing letters back and forth. Annie seems to be very happy now, more than she has been for a very long time. I am happy for her.

I lay in bed at night, when it's real quiet, and I can hear the big trucks down there on highway three twenty one, going up the steep hills, changing them gears and I think to myself, that's what I want to do when I grow up.

It's March, the winter has been rough for our family, but we were able to get through it. Easter is coming soon, and my birthday will be here soon too. I will be six years old, you know.

Brother Burk, and Myrtle and family came up for a few days. We always look forward to their visit in the summer.

There was not a lot of excitement this year, except back in the spring, early night, when the sky lit up real bright with a red glow. Mr. McMurry's barn caught fire. They lost a couple of cows, and a loft full of hay. It burned for days afterward. I don't know if they ever found out what started the fire.

Summer is gradually passing, harvest time before we know it. August is upon us now. I will be starting first grade of school pretty soon.

Unlike Brodus, I am looking forward to going to school. I guess it will be interesting to see if Brodus is ready to start when I do, like he said he would.

Everyone is talking about a big bomb, that the United States dropped on Japan, that killed lots, and lots of people this month. No, I guess there were two big bombs dropped, a lot of people are saying that those bombs will probably help end world war two.

Mama received some very bad news today. Two men dressed in Navy attire came to the house, and brought Mama a big brown envelope. They explained to Mama that Mack had been very seriously injured on a ship, out in the Pacific Ocean, near Japan, and that he was in an Army hospital in Japan. They told Mama she would be notified when more information was available. The mood here is very somber now. Everyone is talking about how hard it is when a person doesn't know what's happening, especially when it's so far away.

It's hard to get life back to some kind of normalcy, and be worried like everyone is, and have life go on as usual.

Today is Labor Day, guess what? School starts tomorrow. I am glad.

"Brodus, are you ready to start to school tomorrow?" Mama asked.

"I am, if Harper goes," he replied.

"Well, Harper is going, so you boys will be in your first day of school tomorrow. I will walk with ya'll to school, and get you in your class, and I will come back home."

Just like she said, Mama is up, fixing our school lunch for today. Mama fixed us biscuits with butter and brown sugar in each biscuit. Two biscuits for each of us, and we are off to school. This is exciting!

We arrive at school, Mama went into some office to find out what room to take us to, she comes back and she takes us to our room.

There are lots of kids here, and some of their mothers are here with them. They have big desks in here, big enough for two children to set in side by side. The teacher took us to the desk that we would be setting at. Mama told us to come on home with Cally and Dallas, when school was out, and she left.

It's time now to start picking cotton. Each day after school, Dallas and Cally have to go pick cotton. Gaither has been out there picking cotton all day. That's about all he gets done now. Picking cotton is one of the worst jobs anyone could have. Having those cotton sack straps over your shoulder, and the more you pick, the heavier the sack gets. A person gets so tired bending over to pick, so you get on your knees, and drag the sack. Your knees get so sore, you cannot stand it, then you stand up again. And finally you get to the end of the row, and empty your sack of cotton on the sheet, thank God your sack is gonna be light, for a little while.

Now, if that is not miserable enough, at the end of the day, just look and feel the end of your fingers. When the cotton bowls open, the end of each five parts of the bowl has a very sharp point, like a knife or needle. When picking cotton you cannot avoid those sharp points puncturing the sides of your finger nails. And that hurts, I mean really hurts.

Brodus and I are going to school every day now. Brodus is my shadow, he will not leave my side, and I don't mind. I like school. ABC's and numbers, it's fun. I believe Brodus likes it also. We can hardly wait to get home from school each day so we can tell Mama what we did at school, and what we learned.

Mama received word that Mack was now at the Navy Hospital at Bainbridge, Maryland. That was some really good news to receive, and that he would be taken to the Navy hospital in Charleston, S.C., after a week of rest.

October, the tree leaves are turning all colors and they are so pretty, the teacher talks about the tree leaves in school.

Down there where our dirt road junctions with highway three twenty one, going north is a fairly steep hill, and going south there is a steep hill also.

Mama and some of the other neighbors went to the school and had a meeting with the principal, attempting to find out if the school bus would stop at our gravel road, and pick up the children that were walking to school. The consensus was that it was very dangerous for the children to be walking along the side of the road that was so heavily traveled mornings, and afternoons, when the children were walking to and from school. The principal agreed to take the parents' concerns to the county schools superintendent. He said it would be his decision. And he would let the parents know the results of his decision.

In the meantime the eight of us will walk along side of the busy highway, a little more than a mile to school every day.

This weekend will bring November in, and a man came by to talk to Mama about butchering two of our hogs. He told Mama he would bring his brother to help. He said we should make sure we filled the big wash pots with water, and get a good fire going around them early, so the water would be plenty hot when they killed the hogs. We heated water in those big wash pots every week, so Mama would have hot water to wash the clothes.

I think we will have plenty of meat through the winter; ham, bacon, and Mama will have plenty of fat back to cook with.

Last day of school for the week, we are at the supper table. Mama brought a letter in and handed it to Dallas.

"Read this," she said.

Dallas said, "Oh, it's a letter from the Navy hospital in Charleston."

Hello, I am a friend of your son, Mack. He asked me to write a letter to ya'll and let you know how he is doing. He says he is doing pretty well, but I don't think he is. His injuries are pretty bad. His right leg is broken real bad, and his left arm is in pretty bad shape. He also has a lot of shrapnel in his shoulders. The doctors say his wounds are not life threatening, which are prayers answered! He said his wife is coming down this weekend and when she goes back home she will come and visit ya'll and tell you

about him. Mack is really looking forward to that. He said
in ending, keep your prayers coming this way, we need
all we can get!

Mama said "It's so good to hear from him, God bless and be with him. I would give anything to go see him, but I don't know how I could. It's a long way and I sure don't have the money to make the trip."

Saturday, and the place is as busy as a bee hive. People are all over the place, roaring fires around the big black wash pots, and big iron tripods over two of the wash pots, with a hog hanging from each tripod. Men are working on them with big knives. I have never seen anything like this. Of course Will Morrison is here helping the men. Do you remember Will from a while back? Will is always willing to help. One of the men told me and Brodus, the best way we could help is to just stay out of the way, so we did.

The men have been working very hard all day. It will be dark soon and the meat has been all salted down and put in the smokehouse. Mama gave the men some pieces of the hogs that they wanted. Mama has a lot of lard now that she will make use of. This was a very good day.

Monday, and back to school we go. I'm beginning to look forward to going to school. I have gained some new friends to play with during recess, and we have a lot of fun. It started raining this morning, guess it will be fun walking home in the rain. We hope the water in the branch will not rise too high before we get there. There are two logs laying across the branch that we walk across when going, and coming home from school, but if it rains hard for a long period of time, the water will rise above the logs. In the summer time we can just take our shoes off and wade through the water, that's always fun, we all hold hands as we walk through the branch, for safety.

Nothing exciting has happened through the winter of nineteen forty five, except a lot of soldiers coming home from the war, everyone is talking about that. Harry S. Truman is president.

Mama did hear from the Lincoln County schools superintendent in December about the reason the school bus cannot stop and pick the children up on highway 321 The letter said,

It was determined that the location you are asking about the bus to stop, is at the bottom of two steep hills. if the bus stopped at that point, it would cause the driver of the bus to not get a reasonable amount of speed up to climb the hill after the stop, which would back traffic up and could possibly be a hazard. So I have to inform you that the bus will not be stopping at that location.

Annie has been corresponding with Bill Bumgardner all winter, Neva has been getting more and more spoiled.

I heard Mamma and the girls talking about what Annie told Bill in a letter she wrote to him. She told him,

Bill, I am going to pack up my and Neva's clothes, and we are coming out there, and when we get there, you and I will get married.

That is just what she did. She found out right away after arriving in Indiana, that Bill was illiterate, and Bills sister Mary had been writing the letters to Annie for Bill. She also found out that Bill was the youngest in the family, and the favorite son of Mom and Dad. And they did not necessarily agree that Bill should be getting married.

Bill and his brothers, and Father "Bum," as they called Bill's Dad, was into visiting the town tavern on a regular basis. That was not to the liking of Annie at all. She was determined that many of Bill's habits, (drinking and smoking) would come to an end after they were married.

One month after Annie arrived in North Manchester, Indiana, Annie and Bill Bumgardner were married August third, 1946. Not very long after their marriage, Annie became a member of the North Manchester Church of the Nazarene, and so did Bill. Annie was very faithful to her religion.

Bill's Dad and brothers began going to the town tavern without Bill. And yes, Bill even quit smoking. Of course "Bum" was not very happy about all the changes that were taking place with his special son. Guess he was not able to do much about the situation, and Annie made sure of that.

Boyd was discharged from the Army a few weeks ago. Boyd, Beulah, and son Jerry are living here in town for now. It is a blessing that Boyd is home, and has no injuries from the war. He did find employment in town, but I don't know what kind of work he is doing now.

Very late on the night of December nineteenth, nineteen forty five, is a night all of the family will always remember. I do not know if everyone was sleeping or not. I know I was sleeping until the sound of a vehicle pulled into our driveway, right up to the front porch. Mama got up, uttering something like "Now who could be coming here this time of the night?"

I heard her open the front door and say "Who is it?"

By this time Cally and I had opened our bedroom door just enough to see the front door, and Mama standing there.

One of the men in the car said, "You ask her."

And the other man said, "You ask her."

Mama said, "What do you want?"

And again, one man said, "You ask her,"

Another voice said, "No, you ask her."

I guess Mama had heard enough. She reached up above the door and removed the rifle, and leveled it, and pulled the trigger. That car spun out of the drive way, I guess, as fast as it could possibly go. We were all afraid of course. All of us sat in the living room in the dark, wondering who they were. Mama said she had no idea who it could have been. We were all wide awake now, wondering if they might come back later. Mama reloaded the rifle; it is a single shot twenty two rifle.

Mama said, "You kids go on back to bed, it will be daylight pretty soon."

We went back to bed, but I don't think anyone went back to sleep. One thing is for sure, Mama is going to watch over her family, and keep all of us safe.

Mama has been getting letters from Annie, they seem to be getting along fine. She sends photos of Neva in the snow, deep snow. We have never seen snow so deep.

Someone knocked on the door, Mama went and opened the front door.

Chapter Eight

"Well for goodness sake," Mama said. "If it ain't Maudie and Sarah May, (Maude's sister,) come on in. I have been praying you would be bringing some good news about Mack. Did ya'll go down to see him, how is he doing?"

Maudie said, "As you might expect, he is still in some pain. Mentally he is very good. He was so very excited to see us, and of course it was just wonderful to see him. He said he was feeling real good, but hates being in the hospital. I don't think he is as well as he thinks he is, but I'm sure he feels much better since he is this close to home. He looks much better than I was expecting him to. I didn't know what to expect, of course all the nurses just love him. He likes to give them a hard time.

Well Molly, I think we better be going on to Shelby, we knew you would be anxious to hear about Mack, so we came by on our way home. We've been gone three days. It's good to see you. We will let you know the next time we hear any news from him."

Mama said, "I just cannot thank you enough for coming by and letting me know about him."

"That's okay Molly, we'll see you again soon, Bye."

It's another cold Carolina winter. It is January, and things are a little quiet, we are feeding the animals, and making sure they have water that's not frozen. Mama is sewing a lot on her old Singer sewing machine. I think Mama is happy when she is sewing. She sings and hums hymns like "The Old Rugged Cross" and "What a Friend We Have in Jesus". She has got that old Singer sewing machine humming. Too cold to play outside so Brodus and I push our little blocks of wood, that we call our trucks all over that old wooden floor.

Well, February is coming up soon, we are making Valentines for everyone in our grade, that's a lot of fun. Valentine's Day will be here soon.

It snowed yesterday, and when we returned home from school, Mama made some snow cream, boy was that good! Yes it was, that was a good treat.

Mama can make a meal out of nothing, she has done that so many times. We have plenty to eat now. Still have a lot of meat in the smokehouse, from the hogs that was slaughtered last fall, and plenty of vegetables that Mama and the girls canned last summer, and potatoes under the house. Nobody can make vegetable soup as good as my Mama can. I mean that!

Sometime just a banana sandwich will fill me up. Did you ever eat a banana sandwich? Oh, it is so good, I can do that myself. We do not get sliced bread or bananas very often. Just take two pieces of bread and smooth out some mayonnaise on the bread, peel a banana, slice thin pieces on to the bread, my, that is so good.

We received some wonderful news in a letter from Annie today. Dallas got the mail out of the mailbox on our way home from school. Mama usually asks Dallas to read the mail.

Mama could not read very well. From what I've heard, Mama only went to school a little while in the first grade. I've seen her sit by the oil lamp, and read the Bible every night. I guess she just reads the words that she could read and understand.

Dallas removed the letter from the envelope and began to read;

> *Dear Mama and family. I hope this finds you all fine and healthy. We are doing well. We have had a lot of snow this winter and people say the winters are like this here in Indiana.*
>
> *Bill and I have been talking about loading up our old International panel truck and moving down there and see if we can find an apartment and a job. Hopefully we will not have to live there with ya'll very long, I realize you don't have a lot of room for us. It will probably be about a month until we can get*

things done here, and be ready to make the trip down there. I am sure looking forward to seeing everyone and possibly getting a job there. And Bill is looking forward to meeting all of my family. Well, I guess I had better close for now. Write back soon. Sending ya'll all our love. Annie, Bill, and Geneva.

Mama said, "I never would have thought that would happen. Can you kids believe that? Sure is a wonderful surprise. Guess they will be here sometime in March."

This time of the year the days seem to be so long, everyone is thinking about spring and summer. One of the reasons we liked summer so well was that through the winter when we took a bath, Mama would heat some water, and we took a bath standing in what we called a foot tub, about half the size of a regular tin tub.

Now when the weather warms up enough, we could take our towel, soap and wash cloth, cross the road in front of the house, go across the field and through some woods to the branch, remove our clothes and set there on that big rock in the branch with the water flowing over the rock and me, and take myself a good bath. Brodus and I do that a lot in the summer.

Maudie and Mack pulled in the drive way today. My, were we ever surprised. Lots of hugging going on. It has been a long time since we've seen him.

Mama asked Mack, "When did you get out of the hospital? We sure were not expecting you to be out this soon."

Maudie said, "He is not supposed to be, he ran away."

"Ran away?" Mama asked. "We are so glad to see you, but why would you run away from the hospital?"

Mack replied, "I just got sick and tired of being there!"

"Well, how did you get home?"

"I put on my uniform, and got my crutches, and walked down the road a ways, and stuck out my thumb. Guess people felt sorry for me or something, but I would get out of one car and someone else would pick me up. It didn't take long to get home, and I'm glad to be here and see everyone."

"Are you well?" Mama asked.

"Oh, I still have a lot of pain of course, pain in my right leg and left shoulder, but nothing that I can't handle."

Maudie has had an apartment in town for Mack, when he was released from the hospital. Brodus and I have spent the night with her a couple of times, I guess to keep her company.

The last time we stayed with her, the sirens went off all over town.

Maudie said, "Turn off all the lights, it's a blackout!"

Then she explained that there were an unidentified aircraft close by, and the civil defense wanted the town to be as dark as possible. That practice had been set up at the end of the war, just in case it might be an enemy from the war. I'll tell you that was awfully scary.

Mack was home for about three weeks, and his pain was just too hard to bear, so Maudie took him back to Charleston, to the naval hospital.

Mama came home with the mail today.

Dallas read the letter.

> Dear Mama, and family, I want to write a short note and tell you our plans are to leave here next Friday. We think we should arrive there sometime Saturday afternoon if God is willing, and we don't have any trouble with our truck. We hope to see you then. We love you all and God bless you all, Annie.

"Well," Dallas said, "that was a short note alright."

Mama has had all of us busy after school every day this week, getting the house cleaned up the best it can be cleaned. The girls are trying to get a bedroom ready for them when they arrive. Mama has been busy baking a cake and some pies. Brodus and I had to try to get the front yard to look a little better, picking up the sticks and sweeping the driveway. We did not have grass.

It's Saturday afternoon, we had our dinner.

I said to Brodus, "Let's go out by the road and watch for them to come, I can't hardly wait to see them!"

Brodus said, "Me either, let's go"

After a little over four hours, we saw that old black international panel truck coming in to sight. Yep, that must be them, haven't seen a vehicle that looks like that on this road before, and it was, Annie and Neva waving at us.

Everyone came out of the house onto the porch. Everybody is so excited to see each other, and hugging each other.

Annie said, "Hey ya'll, I want you to meet my husband, Bill Bumgardner. You will get to know him real soon, and I know you're gonna like him."

Bill said, "I sure do hope you will." He seemed a little shy.

Bill asked Brodus, "How old are you?"

"I'm nine years old, and Hopper is seven".

That's what they called me, Hopper. I don't know why, my name is supposed to be Harper. The family has called me Hopper as long as I can remember. Sometime they call me "grasshopper". They think that's funny, I guess.

Bill said, "You mean you are two years older than Hopper, and he is bigger than you?"

"Yep," Brodus said.

"How did that happen?" Bill asked. "Did they not feed you enough?"

Brodus said, "I've been sick a lot".

I know he has heard the rest of the family tell people that so many times, that's all he knows to say, and he has.

Bill said, "Where did everyone go?"

I said, "I guess they went in the house, we better get in there. Bill said, "They might be eating, and we don't want to miss out"

"No sir," we replied.

Upon entering the house, no one was eating. Mama was in the kitchen getting food around for supper. Annie and the other girls were in conversation with each other.

Cecile asked Annie, "How do you like Indiana?"

"It's a long way from where I grew up, I don't like that, I would like to be a lot closer to my family."

Bill interrupted "Oh, she just doesn't like the cold weather."

"Now you just hush Bill, I don't mind the weather out there at all," Annie said, "I did enjoy the snow!"

Mama came to the door and said to Annie, "Mack was here last week from the hospital. I wish you could have been here then."

"Is he home now?" Annie asked.

"No, he ran away from the hospital, thought he could recuperate at home, but he couldn't, so Maudie took him back. I think he has a lot of healing to do before he is released from the hospital. He looks and acts like he is in a lot of pain."

"God bless him, Annie said, I sure hope he can recover soon, we have been praying for him."

After supper last night, we got ready, and Mama sent Brodus and me to bed.

We, were awakened this morning by Bill tickling me and Brodus under our arms, and he was just laughing and laughing. He thought that was so funny. What a way to wake up!

We did not go to church this morning, I guess because Annie's family was here.

Mama said, "Come on Harper, I need you to catch a couple of chickens for dinner."

"Yes mam," I said. So I went about chasing a chicken to catch, it didn't take long, I had a big fat one.

"This one alright Mama?" I asked, as I handed her the chicken.

"Yes," she said, "Now, catch another one like this."

We were near the wood pile, she held the chicken by the legs and laid it across chopping block where we split our stove wood, and she picked up the ax and whap, there went its head. She threw the chicken on the wood pile, where it started flipping and flopping all over the place. They do that when you cut their head off. They don't do that very long.

"Did you catch another one?" she asked.

"No, I wanted to watch you kill that one!" I caught another one for her to kill, and she did!

She put the chickens in some hot boiling water, she says the feathers are easier to pull out if you put them in hot water for a while.

What a good Sunday dinner we had today, there's nothing quite like a fresh home grown "Mama fried chicken" for dinner, plus all the trimmings. Did you ever have that? You should! Did I mention the fresh homemade coconut cake, and apple pie? All prepared on Mama's old wood burning cook stove. No one could cook like my Mama.

After dinner, when the kitchen was cleaned up, everyone went out on the front porch to relax.

Dallas asked "Do ya'll want to sing a few songs?"

"Oh, let's do," Cecile said.

"What are we going to sing?" someone asked.

"A few songs that everyone knows," Dallas said.

They have been singing for two and a half hours, having fun, and we really enjoyed that. "Amazing Grace," "Farther Along," "Kneel at the Cross." I sure like them old songs.

Brodus and I were able to talk Dallas and Cally into playing tag with us, even Bill played with us, we had a lot of fun. It's funny to watch Bill run.

This has been quite a week, to say the least, it's back to school tomorrow. Annie said she and Bill was going to go looking for a job tomorrow. I am so happy that they will be living close to us now.

Last night before we went to bed, Annie said to Bill,

"Go out to the truck and get that bag of stuff we brought for Hopper and Brodus."

He came back with a bag and set it down there beside Annie. Annie reached in the bag, and pulled out a package that had six yellow pads of lined paper. She handed it to Brodus, along with a package of ten pencils. Then she handed me the same as she gave Brodus.

"I'll bet you kids could use that in school, couldn't you?"

"Oh yes, we sure can. Thank you so much, Annie. That will be so good to have in school, thank you. And thank you too, Bill."

Walking home from school this afternoon, Annie and Bill was on their way home from town. So they stopped and picked us up, and brought us home. That was good. We got to ride in their panel truck. We went into the house, and Mama asked Annie, "Did Bill get a job?"

"Yes, he sure did, on the night shift at the cotton mill. He will be working from ten at night until six in the morning. Light maintenance, sweeping and cleaning. It don't pay all that much, but it's better than nothing. Now, I'm hoping I can find work somewhere. Then we will try to find an apartment."

She did find work and an apartment, about two weeks later. An old gas station out on the Boger City highway east of town had been turned into an apartment, and they rented it. It's pretty nice.

Bill met a man at the mill where he was working that told him where he could find a saw mill.

Bill asked Mama if Brodus and I could go with him to find that saw mill after school.

Mama said we could.

When we arrived home from school, we jumped in Bill's old truck and away we went. Bill located the saw mill off a gravel road away back in the woods. When we arrived there Bill found the man in charge, his name is Mr. Roberts, and asked him,

"Is there a chance that you could let us have some of the slabs that you are cutting off of the logs? We sure could use them to burn in our cook stove and fireplace."

Mr. Roberts asked, "Do you have some way of hauling the slabs?"

"Yes sir, in that panel truck," as he pointed to it setting over there.

"You can have all the slabs that you can haul out of here," Mr. Roberts told Bill. "Just don't expect any help loading the slabs from any of us."

Bill replied, "No sir, we will do all the loading, and I sure do thank you so very much."

Bill backed the truck over to the slab pile, and started loading the truck. Brodus and I was trying to help, but I doubt we were very much help. Bill just kept on pushing those slabs into the back of that old truck. The slabs were very long, and sticking out the rear of the truck a good ten foot. Bill finally loaded as many of the slabs in the truck as he thought the truck could haul. It was a load. We are going home.

We finally returned to the gravel road we came in on. Starting down the road, Bill said "We have us a big load in here now, feels like the front end of the truck is leaving the ground! I better not drive too fast."

I am sure it did! When we started up the long steep hill that goes up to our house, the front of that truck kept coming up off the ground, it was like a rocking horse. We could hear the slabs dragging on the road, I guess that's the reason we kept going straight. Brodus got real scared, I thought it was fun!

Bill was driving really slow.

"Everything is alright," Bill told Brodus, "We will be home in just a few minutes. When we go after another load, I'm not gonna get as big a load as we have on here now!"

"Here we are," Bill said, "We made it home, Mrs. Garris will have plenty of wood to burn for a while."

It is May, nineteen forty six.

Brodus and I received our report cards today, and both of us passed to the third grade. No one is here working in the fields. Mama has started planting some vegetables in the garden. I wonder if anyone is going to work the fields this year. I have not heard anyone talking about it.

The weather is warming up pretty good. Bill and I have hauled a couple more loads of slabs, but not as big a load as the first load we hauled.

Bill gets off work every morning at six, and comes home and tickles me and Brodus awake. Then he goes to bed, but he's always up when we get home from school. I'll be glad when they get moved in their apartment.

At the supper table tonight, Bill says to Mama,

"Mrs. Garris, would you like for me to use some of those slabs and build ya'll an outhouse?"

"Well sure Bill, all of us would love to have an outhouse. Do you think you could build one?"

"Sure I can, that would not be all that hard to do. That sure would be a lot better than just going down there in the woods!"

"Oh, yes Bill, that would be great."

"Okay then," Bill said, "I will start on it tomorrow."

When we arrived home from school this afternoon, I saw Bill dragging a couple of slabs across the back yard. He must be trying to determine the area where he will start building the outhouse.

I'm gonna go in the house and eat me a biscuit, before I go out there to see if I can help him.

Out the door I go.

"Hey Bill, is this all you've got done today?"

"I had to work last night, I went to bed this morning when you kids went to school, I have to get some rest, you know!"

"Yeah, I know. I was just kidding you."

Bill said, "Well, let's get busy."

We went looking for some tools, and there were not a lot of tools to be found. We found an old hand saw, and a hammer, and some nails in the car shed.

Bill said, "This will give us something we can use to get started with." We did find one of those old fold up rulers to measure with.

Bill said, "We have to find something to put the slab on, so it will be easy to saw the pieces off, so we went looking. Bill found an old table in the barn. He set it outside the barn.

"Hopper, do you think it will be alright to use this?"

"Oh yeah, that's ok," I told him.

He brought the table out here where I am and put a slab on it.

"I guess we will start by making a wall," he said. "I think I will make the side wall six feet, front to back," he said as he was unfolding the ruler.

He measured six feet on the slab, and made a mark on it; he picked up the saw and began to saw. He sawed one piece off and said, "I guess we will need four pieces this long." Then he sawed three more pieces that was that long. "We will need two for each end. I suppose we should make it seven foot high," he said.

He began to measure and saw pieces off seven feet long. He picked up one of the pieces that was six foot long and placed it on the ground out of the way. He then picked up a seven foot long board, placed it on the end of the six foot board, with the end of that board flush with the top of the six foot piece, and flush with the end of the six foot board.

"Hopper," he said, "Hand me that can of nails and the hammer." He nailed that board to the board that will eventually be the top of the wall, and he nailed seven foot boards all across the six foot board, to the end of the six foot board.

Then he placed a six foot board under the other end of the seven foot boards, placing the board flush with the left and bottom end of the seven foot board on the left side. He nailed all the boards along what will be the bottom side of the wall. "There," Bill said, "that's one wall finished."

"Bill," I said. "It didn't come out flush on the top or the bottom of the right side."

Bill remarked, "It's good enough."

And I said, "There are some pretty big openings between the boards."

Bill said, "Well it's better than going off down there in the woods, and just having to squat down on the ground."

"You are right about that," I said.

"We had better quit for today," Bill said. "Supper will probably be ready soon. Maybe we will get another wall put together tomorrow evening."

"Alright, that's a good idea," I said.

I had me a glass of cornbread and milk for supper, that's all I wanted.

Mama asked Bill, "How are you coming with the outhouse?"

"It's coming along," Bill told her. "I got one wall put together this afternoon. I will get another wall finished tomorrow evening."

Bill did get the back and other side wall finished the next few days. On Friday, and Saturday we finished a wall that left an opening for the door, which was on the back side of the building from the house. And then he nailed a couple of slabs, smooth side up, from one side wall to the other for a seat. He cut an opening that a person would set over to use the toilet. He did cover the front of the seat, where your legs would be, when and if, you chose to use the toilet. There was never a roof or door put on the "toilet".

If you know what slabs are, you know that the edges of slabs are not straight or even. Therefore, there were some pretty big cracks in the walls, fortunately enough, the building was far enough away from the house that it did serve as a certain amount of privacy. O.K. so the building was not perfect by any stretch. But, as Bill said, it will be better than going out into the woods. He was right about that.

Bill remarked many times that he was not a carpenter, and I found that to be true. However, he did do the best that he could do, he was trying to do something for us, and we were very thankful for his efforts. I know the ladies were glad to have the "toilet" to use.

If you did not know, a slab is the first piece of wood that is cut from a log at the saw mill, before they began to cut the log into lumber. Of course, one side of the piece is round, and there are four slabs from every log.

Brodus and I sure do like Bill, he plays with us, teases us a lot, and he loves to tickle us on our knees, and under our arms, he is kind of like a kid himself, and a good person.

Annie and Bill finally got moved in their apartment east of Lincolnton, on the Bogor City Highway. They seem to like it so far, it gives us more room here at our house.

It's June 1946. School is out until the day after Labor Day. It is kind of boring around here now. No farming going on. We have to tie the cow out by the road so she can eat some green grass every day. That's Cally's job, because she likes to ride her out to wherever she is going to tie her out.

Mack slipped away from the hospital again last week. Maudie brought him out to see us. Sure was good to see him again. He says he is feeling pretty good.

Mack said, "Well, I have to go down in the woods, I guess."

Mama told Mack that Bill had built us a outhouse.

"Really?" Mack said, "I guess I will go to the toilet." He walked out the back door, and down to the outhouse, turned around and came back to the house.

He said, "I cannot use that, because I cannot bend my right leg, and the wall is too close for me to stretch my leg out in front of me. I guess the boys are gonna have to go to the woods with me, and help me bend over a real small tree, so I can hang my butt over it, and do my business."

As we walked across the barnyard, Mack told me and Brodus to pick up some corn cobs for obvious reasons, and we did. When he finished his 'business', he hollered at us, and said bring me some more corn cobs. We brought him more corn cobs. And he hollered again and said, "I need more corn cobs." Finally he was done!

We went back to the house, and went in the front room where Mama was sitting. Mack said to Mama, "When the boys were getting corn cobs for me, Harper said to me, my goodness, you must have a big ass!"

Mama looked at me and asked, "Did you say that?" Well, I could just feel that hickory switch hitting my rear end. I knew Mama would believe him.

Then, Mack spoke up and said, "Mama, I was just kidding, he didn't say that, I was just kidding around." I'm sure glad he said that, or I would have surely got my tail warmed up good.

In our house, we had better not use words like, ass, durn, darn, butt, heck, dang, shut up, or any word that sounds like a curse word.

Last night Mack was telling us about one time when he got one of the worst beatings that he ever got from Daddy. His story went like this.

"Daddy went to town one day for some reason, and took along the cross cut saw. He knew a man in town that did a very good job sharpening saws. After taking care of what he wanted to do in town, he headed back home. About a mile out of town, Daddy remembered that he didn't take the saw to get it sharpened. He didn't want to turn the wagon around, and go back to town. So he stopped at a blacksmith shop just a little ways up the road, and asked Clyde, the man that owned the shop, to sharpen his saw, and that he would pick it up later, and he came on home.

Three days later he says to me, Mack, I left the crosscut saw at Clyde's blacksmith shop a couple days ago, he should have it sharpened by now. He is as slow as a snail and he can't sharpen saws worth a damn, but I left it there anyhow. Daddy told me, I want you to go get that saw and get back here as soon as you can! We have a lot of work to get done today.

So I'm on my way to Clyde's blacksmith shop. Upon arrival, I told Clyde I was there to pick up Daddy's crosscut saw that he left here to be sharpened. He said, you must be Harper's son. I told him I was.

Clyde said it wasn't finished yet, if you have a few minutes I will get it finished. I told him I did not have much time because Daddy told me to hurry back. Oh well, he said it will only take a few minutes.

The longer I waited, I was getting more worried about getting my ass torn up by Daddy when I returned home, because it took me so long. So I walked over to where he was working and said, Mr. Clyde, I don't think I can wait any longer. Daddy told me that you were as slow as a snail and that you couldn't sharpen a saw worth a damn.

Clyde said Okay, okay, it's all finished, take it and get out of here.

I got the saw home in good enough time. Daddy seemed to think everything was good.

But when Daddy happened to see Clyde about a week later, Clyde told Daddy what I told him, that Daddy had told me about him. I guess it must have really pissed Daddy off, I swear he turned in to a mad man. I had never seen him like that.

I said Daddy, you told me to hurry back home and I was trying to get him to hurry, I didn't know what to do. Daddy just said, shut up and kept on beating me. When he finished whipping me, I knew I was going to Heaven, because he beat the living hell out of me. I just can't seem to win for losing."

Mack always has plenty of stories to tell about his early days growing up.

Mama would let me and Brodus stay up late when we had company. We stayed up late tonight, I think we stayed up until about eight thirty. That was after Mack told one more story.

Mack said, "Of course we only had one car to use. Boyd had been driving a couple of years before I was old enough to get my license to drive, and we had some fights about who was gonna use the car for a date or whatever!

Daddy made a rule. You boys will have to alternate the times you use the car. On this particular night, it was my turn to use the car. I had made a date with a girl that I was fond of. Now, let me tell you, when either one of us had the car for an evening, we had better be home by ten-o-clock. I was the first one to break that rule. As I pulled in the yard, I saw Daddy standing on the front porch. The time was ten thirty. As I got out of the car, he was walking toward me with his buggy whip in his hand.

I said to myself, I think I am a little too old, and a little too big to be whipped with a buggy whip. I said Daddy, you are my Father, and I have always tried to obey you, and you gave me many beatings that it took days to heal from. Now I am telling you, no more! I know you are an old man, but if you hit me one time with that whip, you will never hit me or anyone else again. Now you decide what you want to do.

Daddy just stood there for what seemed like hours and he dropped the whip on the ground, turned around, and walked back in to the house. And I just stood there shaking, but, he never whipped me again after that!"

I think Mack was home with Maudie for about a month, until he was just overcome by the pain. Maudie took him back to the VA in Charleston, SC.

The summer is just flying by. Burk and Myrtle was here for their summer visit, Annie, Bill, and Neva came over on Sunday afternoon when we made ice cream. They sure did enjoy the ice cream, and getting to see Burk and Myrtle. Guess it's been a very long time since they have seen each other.

The dog days of summer, I heard someone say, and it is hot. At least there is not any cotton to pick this fall. The family is happy about that.

School will be starting after Labor Day. I will be in the second grade. I am looking forward to the second grade.

Mack was officially released from the VA hospital a couple weeks ago. His discharge said he was totally disabled. He will receive total disability from the U.S. Navy, and also he can receive medical treatment from the VA as long as he lives.

Brodus and I are back in school again. We started back yesterday. September and October are beautiful months of the year. And we don't have too many chores since we have no crops to harvest. So we have time to play awhile after school. Dallas and Cally play with us sometimes. We usually play ball, tag or hide and seek after dark.

Brodus and I are going to spend the night with Annie and Bill Friday night, we are looking forward to that. They are going to eat supper with us, and then we will go home with them.

November, 1946

Brodus and I, and the girls, are busy cutting up the slabs to burn in the cook stove and fireplace this winter. They say it's going to be a cold winter again this year. Bill, bless his heart, has hauled a great big pile of slabs for us to burn this winter. We are very thankful for that. He just loves to do that I guess.

Christmas is coming up soon. Lots of preparations are being made for the holiday season. The girls are getting very excited.

I asked Mama, "Do you think I could get one of those little red wagons that I saw in the Sears Roebuck catalog?"

Mama replied, "Son, we will just have to wait and see. I don't know what Brodus wants for Christmas."

Today is Christmas Eve, everyone is busy, rushing around, Mama is making a fruit cake, she bakes one every year at Christmas. She baked a coconut cake also. She has baked a couple pies.

Annie, Bill, and Neve will be here for dinner tomorrow. I think they will be here this evening for Christmas Eve celebration.

I asked Brodus, "What did you ask for, for Christmas?"

He said, "I asked for one of those little metal dump trucks that would actually dump stuff out."

"Yep," I said, "that would be fun to play with."

Cally, Dallas, and Cecile decorated a Christmas tree that we found out in the woods, it is real pretty. I'm sure Mama will fix us all a poke with all the goodies in it, like hard candy, apple, orange, and some chocolate candy, and all kinds of nuts, after us kids go to bed. She always does that on Christmas Eve. It's the only time of the year when we get goodies like that, and we look forward to that. Mama made a cake, and some cookies, and Cally and I took it up to the McMurry's on Christmas Eve. They sure did appreciate it.

January, 1947

Christmas has come and gone. We all had a wonderful Christmas. Santa Claus brought me a flatbed metal truck, and Brodus a metal dump truck, that really dumps, that's what he asked for. We got a little Radio Flyer wagon. We are so happy about what we got for Christmas.

Oh yes, and we did get our pokes, Christmas morning. Wow, what a Christmas!

Mama said, "Now boys, you can use that wagon to haul the wood from the wood pile to the front porch, to burn in the fireplace."

My, my, how time flies, here it is the end of February. It's Friday evening, and Annie, Bill and Neva are coming for supper.

At the supper table, Annie said, "I'm glad all of you are here. I have something to tell ya'll. We hope, what I'm gonna tell you won't upset you. Bill and I have decided that we are going to move back to Indiana. We think the employment opportunities up there are a lot better than they are down here."

Mama said, "Oh my goodness, we sure hate to hear you tell us that. But, I guess we can't blame you, if you think there are better jobs where you can make more money. But you are so far away up there. I guess that's the reason I hate to see ya'll move.

Cecile said, "I guess I had better go ahead and tell you now, I am going to Indiana with them, and see if I can find a good job.

Mama replied, "You know I hate to see you go Ceicle, well, of course I hate to see all of you go. If your mind is made up, then what can I say? I guess all I know to say is, I wish you the best of everything."

That was a lot of bad news for us, and especially Dallas, and Cally.

"We will be okay," Mama said. I know Mama was hurting inside, but Mama never showed her emotions, she never did show how she really did feel.

Two weeks later.

They all left for Indiana today. We sure hated to see them go, especially not knowing when we would see them again. Everyone wished them well. Dallas and Cally was crying as they pulled out of the driveway. It will be a big void around here with them gone. I tried to be a big boy, but I went around to the side of the house and shed tears myself.

Our time is spent now going to school every day and coming home and doing our chores. My birthday is coming up pretty soon, I will be eight years old on April nineteenth.

When we came home from school today, Dallas and Cally was in the kitchen talking to Mama.

At the supper table tonight, Mama told Brodus and me what they were talking about earlier. She said Mack came by today, and told her that Maude's Father, Odell Parker was a contractor, he builds houses. He told Mack to tell Mama if she could sell the farm, he would build us a house in Shelby, North Carolina, at a very reasonable price. That's where the Parkers, and Mack and Maude live now.

Mama said, "So, I will try to sell the farm, and see what happens."

Mama and the rest of us sure are hoping that the farm will sell pretty soon. That would be just wonderful to move into a new home, we cannot even imagine that.

It hasn't been very long now since Mama put the farm up for sale, and today some men came to the house and wanted to look at the farm. They were here for a couple hours, I guess.

At the supper table tonight Mama said, "We have been blessed, God answers prayers. The people that were here today were from the County Home. They are going to buy our farm. They said it would be ideal for the able bodied men at the Home, to work the ground, possibly planting and growing some of the food for use at the Home."

Mama let Mack know that the farm was sold, and that Mr. Parker

could go ahead and start building our house. It was agreed that we
could live here in this house until we could move in to our new house
in Shelby.

No one could begin to imagine how excited our family was. Living
in a new house, our family, just a dream? No, it's going to be a reality.
Mr. Parker told Mama if the weather permits, we could be moving in
by early fall.

First of March, 1947

One month later when we came home from school, there were
several men here working on the house, repairing the front porch,
they brought a tractor, and a man was plowing in the field. Many
things were going on. The man working on the porch said his name
was Ralph, he was very friendly.

It's not too far to Shelby where our house is being built, Mama said
that we might be able to go over there sometime this summer and see
how it's coming along. Sure looking forward to that.

Just wondering how it will be going to a different school when we
are living in Shelby, for that matter everything will be different from
living on this farm.

Mama received a letter from Mr. Parker today, telling her that we
could move in the house any time. He said that there was some work
he had to do yet, but on rainy days, when he couldn't work outside, he
would come and finish up on the inside of our house.

Chapter Nine

So we moved in, with the help of Mack and neighbors. Mr. McMurry used his fertilizer delivery truck, and hauled all the furniture that we had in our house on that truck, to Shelby. We had already sold our mule and cow.

The new house did not have electricity, or running water, no bathroom, but we did have a outhouse, which was built by a real carpenter. There was a room that would have been our bathroom, if we would have had running water in our house. I guess Mama could not afford that at the time, Mama said we could use that little room for the closet. All of us hung our clothes in that room. Anyhow, there were no closets anywhere else in the house.

Mama had to buy a kerosene burning cook stove. She did not like that stove at all. Of course we did not have a sink in the kitchen. We had a table under the window, with two big pans to wash and dry the dishes. In our living room we had a fireplace, where we had a small "Warm Morning Heater" set up. That little heater sure will keep us warm. We did not have any doors inside the house. Mr. Parker told Mama to just hang curtains over the open doorways, and she did.

We had a small front porch, and a back porch, that was all the way across the back of the house, that will be very handy, Mama said.

We just don't know for sure, but most all of the children think Mama got taken advantage of.

Mama received a letter from Ceicle today. At the supper table Dallas read the letter to the rest of us.

Dear Mama and family, not very long after I came to Indiana, I met a man where I was working, and we have been dating ever since I met him. He is a wonderful man, and we will be getting married next month. I know you will like him when ya'll meet him.

Shortly after we moved in our new home, Mama found out that several of the neighbors tried to get a petition to keep us from moving in, before we had indoor plumbing. Guess they did not get enough signatures.

There was a house behind ours. Their property line bordered ours. There was a lady living there, Mrs. Evans, with her two sons Jack and Bobby.

Mama went down to Mrs. Evans to introduce herself, and get acquainted with her, and to ask her if there was a chance we could get water from her outside water faucet, until we got our city water hooked up to our house. She told Mama that we were welcome to take all the water we needed. Mama told us that she was a very nice lady.

If you left our house going west about a city block, and turn left on Cleveland Ave. that street would curve around, and go east past the front of the Evans home. If you continue down the hill you will come to Park Ave. You have to turn right on Park Ave. and go about a city block, and you will come to highway 74.

I could walk out our back door, and walk across our back yard, and walk through the woods, and get to Cleveland Ave. very quickly. If I would walk down to highway 74, and go across the highway, on the left was an old gas station building someone was living in. If I continued walking down that dirt road I will see one room cottages on the left, and houses on the right. All of these houses belonged to Mr. Patterson, and the people that lived in these houses worked at Patterson's greenhouses. Continuing down the dirt road to a sharp curve around to the right I will see a line of greenhouses to my left, and a few on the right. And back to highway 74 again. I just wanted to give you an idea of the area where we lived.

Although there were many issues about the house, we are so happy to be here. We have never lived in a house that had such conveniences as running water, and electricity anyhow!

For our family, living here was a whole different world, especially for Brodus and me. Our house was surrounded by trees, and a lot of them. We sure have a large area to play in.

Going west down the road, about a quarter of a mile, there were additional greenhouses that belonged to the Pattersons, a large flower farm. There must be about fifteen or more green houses on both sides of highway 74.

Cally said, "Tomorrow I am going down there to the greenhouse, and ask for a job. I guess it won't hurt to go and ask."

Cally did go down there this morning, and yes, she got a job. She starts to work tomorrow morning. The flower farm is classified as agriculture, so they don't even have to pay minimum wage. But as she said, whatever I make, will be better than nothing. That's what I was making.

She said the owner of the flower farm was a Mr. U.L. Patterson, and they wholesale flowers throughout the south eastern United States.

Dallas has been living in Shelby for about nine months, with Mack and Maudie. She has been working at the F.W. Woolworth Dime store. She works behind the candy counter. She really likes that job, yeah, I would too!

About a month after we moved into our "new" home, on a Saturday after dinner, Mama was getting ready to go to town and she said to Brodus and me, "You boys are going to town with me."

We haven't been to town since we moved here, and we were very excited about going. It is three miles to Shelby.

Mack picked us up, and drove us to town. He let us out at the dime store where Dallas works, and told Mama he would pick us up here at four thirty.

Mama said, "Okay, we will be right here waiting for you, thank you very much."

We went in the dime store, there's Dallas right there behind the candy counter. I have never seen so much candy in my whole life.

Mama said, "You boys pick out what kind of candy you want." Sure is a lot to choose from!

Dallas said, "I can help you choose a real good kind."

"Okay," we said, "what would be the best?"

"Right here," she said, as she pointed at a certain kind, "this is chocolate covered peanuts, you will like them."

Mama said, "Just give us a half pound of them."

Wow, I never knew a half pound was so much!

Mama gave us some of them, and boy, they were good, we have never had any candy like that before.

Mama said, "I am going to look in some other stores down the street. Dallas, could the boys stay here at the store until I return."

"Sure," Dallas replied, "if you are not gonna be gone very long."

"Oh I will be back soon."

Dallas said, "Brodus, you and Harper can look around in the store if you want to, but don't touch anything."

Off we go, boy this is an awful big store. They have everything in here, all kinds of toys. Guess we can only dream about some of those.

It wasn't very long until Mama came back to the store to wait for Mack to pick us up. We know how Mama is, she likes to go in a dime store, and she will look at every item they have in the store, and leave without buying one thing! Guess it's cheaper doing that.

Dallas told Mama to leave me and Brodus at the store, when she leaves with Mack, and that we can ride home with her on the bus. That's how she gets home every day.

Dallas gets off work at five thirty every day. She said when she gets off work, that we will go next door to the drug store, and get a sandwich before we go to the bus station.

At the drug store, the girl came over to our booth and asked, "Can I help ya'll?"

Dallas asked Brodus, "What kind of sandwich do you want?"

Brodus looked straight up at that girl, and said politely, "Peanut butter."

"Oh Brodus," Dallas said, "they don't have peanut butter sandwiches in here."

"That's what I have at home," Brodus said, "Okay then, I'll just have a banana sandwich."

"No, no," Dallas said, "they don't have bologna here, either!"

"Well then, what can I have?"

"Dallas said, "How about a grilled cheese, you like that, don't you?"

"That'll be good," Brodus said, looking up at the waitress and smiling.

"What do you want, Harper?" Dallas asked.

Well, I'm thinking I had better not order peanut butter, or bologna, so I said, "I'll just have a grilled cheese sandwich."

Mama buys sliced bread now and then. At home, we make a bologna sandwich, or a peanut butter, or even a banana sandwich.

I do know Dallas was very embarrassed at us, however, in our defense, this was the first time we had ever eaten in a restaurant.

There is so much going on around here, we are trying to learn all we can about the area, and there is so much to learn.

I have learned that to get to our house from Shelby, go east on U.S. Highway 74, continue on to the Cleveland Country Club. Turn left on Elizabeth Church road, you will see part of the golf course on the left, go past the green houses, and go past Cleveland Ave. and the next house on the right is where we live. There is a small ditch you drive through, into to our driveway. There is a big embankment in front of our house down to the highway.

In order to get rid of the embankment, someone told Mama that she would have to have water tile put in the ditch, the length of our lot, and have it all covered with dirt. And that would be very expensive. That was out of the question, because Mama could not afford that.

At the junction of Highway 74, and state road 180, there is a small grocery store. It is known as Dad Blanton's store, and he does a big business.

This morning we are on our way to school. Mama bought us brand new overalls, and we are looking good for our first day of school.

Just beyond the new brick school building, there is an old school building, very old. We walked in there, and a very nice lady asked us what grade we were in?

I told her, the third grade.

She asked, "Are you boys new students?"

"Yes 'mam, we are," I told her.

"Are you brothers?" She asked.

"Yes 'mam," I replied, "My name is Harper. And this is Brodus, my brother. Our last name is Garris."

She took us to the third grade class, and showed us the desk where we would set. The building was really big, and the grades are separated by great big curtains.

They made an announcement that the new school building would be finished within three to four weeks, and then we would be attending classes over there.

We got acquainted with a lot of boys and girls today. I'm sure I will really like this school. Mrs. Holbrook is our teacher, she seems very nice.

Our school (Elizabeth) is located on highway 180 that runs north and south. As you leave the school traveling north, you will pass the county home. Then you will come to highway seventy four, that runs east and west. That road goes north east to the prison camp. Also at this intersection is Blanton's grocery store, and the fairground grill. As you continue north thru the intersection, you will pass Donald Cook's house, and the next great big house is where Mackie Poston lives. There are many pecan trees in their yard.

When school let out today, there were several students who walked home the same way we were going. We talked to Mackie as we walked along. He seems to be a really good kid. I think we could have a lot of fun playing together, maybe he could come to our house sometime after school, and play for a while.

At the supper table tonight, Cally was talking about being real tired. She said they were potting mums all day long. At least she was working in the shed where it wasn't nearly as hot as it was in the greenhouses.

The shed was a large building about 75 foot wide and 200 feet long. The cooler was in this building

She said there was a man that would mix the soil, and keep her potting bench with plenty of potting soil. She was telling us that they would fill up a flat with eight flower pots, and another man would put the flats on a small cart, and push the cart up through the green houses. He would empty the cart of flats on a empty bed, and the pots had to be placed on the bed just a certain way. That was called "off bearing".

There was a big door in the middle of the shed. Go through that door and there was a wide cement walkway. On each side of the walkway there were flower beds. All the flower beds were about two and a half feet high, and four feet wide and about seventy feet long, and the isle between the flower beds was about two feet wide.

There was a great big fan at the end of each green house, blowing out, and a door at each end of every green house. As you went up the walkway, you would go out of one green house into another one. And there were about fifteen glass houses.

They grew just about all the different kinds of flowers that you could think of. I'm telling you it was a very large flower farm all under glass.

They grew all the holiday flowers, Easter, Christmas, and Mother's Day, and that was very busy times, to get the flowers delivered to all of the customers before each holiday. They also grew many other flowers all year around, such as hhydrangeas, gardenia gloxinia, gladiolus, chrysanthemums, as well as many other cut flowers and stem roses.

As we were to learn later, Patterson Flowers would be the source of our income for many years. After leaving the farm and coming to Shelby, I guess Mama and the girls were happy to have a job with a steady income. Yes, I said Mama, because she went to work in the greenhouses too. Life was very rough in the late forties, but they knew with their jobs at the greenhouses, we were so much better off than when we lived on the farm in Lincolnton.

Mama and the girls were talking last night.

Dallas said, "You know, if I could get a job at the greenhouse where ya'll are working, all of us would be working together, and go and come to work at the same time."

And just like that, Dallas went down there, and sure enough, she got a job.

Mama told Brodus and me that we would have to wash the dishes every day when we came home from school, and every Wednesday we had to wash our overalls when we got home from school, and hang them up to dry, so we could wear them to school the next day. Needless to say, we were not real happy about that rule, but we knew better than to argue, and we didn't!

However, that was not all. Mama and the girls asked us if we would like to make a quarter every week. Sure, we told them.

"Okay" Mama said, "You wash the dishes after every meal, except Sunday. "On Saturday, put furniture polish on all the furniture, sweep all the floors, and mop. Sweep the back porch, and yard. Then you will get your quarter."

That is more money than we have ever had. For that matter, I didn't think it was a question, I'm sure she meant we would be doing those chores, and we do!

We started to school this week in the new school. Boy, is this a nice, brick building, and it is big. We enter the front door to a very long hallway, with classrooms on both sides of the hallway.

As the weeks go by, we go to school, come home and do our chores.

When we left school today, we asked Mackie if his mother would let him come to our house and play awhile.

He said, "Ya'll come in the house with me when we get there, and I will ask her."

In the house, his Mother was in the kitchen working over the sink.

"Mama," Mackie said, "these are my two new friends I have been telling you about. This is Harper and Brodus Garris."

"Hey there," she said, looking at us.

"They asked if I could go home with them, and play a little while."

"Where do you boys live?" she asked.

We told her, and she asked if it would be okay with our mother.

I said, "I'm sure it will be okay with her."

Mrs. Poston said that he could come over, and that he would have to be home by five-o-clock.

Mackie said, "Thanks Mom, I'll be home by five-o-clock for sure." And away we came. We have never had anyone come to our house to play with us before.

Of course we had a lot of fun until Mackie had to leave at about four forty five. We played cowboy all the time he was here.

As the days and weeks passed, we began to know each other quite well. His real father had passed away several years ago, and his mother had remarried a man named Grady Poston. After they were married for some time, Grady adopted Mackie, making his last name Poston. Grady had a brother who lived with them, his name was John D. Everyone knew John D, he did not talk, John D was retarded. He was never seen without his leather strap; it measured about fifteen inches long and about one half inch wide. He twirled it around his finger, all the time. John spent a lot of his time up at Blanton's Grocery store.

He would just stand around, watching the people come and go, never bothered anyone.

Some men liked to tease him, they would take his leather strap from him, and that would make him oh, so angry. He would chase them around, trying to get his strap back. They would always give it back to him. They just liked to tease him. I always felt sorry for him.

Grady has a lot of cows, and a great big barn. He milks his cows, and processes the milk and sales it. He has a regular milk truck that he delivers milk every morning house to house. He uses them big heavy milk bottles, and puts the cardboard lids in the top of each bottle. He picks up the empty bottles on his route, and brings them back to his milk house. He washes them every evening, and uses them over and over. He is a hardworking man. He delivers milk to our house every Monday, Wednesday, and Friday.

We celebrated Thanksgiving yesterday, just our family, and we are truly thankful for the new house we are living in.

Just last week, Mama and the girls went to town, and paid to have our electricity hooked up. Now we have a light bulb in the center of the ceiling in every room, and on the front and back porch. This is the first house we have ever lived in with electricity. We are beginning to think we are wealthy, well, at least I am!

Christmas has come and gone and we celebrated the birth of Jesus more, and better than we ever have. Brodus and I got a cap gun, belt and holster, and a cowboy hat. Wow, we have never had a Christmas like this before. We can hardly wait to show Mackie what we got for Christmas, and of course we are wondering what he got for Christmas. He got a horse!

My goodness, another year is here. I will turn ten years old this year. I'm hoping we will have as good a year as last year. Harry S. Truman is our president now. We are hearing a lot about him.

Mama and the girls are working every day at the greenhouses. Brodus and I are in school every day.

Sometime Brodus and I walk down to the greenhouses to see Mama when we get out of school. We have come to know many of the people who work there.

Traveling east on highway 74, at the junction of highway 180 there is another road that angles off to the north east. (Guess this would be called five points) This road is called the prison camp road, it only goes about a mile and at the end is a large prison camp. It's big. Every day they load truckloads of prisoners, and go out and work alongside the road. The prisoners always wear striped clothes, and leg chains, and usually have two guards with each crew.

Somehow, Mama found out that there was a prisoner there who was a barber, and he only charged twenty five cents for a haircut. Mama decided that Brodus and I could go up there to the prison camp, and get our haircut. Other barber shops charged fifty cents. Of course, we were not happy about that, and we did not want to go to that prison camp to get our haircut, having no idea what to expect. So here we go, walking up to the prison camp.

"Wonder where he will cut our hair?" I asked Brodus.

Brodus said, "I don't know, but I hope we don't have to set in his cell while he cuts our hair. If that's what we have to do, I'm going back home. I just won't get my hair cut."

I said, "Oh I don't think we will have to do that, I'll bet he will have a special place where he cuts hair, at least I hope so!"

Well, here we are, there is a sign that says "office".

Brodus said, "I guess we can go in there, and find out where the barber cuts hair."

Upon entering the door, looking across the room, an older man set behind a desk.

"Come on in," he said. "And what can I do for you boys?"

Of course we are very nervous, but I replied, "Mama said she heard that there was a barber here, and she sent us up here to get a haircut." Nervously, I asked, "Are you the barber?"

With a broad grin across his face, he said, "No, I am not a barber, but we do have a prisoner here that is a barber. Let me get his clippers, and stool out here, and I will go get him."

"Is he a nice man?" Brodus asked.

"Oh yes, he is a very nice man," he said. Unlocking the door behind him, he said, "I'll be right back."

The door opens again and all we see is the biggest black man that we had ever seen. My heart dropped down to my waist, and then I saw the guard behind him. Scared us half to death! The guard is the man we saw behind the desk when we walked in.

"Hey boys," he said, "you in need of a haircut, huh?"

"Yes sir," I replied.

"Oh," he said, "Don't "sir" me, just call me Al," as he motioned for one of us to climb up on the stool. "And don't be nervous or scared. No one here is gonna hurt you, I'll see to that. I've been in this prison camp for thirty three years, and always will be. I am regarded as a trustee. I will not tell you why I am here."

We did relax then, he seemed like a very nice man, soft spoken, and he looked to be maybe sixty five or so. We are leaving here feeling pretty good about the experience.

As we were leaving, Al said, "You boys come back to see me now, okay?"

"Okay" we said.

When we returned home, Mama asked us if we got along alright at the prison camp.

"Yes," Brodus told her, "Everything went real good. They were very nice."

"Well, I'm glad to hear that!" Mama said.

Here we go again. We received a letter from Cecile today. She said her and Jack would be coming down here in May. She said her and Jack was going to try to find a job, and live here.

The weather is warming up here real nice now, a lot of kids at school are playing marbles at recess, including me, and I am one more marble shooting fool. Mackie was real good at it too. Sometimes other kids from school would come to our house just to play marbles.

We always played what we called "for keeps." Meaning that if a player shot, and knocked a marble out of the ring, that was his marble.

Draw a circle about two feet across, and each player would put the same amount of marbles in the center of the ring. One of the players would "jack" them up, meaning make his fingers in the shape of a triangle, and make all the marbles in the shape of the triangle, if there were enough marbles to do that, there usually were. I have played with as many as two, to ten marbles from each player, in the ring. Every time a player would shoot, and knock a marble out of the ring, and the marble we were shooting with, (we called that marble our toy) stayed inside the ring, we called that "stuck", then we could shoot again. That player could keep shooting, as long as he knocked a marble out of the ring, and his toy stayed inside the ring.

Usually, I would go to school with no marbles at all. I would ask another kid to loan me three marbles, and I would pay him back six, at the end of recess.

I would ask some other kid to play me a game of marbles.

"Let's play twos," I would say, "and you can shoot first."

"Okay," he would say.

Well, he would shoot, and not knock a marble out. Then I would shoot, and usually shoot, until I knocked all the marbles out of the ring. So I would pay back the six marbles that I promised, and usually have fifteen or twenty marbles in my pocket that I won. By the end of the school day, I would have fifty or sixty marbles, and I would sell them, two marbles for a penny.

On the way home, there was a restaurant called the "Fairground Grill". I would go in there and play the juke box. On the juke box they had songs by Lester Flatt and Earl Scruggs, I really like their music, especially "Flint Hill Special" and I spend all my money that I won playing marbles, playing that song. Each play cost a nickel.

You see, Earl Scruggs was born and raised between Shelby and Boiling Springs, North Carolina. He lived on a road that was named Flint Hill Road.

Jack and Cecile finally arrived here a couple of days ago. Sure is good to see Cecile, and meet her husband Jack. He is a pretty big fellow, and seems to be very nice. Cecile seems really happy to be back in North Carolina again.

At the supper table tonight, Jack said, "I think tomorrow I will go for a ride and see if I can find any place where they are hiring. I'm gonna have to find a job. Ya going with me Ceil?" That's what he called Cecile, Ceil! We didn't really like that, she is his wife! After supper we just sit in the living room and visited.

Mama asked, "How is Annie's family getting along?"

Cecile replied, "They were just fine when we left, they are working every day. Annie is working in a big factory, where they make all kinds of wiring products for the automobile industry. Bill is working in a factory where they manufacture ceiling tile. The name of that company is Celotex."

Mama said, "Sounds like they are staying busy."

It's getting late, so I guess I had better go get, what we call "the bucket" and bring it in, just in case one of the girls have to pee during the night. We put it in what is supposed to be the bathroom. As you know, we have no indoor plumbing, and oh my, the girls could never go out to the outhouse at night! So, here's the deal, I bring it in, and take it out and empty it, for a week, and Brodus does the same, every other week. What a chore, and that's the way it is. At least we have a real outhouse to take it to. Yes sir.

Up early, go to school. Learn stuff, and play marbles.

Mama has been telling me if I didn't quit crawling around on my knees playing marbles, and wearing holes in my overalls, that she was gonna sew buttons on the inside of the knees. She hasn't yet! I won forty one marbles today. Came home, washed the breakfast and dinner dishes, swept the kitchen, well, Brodus and I did.

Jack and Cecile came home about four thirty. Jack said he found a job, that's good. He starts to work tomorrow. He didn't tell us where.

While we were eating supper, Jack said, "I got a job today."

Mama asked, "Where?"

Jack replied, "We stopped at a gas station in town, and while the attendant was putting gas in my car, I asked him if he knew of any place where a fellow could get a job. He said his brother-in-law works out at the big cemetery here in town, and he said they were hiring. So I left the gas station, and went out to the cemetery, and located the man in charge and talked to him. He said, "You are just the man I am looking for. Bet you could mow a lot of grass in a day."

"I'll do the best I can," I told him. He asked if I could start in the morning, I said I sure can. He said, "See you at six in the morning. We like to get as much done as we can before that hot sun starts bearing down on us, and we knock off around two thirty. We take one half hour for lunch at eleven."

"I told him, that sounds good to me. Ceil, you can drive me in there in the morning, that way you can bring my dinner at eleven."

Later this evening I heard Mama ask Cecile. "Why can't you fix him some sandwiches to take for his dinner? That would save some trips driving to town and back, two or three times a day."

Cecile said, "Oh Mama, he won't eat sandwiches. He has to have a hot meal at noon."

Mama said, "If he was my husband, he would eat sandwiches!"

It's getting late, and I'm sleepy, guess I had better go grab the bucket and get to bed. I'll be getting up at six.

Up at six, Cecile has already left to take Jack to work. Brodus is still in bed, guess he is not feeling well. Mama told him to stay home from school today.

That sun sure is hot today, almost too hot to play marbles, and I didn't play very much. Some of the students were playing baseball, so I played with them the second recess, and that was fun! And boy, it was hot out there on that baseball field today!

Returned home from school, and found that Jack, Cecile and Brodus were here.

"Did you work today?" I asked Jack.

He replied, "Don't you know that I get off at two thirty?"

"Oh yes," I said, "I forgot that."

Brodus and I are out in the woods playing, and Brodus said to me,

"Would you like to know what really happened, when I went with Cecile to take Jack's dinner to him this morning?"

I said, "Yeah, tell me!"

Brodus said, "You better not tell anyone I told you!"

"I won't tell anyone, now tell me."

Brodus said, "We went over there to the cemetery where Jack works, and we set down under a tree. Jack came over where we were, and Cecile opened up his dinner basket, Jack set down beside of Cecile and ate his dinner. Everything seemed to be okay. When his lunch time was over, he stood up and started to stagger around a little bit, Cecile said to me, "Oh Brodus, he's gonna faint. Don't let him fall." So I jumped up and grabbed him the best I could, trying to keep him from falling down in the grass. And I was able to hold him up. His boss, and a couple other men weren't very far away. Cecile motioned for them to come over. They came over, and by that time I had helped him set down by the tree. One of them asked what happened. Cecile told them,

"I guess he fainted, he is not used to working in this hot sun."

"Yeah," the man said, "Are you gonna be alright?"

Jack said, "Oh, I think I will."

His boss said to Cecile, "Just take him on home now. It will take a few days for him to get used to this work, we'll see you tomorrow, Jack."

Jack said "o.k."

"So we came home," Brodus said.

"As big as he is, I cannot imagine you holding him up," I said. "He must weigh over two hundred pounds."

"Well I did," Brodus said.

"Okay, I did not say you didn't. I am saying you are pretty small to be holding up a man as big as him, I am glad he didn't fall on you."

At the supper table tonight, Cecile was telling what happened today. Just about the same story that Brodus told me when I returned home from school.

Cecile told us when Jack gets really hot, he might pass out. Cecile said Jack had passed out many times since she met him. Wow, I think that begs a big question!

Mama remarked, "I don't understand why he took a job mowing grass, as hot as it has been."

Cecile said, "We talked about that the other day, after they hired him. He said he thought he could handle it, because the cementary had an awful lot of trees for shade."

Jack is not working now, I guess you might say that he is just not too energetic. He says he can't seem to find a job around here.

School is out for the summer, we are happy about that! Brodus and I will be in the fifth grade in the fall.

Jack is still not working. I wonder if he wants a job.

Mama stayed home from work this morning to wash the clothes. Cecile, Brodus, and I are carrying water from the neighbor's house to wash the clothes. Jack is sitting on a chair on the porch. Mama is scrubbing clothes on the wash board.

Mama just quit what she was doing and walked in to the house.

About two minutes later Mama came out of the back door with the rifle. She looked straight in the face of Jack and said, "If you don't get off of your lazy ass, and get out there and help your wife carry water, I will shoot you."

Jack did not say a word. He did start carrying water, one trip after another. He carried a lot of water, I'm sure he got hot, and he did sweat, but he did not faint, or pass out. There was not much conversation the rest of the day, with anyone, I'm sure Cecile felt sorry for him. I think Mama just got fed up with him.

Later this evening, Cecile was in the bed room putting clothes in suitcases, and I asked her, "Are ya'll going somewhere?"

And she replied, "Yes Harper," she said, "we are leaving early in the morning, and going back to Indiana."

"Is that because of yesterday, when Mama came out with the rifle?"

Cecile said, "That may be some of the reason, but Jack could not seem to find a job here, so we thought it would be the best thing to go back up to Indiana. Maybe he can find employment up there."

I said, "Well, that could be true, but I sure hate to see ya'll leave."

Here we go again, Mama has found places for me and Brodus to pick cotton on farms around the area. In the fall when the cotton is ready to pick, I guess me and Brodus will be picking cotton.

It's the middle of August. Mama and the girls got laid off at the greenhouses, so Mama and the girls and me and Brodus are picking cotton. The farmer picks us up at 5:30 every morning and takes us to the cotton field. Mama has our lunch packed which consisted of potted meat, sardines, peanut butter, and biscuits. We also usually take two or three gallons of water. We pick 'til noon and take a dinner break for a while, if we can find a shade tree to sit under. Then we pick cotton again until around six-o-clock, or when the farmer comes to get us. He arrives, weighs our cotton sheets, and then takes us home. As it turns out, when all the family picks cotton, at the end of the week, we end up with more income than Mama and the girls made working at the greenhouses. But the cotton picking season only lasts so long, and greenhouse work wasn't nearly as hard.

Well, by golly, Mama and the girls went to town to pay to have our city water hooked up. We have one cold water faucet under the kitchen window now, and a faucet outside. We are so happy about that. The first house we ever lived in that has running water in the house. Oh man, we are so blessed. No more carrying water from the neighbor's house.

There was a man, Mr. Carpenter, who lived down on highway seventy four, that owned Carpenter's Furniture and Appliance store in Shelby. He showed up recently with a refrigerator. Mama was in town, Dallas and Cally was here. He said, "I've got a real nice refrigerator on the truck outside, and I wonder if your family might be interested in buying it."

Dallas said, "I don't know, I guess that is something Mama will have to decide."

He said, "How about I just leave it here, and when Mrs. Garris returns from town, see what she has to say about it. I will set the payment amount where you can afford it. And, if she says absolutely not, I will come and pick it up, no questions asked!"

"Okay," Dallas said, "that's fair enough."

They brought it in, and put our old ice box on the back porch. He plugged it in, and showed Dallas and Cally everything about it. Man, what a beautiful sight it is. Open the door and the light comes on, wow.

"Just let me know after the first of the week what you have decided."

Mama is home from town.

"What is this?" She asked. when she saw the refrigerator.

Dallas said, "Mama, this is something we need!"

Mama asked, "Did y'all order it, or where did it come from?"

"No Mama," Dallas replied. "Mr. Carpenter brought it here from his appliance store. He said that if you absolutely did not want it, he would come back and pick it up the first of the week."

"He will just have to come back and get it, because we cannot afford it!"

"We would not have to buy ice anymore, and would not have to worry about the meat or milk going bad."

"I said No, and that's it! I don't want to hear another word about it."

There it sits, all Saturday evening, and all day Sunday. Mama was using it quite a bit. Dallas and Cally was hoping and praying, that she would change her mind.

This evening after supper, relaxing in the living room, Mama asked the girls, "Do ya'll really think that we could afford to buy that refrigerator?"

Dallas replied, "Mama, I'm sure we can afford it. With all of us working like we are, I know we can, it would be one of the best things we could have."

"Okay," Mama said, "We will keep it."

Boy, you should have seen Dallas and Cally's face light up like a light bulb, they were so happy.

Dallas and Cally met a girl at work by the name of Geraldine, I don't know her last name. They became very good friends. I guess she lives in that old gas station building down on seventy four, that I was telling you about earlier.

Several people live there I guess. An older man they call Grandpa, his son Hubert, and his two sons, Howard, and a young boy about my age named Billy Ray, all their last names were Addington's.

Geraldine told Cally, "I will have to introduce you to Howard, he is a good looking man, and he works here at the greenhouses. He is a salesman."

Cally met Howard, 1949

I believe it was love at first sight. He is all Cally talks about. Cally said he takes a truck load of flowers and wholesales them to the flower shops in Georgia, North and South Carolina. He leaves on Sunday morning and returns on Tuesday evening. He loads his truck on Wednesday with the best looking flowers they have and leaves Thursday morning and returns Friday evening.

Cally began dating Howard on the weekends, if he was in the area.

From the way they talk, Howard is a pretty heavy drinker.

Cleveland County, where we live is a dry county, however South Carolina is only eleven miles south, and a tavern just inside the state line, which makes it easy to get all the alcohol you want to drink pretty fast, and he does.

Howard moved out of that old gas station building, and moved in one of the houses just a little ways down that dirt road on the right.

If Howard was home, his car would be parked in his drive way. Now here's the story about that. Every weekend, Friday, and Saturday, Cally would ask me to ride my bicycle down the hill on Cleveland Ave. to the curve, where I could see Howard's house, to see if his car was in the driveway. Not once, twice or five times, but many times. I always did! Cally and I are very close. She wanted him to be home so bad, and I feel sorry for her. When I would return and tell her his car was home, oh, she would be so happy. I thought I would wear that street out.

It's back to school in the fall. It has been a summer of doing chores. We've had a lot of fun playing games with Mackie.

Cally is spending a lot of time with Howard. He would usually come to see Cally on Wednesday and Friday.

Howard came to see Cally last night. We were all setting in the living room, when Cally got so mad at Brodus, that she was about to have a "hissy." He brought the bucket in, and stopped in the living room, he wanted to say something to Howard. He stood there swinging the bucket, and it smelled awful. Cally screamed at him, "Brodus get that bucket out of here right now." Oh, she was so embarrassed, and mad. Howard just set there laughing, I'm sure he probably knew what the bucket was used for.

We started back to school the day after Labor Day as usual. It's good to see all the classmates again. I am in the sixth grade, and there are two new students in our room. I don't know them yet.

I am eleven years old, and Brodus is thirteen, and a lot of kids ask us why we are in the same grade. We tell them that Brodus didn't start to school until I did, because he suffered a lot of illness when he was six and seven years old. Well it's back to playing marbles, and ball, at recess time. In class, its arithmetic, history, spelling and geography. I like history, but I don't understand a lot of arithmetic, especially divisions. Hopefully I will be able to learn it better! I do really well in spelling.

The grower, Mr. Stitz at the greenhouses, asked Mama if Brodus and I would like to come down to the greenhouses and cover some flower beds with black cloths.

The reason for that was to slow down the growth of the flowers, by making the day shorter for the flowers. We began doing that every evening at five thirty. We did that for all the flowers that would need to bloom, just in time for a holiday. Mr. Stitz was a very good grower. He sure knows how to grow flowers.

We met Howard's brother, Billy Ray Addington, a few weeks ago. He is a year or so younger than me. He is spoiled by his dad, and Howard. Each one of them give him a dollar a week allowance. He doesn't even have chores to do, like Brodus and me. He has been spending a lot of time at our house. I think Mama kind of feels sorry for him. His mother is in a mental hospital up at Marion, North Carolina. I've heard Billy's dad drove her crazy with his drinking.

Howard and Billy's dad was a barber at one time, when he was younger. People say, one of the best in the area, but he started drinking, and it got the best of him. He works down at the greenhouses, watering plants, for around sixty cents an hour.

This year, I met Robert "Red" Sullivan, (1950)

The Evans family who live behind us have a three car garage, that borders our back property. I have been hearing a lot of banging and bumping in there for the last few days, and I cannot help but wonder what's going on. I am very curious. Maybe I should go around there and find out! I am on my way. Before I get there I see a big, strong looking, broad shoulderd man, with bright red hair.

"Hey," I said to him.

He said, "Hey, who are you?"

"Harper is my name. I live in the house right behind here."

"What is your first name?" he asked me.

"Harper is my first name," I replied, "my last name is Garris."

He said, "My name is Robert Sullivan, you can just call me "Red" if you like, everyone else does."

"Are you relatives of the Evans family who live here?" I asked.

"Surely, you know that Mrs. Evans passed away some time back, and Bobby lives far away. Jack is the only one that lives here now. He is my cousin and he invited my family to move in here with him. It is a pretty big house for one person to live in."

"Yeah it is," I said. "Are you cleaning out this garage to park your cars in here?"

Grinning, he said, "No, I am a sign painter, and this will be my sign shop when I get moved in."

I go down to visit him in his shop every day, he is always nice to me. Sometimes I ask him if I could help him with anything, and he says no, not now.

And then, I walked down to his shop a couple days later. He had built an easel along the back wall of the shop. It must be fifteen foot long. He was lettering a sign on the easel. I have never seen anything like that. He was really good. He sure is a sign painter.

"Harper," I hear my name called in the distance.

"That's Mama calling," I said, "I better go."

Robert said, "See ya later."

"What was you doing down there?" Mama asked.

"I was watching Robert letter a sign, he is really good."

Mama said, "Don't you be going down there and bothering him, he probably has a lot of work to do."

Chapter Ten

Mr. and Mrs. Mauney live across the road in front of our house. They have two boys. Their names are Bob and Bill. Bill is about five years older than me. He goes to high school in Shelby. I don't know Bob very well, and I very seldom see him. Bill said he goes to college.

We have visited with them several times. They are a real nice God fearing family, at least the mom and dad are! There's more to find out about Bill.

The custodian of the golf course, Mr. Glover is close friends with the Mauney's. He lives on Elizabeth road, across from the golf course.

Bill came over to our house this afternoon, and asked if Brodus and I could go with him to the golf course lake, and get some golf balls, that the golfers knocked in the lake by mistake.

We asked Mama if we could, and she said, it's okay if you go, just stay out of trouble.

Bill said, "Oh, there will be no trouble to get in to."

It was about dusk when we walked over there, there was no one playing golf. The lake was located at a rather low place on the course. I had never seen the lake before.

Bill said, "Now Harper, I want you to go up there on top of that hill, where you can see a long way, if anyone is coming. When you get up there lay down, so no one can see you. If you see old man Glover coming, let me know so we can leave before he gets here. The lake was close to some trees.

"Okay," I said.

"Brodus," Bill said, "you go up there on the other side of the lake, and do the same thing that I told Harper to do."

Bill pulled all of his clothes off, he was naked, not a stitch on, and went into the lake. The lake was not real big, maybe one hundred and twenty five foot long, and one hundred foot wide, and not very deep.

Bill got down on his knees, and crawled back and forth across the lake. He kept finding golf balls, and throwing them up on the bank of the lake, to be collected later.

Bill found a lot of golf balls, he got out of the lake, and we picked up all the balls, and he got dressed and we came home.

Bill said, "That was a good haul, we will do that again soon."

This has been a good summer, I have had a lot of fun getting to know Robert. He is very interesting, and very smart.

His wife's name is Marie, sometimes he calls her "Choc", I don't know why, just a nick name, I guess. They have two girls, Sherry, and Shelia. They are a few years younger than Brodus and me.

From the time I can first remember, Mama and Daddy did not allow any cussing, by any of the children. We were forbidden to use such words as dang, darn, daggum it, or heck. These words would get us a whipping, and you sure had better not use the Lord's name in vain, or son of a bi#%@, or worse. Most of those words I had never heard any how! I would feel sorry for anyone of the kids in our family getting caught saying any of those words.

On the other hand, Robert used all of those words and more, he cussed all the time, when things didn't go well, or if things went well. Sometimes it was funny, and other times he would scare me, when he pitched a cussing fit.

Summer is over, and it's back to school. Brodus and I are going in to the seventh grade. Mrs. Laidlaw is our sixth and seventh grade teacher.

Dallas told Brodus and me, she was going to give each one of us a nickel to buy milk to drink when we ate our lunch, that we carried from home. Mama could not afford for us to eat in the lunch room every day.

A couple of weeks after school started, Bill Mauney came over and asked if we wanted to go back to the golf course lake, and hunt for balls again. We'll go after supper.

We asked Mama if we could go and she said we could.

After supper, here we go back across the field, and through the woods and there's the lake.

Bill said, "You boys know the procedure, go get in position," as he began removing his clothes right down to his bare butt. I'm up on the hill watching for old man Glover, confident that he would not show up.

I turned around watching Bill. He is finding a lot of golf balls again.

He saw me watching him and he hollered, "Keep your eyes open, Harper!"

I don't know how long I was watching Bill, and when I turned around, I saw Mr. Glover coming toward me. He was carrying a shotgun. I jumped up, and took off running as fast as I could toward the lake. I was scared almost to death. It was like a dream when you are trying to run, but can't!

I screamed. "Here comes old man Glover with a shotgun!" Bill is out in the middle of the lake, and he is trying to get to the lake bank as fast as he could, and Brodus and I was headed for the woods.

Then the sound, I heard the shotgun being fired!

My legs got so weak, I just fell down on the ground. Brodus was already in the woods.

Bill climbed out of the lake, hollering for Brodus and me to come back here.

Keep in mind that Bill's Mom and Dad was friends with the Glovers, Mr. Glover is a pretty old man.

Bill was steaming mad! He walked up in Mr. Glovers face, naked as a jay bird and began cussing him out. "G** D+* you old man, who in the hell do you think you are with that shotgun? The next time you come around me with that gun, I will wrap the son-of-a-b*#+h around your G** D++ neck!"

Well, by now Mr. Glover knew it was Bill, and he got scared.

He started stuttering, "Ba, Ba, Ba Bill, I, I, didn't know it wa, wa was you. If, if, I had known it, it was you, I never would have come down here. I tho, tho it was some of them niggers that come down here and hang around after hours, and I have to stop that. I've been getting complaints about them, from some of the golfers. You and your buddies can get all the balls out of the lake that you want to."

With that, Bill put his clothes on and we went home, after we picked up the balls. We did not tell Mama about that!

Last night, Cally was telling me about something that happened when she was a lot younger. She said she had been watching a young lady at church every Sunday, and it appeared to her that the lady was getting big in the stomach pretty fast, and as she was walking home from church one Sunday with Mama, she asked Mama why, when young women get married, after awhile they get so big in the stomach? Mama turned, and slapped her across the face, and said, don't you ever ask questions about people like that again!

In our home, the word sex, was never to be mentioned, never. If we learned anything at all about sex it was away from home, maybe from other children, or what we might read somewhere. My older brothers and sisters say Mama never, ever taught them anything about the subject of sex. I guess being eleven years old, as I am, I never think about it, perhaps I will in time to come. My, the things that cross my mind during idle times, when my mind wonders!

We have lots and lots of pictures that have been taken over the years, of our family members, reunions, and relatives. Mama keeps them in a big cardboard box. I love to get that box out and look at them.

Here is a picture of Mack in his uniform, when he was released from the Navy hospital. He is a very crippled man, I cannot help but feel so sorry for him, that the tears began to burn my eyes.

Here's one I like a lot of Brodus and me, all ready for school, when we started in the first grade.

Oh yes, here is the old stereo photo viewer, that you set the older photos in to view. It makes the photos look so real.

Boy, this is an old one, Mama's Mama and Daddy setting on their front porch.

Here are some pictures of some of my half brothers and sisters, Rome, Willy, Marion, Agnes, they are all there. I like to look at the reunion pictures through the stereo viewer, and see if I can name everyone there.

I guess I had better put these away and get busy before everyone gets home from work.

Going to school is consuming most of my time now, and our chores, of course.

Walking to school, it's a cool fall morning, I'm gonna walk in to Blanton's Grocery store and warm up for a minute. Adrian Littlejohn is working as usual, John D. is in here twirling his strip of leather. I'm just looking around at the different products on the counter and the pipe display caught my eye. I just stood there looking at them.

Adrian asked, "You wanna buy a pipe?"

"Gosh, no" I said, "I can't afford anything like that!"

He said, "I'll tell you what," as he was reaching under the counter, "I'll bet you could afford this one." Opening his hand, he was holding a very small pipe, about three and a half inches long. "Would you like to buy this one?" he asked. "I have smoked it a few times, but it is a good pipe."

"How much do you want for that one?" I asked.

"I'll sell it to you for a quarter."

"Really?" I asked. "I will buy it, if I can pay you a nickel a day 'til it's paid for."

"Sure," he said, "I will keep the pipe until it is paid for, then I will give it to you."

Reaching in to my pocket, I hand him the first payment on my pipe, the nickel that Dallas gave me for my milk today.

This is Monday, so I guess I will have my pipe Friday. Boy that will be pretty cool, I'm thinking!

The days have been dragging by, but Friday is here. I made my last payment this morning, and I've got my brand new used pipe. I kept it in my pocket all day. Walking home from school, I found some cigarette butts, and removed the tobacco, and put it in my pipe and smoked it. Yes sir, I am just like a grown up.

When I get home from school, I will have to hide it, where no one will ever find it. Right here on the back porch will be the perfect place, inside one of these old work shoes, with all these old flower pots setting around them.

Saturday morning, and I can feel the blanket being jerked off my body, and I feel the stinging hits on my legs of a hickory switch, Gosh, that hurts, Mama is hollering at me, and just tearing my legs apart, I'm thinking I will never walk again!

"Oh Mama," I said, "that hurts!"

"You're gonna hurt," she said, "Where did you get that pipe?"

I told her, the best I could, being out of breath from the whipping, like I was.

I will never know how she ever found that pipe, I thought it would be impossible for anyone to find it, I was wrong. And I guess I will never see that pipe again, at least I hope not!

How time flies! Christmas has passed and this is January.

Walking to school is pretty cold, guess it doesn't matter, I have to go. As I walk, I think of many things, when I grow up I will have my own car, to go where I want to go. I will be married to a most beautiful girl. I will have a good job, and buy things like a television, and really nice clothes.

I am about home, I think I will stop in and see Robert for a couple minutes.

"Hey Red, what's going on today?"

"Same old s##t" he says, "Trying to stay busy."

"Do you have anything I can do for you?"

"Well," he says, "there are two or three lettering brushes you can wash out, and oil."

After I clean the brushes, I have to put oil on them so they won't get all dried out and stiff. I enjoy doing that.

"Guess I better get on home, I have to wash out my overalls, so they will dry by morning. I'll see you later Robert."

"Okay," he said.

Mama and the girls came home from work, Mama said she was tired, and gonna set down a bit before she starts supper.

Dallas said, "That's okay Mama, Cally and me will fix supper tonight."

Cally told me and Brodus to straighten up the living room, because Howard was coming over to eat supper with us.

As it turned out, Cally cooked supper, I guess she wanted to try to impress Howard, and show him that she could cook.

She did cook a very good meal, Howard liked it a lot. He said, "This is the best meal I've had for a long time! I loved the chocolate pie."

After supper they went into the living room, of course Brodus and I had to wash dishes.

We finished washing the dishes, and went to the living room with everyone.

Brodus got in trouble with Cally again.

When we went in the living room, Brodus sat down on the floor, he was barefooted all day, and got dirt between his toes. There he sat in front of everyone, including Howard, rubbing the black dirt out from between his toes with his finger.

Cally was just furious, "Mama," she screamed, "Make Brodus get out of here!" Oh, she was so mad!

"Brodus," Mama said, "Get out on the back porch, and wash your feet. No one wants to see you doing that!"

Spring will be coming on pretty soon, Cally is seeing more and more of Howard, and I am seeing more and more of Robert.

Mama let me go with Howard on one of his overnight trips, selling flowers, Boy, that was a lot of fun. We left at four-o-clock in the morning.

Howard said, "By the time we get down to York, S.C., that little café will be open on main street. We will stop there and get us some pancakes, they make the best pancakes there, that you have ever eaten."

Well, I have never eaten pancakes, so I guess they will be.

We arrived at the café about an hour later, walked in, sat down at the counter. We were the only ones in there at the time. The grill that he cooked on was heated by wood, the cook was putting wood underneath the grill, I guess to get the grill heated up enough to cook on. He said, to us, "I'll be with you pretty soon, I just got the place opened up."

"Take your time," Howard said. "When you get 'er fired up, we'll have a couple orders of pancakes."

He turned around and said, "Oh, it's you. How are ya Howard? You got a helper today, do ya?"

"Yeah, he wanted to see somewhere outside of Shelby, but he will have to work for it," as they chuckled a little bit.

"How do you like that?" Howard asked, after I took a couple of bites of pancakes.

"Boy, this is really, really good," I replied. "I've never had anything like this!"

We finished breakfast and headed on south, and began stopping at retail florists, to sell flowers. The florist owners would come out to the truck, and pick out the different plants that they wanted, and I would help Howard carry them in, and that went on all day. By evening we were in Georgia. All florists' were closed for the day.

(And another new experience I had, as we pulled into a motel in Augusta, Georgia.)

I had never been in a motel before.

Howard said, "We will go in here, and get a shower, clean up a little bit before we go eat." The restaurant was attached to the motel.

I have heard about showers, but I have never had one. Howard had to show me how to operate it. Man, this is really something, I'm thinking, wow!

After supper we went back to the room and watched television for a little while, and went to bed. I can hardly go to sleep for thinking about everything we did today! What a day!

We were up early this morning, we had our breakfast, and off we go to sell flowers. We are all over Augusta. There are a lot of flower shops in this city, and Howard knows where every one of them are.

It was after noon until we left Augusta. We stopped at many florists, working our way back up to North Carolina. We returned home about five thirty today, with a lot of memories for me. I sure did enjoy these last two days. I could hardly wait to tell everyone about my trip.

Springtime is upon us, it's warming up some, and Robert is giving me more and more stuff to do. He seems to get busier every day. I have been sweeping, and keeping the shop cleaned for him. He makes a lot of menu boards that are mounted on the outside of drive-ins. The way he makes them is;

He gets a four by eight foot sheet of Masonite at the lumber company, he usually splits it in the middle, for two pieces, four by four, and then puts a three and one half inch frame around it, and attaching three quarter inch molding to the inside of the frame, that makes it look really good. Then he puts two or three coats of white paint on it. And that's a job he has been teaching me to do. I'm learning!

He does so many things that are so interesting to me, especially the sign lettering.

Robert bought a television for their home. There are not too many people around our area that have TV's.

Dallas has a friend, Jeannie Pruitt, who lives up the road about a block or so, and she has a TV. We go up there sometimes in the evening, and watch the Milton Burle comedy hour, and Red Skelton show.

The Lone Ranger show comes on every evening at five –o–clock. I asked Robert, if Brodus and I could watch that on his TV sometime. And he said he would have to ask Choc, his wife. He did ask her and she said, if we would take a bath, and put on clean clothes, we could come and watch the Lone Ranger on their TV. We did one time. She is not as friendly as Robert is.

School is out for the summer.

I am still taking a lot of trips down around the curve for Cally, to see if Howard is home yet! If they are going to get married, I hope they will hurry up and do it. I'm getting tired of all this riding my bicycle down to the curve, to see if he is home.

I walked down to see Billy Ray this morning, to see what he was doing. We sit under the roof out front, that used to cover the gas pumps years ago, when this was a gas station. We do this a lot, sit here and talk, Bill's grandpa is sitting out here, talking about his younger days as a kid, when he saw "Buffalo Bill's Wild West Show". He has told us about that several times. We like to hear him tell stories about his years growing up, very interesting.

Howards making his trips down to the taverns in South Carolina, and Cally can hardly stand it, but she hasn't been able to get him to stop, at least she hasn't yet. He is such a good looking man, and a very hard worker, everybody likes him a lot, it seems. I just wish he did not have such a desire to drink beer the way he does, as they say, like father, like son.

Howard's sister, Helen was married to James "Jay" Kennedy, everyone called him Jay. There was times when Howard and Jay would take off on a Friday evening, and not return home until Sunday. I wondered a lot why Cally didn't just quit seeing Howard, seems like he will never quit drinking. He was in the Navy, stationed in the Philippines, where he saw a lot of action. I just wonder if that is some of the reason for his drinking like he does.

Howard grew up outside a small town, twelve miles south of Shelby, Boiling springs, N.C. He had a friend down there, named Earl Skinner. He brought him up here one weekend, and introduced him to Dallas, and Dallas began to date him on the weekends, with Howard and Cally. They seemed to hit it off quite well, Earl liked Dallas a lot, at least it looked like it to me.

On a Wednesday evening, August thirty first, 1951, Howard and Earl came and picked up Dallas and Cally, they went down to York, S.C. and Howard and Cally exchanged their wedding vows, and was married by a Justice Of The Peace.

In spite of Howard's heavy drinking, Cally was still determined to be his wife. I guess she believed that she could change him. Time will tell, I sure hope she can!

Howard bought a set of horseshoes, and brought them up here, because we have more room in the yard to put the staubs in the ground.

Now, these woods around here are alive with the sound of clanging horseshoes. A few of Howard's friends came up here to play horseshoes with him in the evenings.

After a week or so, Howard's Uncle Horace and Jay and the two sons of Mr. Patterson, (who owns the greenhouses) Knighton and Pat Jr. began coming up to play. Two young black guys that work down at the greenhouses, stop by to play. Mama keeps plenty of ice cold tea ready, for when they get thirsty.

I'm telling you they do have a good time. They play partners, when a team gets beat in a game, they have to sit down, and another team plays. They decided to count a ringer as five points so the game would be over sooner, that way all the teams would get to play more games.

Many times, when Howard and Jay were playing against Pat Jr. and Knighton, you would more than likely here something like this; Pat would throw a shoe, and while it was in the air, he would say "there's five" and it would be a ringer. He threw the other shoe and say, "Five makes ten". And it would be a ringer.

Then Howard throws a shoe, and while it was in the air, he would say, "Five from ten leaves five", throws the other shoe and says, "Five from five leaves zero," and that would be a ringer, and "that's what you got," he would say.

Pat Jr. says, "Damn you, Howard!" And this would go on for two or three hours, three or four nights a week. We had light bulbs hanging from the tree limbs so we could see after dark. I'll tell you them fellers can pitch some horseshoes.

There were several teams that were really, really good horseshoe pitchers. I cannot say that about Brodus and me. We go out there after school, and practice. Maybe we will get good enough sometime to play with them.

Mama said I could ride over to Charlotte today with Robert, to take some neon to be repaired, and pick up some neon that is repaired.

It sure is interesting how he can bend a piece of glass tubing into letters, and numbers, that is really something. I asked him, "Eddie, how long have you been doing that?"

Eddie replied, "I've been doing this for so long, I don't even remember when I started".

"Do you make the different colors in the neon?" I asked him.

"Just hang on a few minutes here, and I will show you how I do it." He melted a real small piece of glass tubing to the underside of the piece of neon.

There were several tanks, like propane tanks, lined up beside his table. He had a real small rubber hose, that he hooked to one of the tanks, and the other end of the hose to the small tube, that he put under the neon. Then he very carefully turned a valve open on the tank, and filled the neon with some kind of gas. I don't know how he knew when there was enough gas in the neon, before he removed the hose from it, and melted the hole shut.

The piece of neon he had bent said "Café". There was a transformer setting close by, and he ran an electric wire from each end of the neon, to each end of the transformer. Then he flipped a switch that supplied electricity to the transformer and, just like magic, the café sign lit up in a bright red glow, WOW!

The entire time that he was working, he held a blow torch instrument, with a very hot flame in one hand, and a small rubber hose that attached to one end of the neon, and the other end he kept in his mouth. I guessed that was so he could blow through the glass, each time he heated the tube to make a bend, to keep the neon from collapsing.

We said our good bye and headed back to Shelby, and I'm thinking, boy, that was quite an experience, never seen anything like that before.

The tree leaves are so pretty, with all the different colors, here in the foothills of the Blue Ridge Mountains in North Carolina. Walking to school makes me so proud to be growing up here in North

Carolina, just a little chill in the air, but it feels good. It will warm up in the afternoon.

Well, I am in the seventh grade this year, and Mrs. Laidlaw is our teacher again this year. She is real nice, I like her a lot.

One of the new students that started to school here this year, is a boy, named Jack Cogsdale. He is sixteen years old, and has his driver's license. He has missed a few years of school, on account of illness. He is a great student, and very smart kid. His Dad bought him a brand new Henry J car. That's what he wanted! The Henry J is a new model of car, that just came out this year. His Daddy is the caretaker of the county home. Jack walks to school, because he lives so close.

After school is out for the day, I usually spend my time down at Robert's shop, there is always something to do down there. If nothing else, I just sit and watch him letter a sign.

Today he was lettering a sign that had the word, piedmont, on it. It was spelled correctly, I said, "Robert, how do you spell piedmont?"

He jumped up from his stool, "s**-of-a-b****h" he said! Looking at it he said, "That's spelled right!"

I said, "Yes, it is, I was just kidding you, gotta keep you on your toes."

"G++ D** you Harper," he said, "You scared the living hell out of me."

And I am standing there laughing.

"You better quit doing that," he said, "you're gonna cause me to have a heart attack."

At the supper table tonight, Dallas said, "Mama, you know we got the refrigerator paid off about a month ago. I think we could afford to buy a television. What do you think?"

"Oh, I don't know about that," Mama replied. "Let's just think about that for a spell."

"Sure would be nice," Dallas said. "We could stay home in the evenings, and not have to walk to a neighbor's house to watch television, anyhow, maybe they don't really want us coming over to watch their television."

"Dallas," Mama said, "I think we should think about that for a few days. Maybe we will."

Of course Brodus and I got real excited about that, Brodus said, "Yeah, and we could watch the Lone Ranger show right here at home".

"Don't get too excited," Mama said, "we haven't made a decision yet. Y'all will have to wait and see".

Well, here it is Saturday. I saw Howard this morning.

"What are you gonna do this afternoon?" I asked.

"I guess I'll carry Mrs. Garris to town. She asked me this morning, I told her I would."

That's what he always said if he was gonna take someone somewhere. He would say he was gonna carry them somewhere. I never heard anyone else use that phrase. So Brodus and I would get the biggest kick when he would say that. Just to imagine him carrying Mama in his arms, we thought that was so funny. Mama was pretty big and heavy.

Howard did take Mama to town this afternoon, in his car.

When they returned home pretty late, we helped carry the groceries in, and there was no television. Brodus and I was pretty disappointed, but we did not say anything. But we thought for sure Mama and Dallas was gonna bring home a television today.

About a half hour later, Mr. Carpenter pulled into our driveway in his pickup truck, and began unloading our television.

"Are you kids ready to watch some television?" he asked, as he was unloading it.

"We sure are!" we replied. "This is a great day for us," we told him.

He brought it in the house, and plugged it in, and put a funny looking thing on top of the television.

He said, "Mrs. Garris, this is what they call "rabbit ears". You have to move this around, until the picture on the screen is real clear. In this area, you can usually pick up three TV stations. There are two stations in Charlotte and one down in Spartanburg, S.C. that comes in pretty clear. Guess I had better be getting on home now, y'all enjoy your T.V." he said, "And thank you folks very much."

I thought we would never, ever, have a television in our home.

Mama said, "This might be an early Christmas present for all of us."

Dallas replied, "It is the best Christmas present that we have ever had, and will have." All of us are so tickled about this.

Howard and Cally just walked in.

"I see you have got 'er all plugged in and cranked up," Howard said.

"Oh yes," Dallas said.

Howard said, "I think Arthur Smith and the Cracker Jacks comes on at nine-o-clock tonight. That's a good show to watch."

We are just having a ball talking about all the different shows that we want to watch. I don't think I've ever been so excited before.

Thanksgiving Day, 1951

Howard and Cally are here for dinner. Dallas said Earl was coming also. There is a parade on television, it is a long one, they said something about Macys a while ago, I don't know who she is, or what she does.

We sure had a wonderful Thanksgiving dinner today Mama and the sisters cooked. All that food, oh boy! Turkey, corn bread dressing, mashed potatoes, gravy, slaw, and butter beans. And that fresh coconut cake and the chocolate pies that Cally made.

Robert went to the metal shop in Shelby, and talked to the owner about allowing us to construct the metal works, of a neon sign, in his shop, and using some of his tools.

The owner gave him permission to do that. Robert will have to pay him so much an hour, and if we need one of his employees to assist us sometimes, he would have to pay an additional $10.00 an hour. So the deal was made.

We were going to make a big sign for a motel, located between Gastonia and Charlotte. It would be called "The Twins Motel". It will have a picture of twins, at the top of the sign. Robert had already made the pattern for the sign. The sign will be fifteen foot tall, and four foot wide. I went to the metal shop when I could, to help Robert, but I was going to school every day, and I didn't get to help very much.

After they finished making the metal box of the sign, Robert brought it back to his shop to finish it up. Robert had the pattern perforated, and he used a pounce bag, and pounced the entire pattern on the metal sign. He had sent the pattern to Eddie at the neon shop in Charlotte, and Eddie used the pattern to bend the neon for the sign. He just received the pattern back today.

Eddie had marked on the pattern where glass housing should be installed on the sign. The glass housing is the place where each end of the neon is installed on the sign. He also marked the places where the neon tube supports should be.

Now Robert has to treat the metal with a substance, that will make the paint stay on the sign for years, without cracking or peeling, and then he will spray several coats of white paint on it. And then we can begin to install the glass housings and tube supports.

When that is finished, we will install the transformers, and wire the sign. Then, Robert can letter the sign, and then we can erect it at the motel.

Christmas has come and gone, and of course, it is such an exciting time of the year, Mama and the girls sure baked and cooked up a lot of good food to eat on Christmas Eve and Christmas day.

Well, it's back to school, after the Christmas and New Year's break.

A new kid started to school today in the seventh grade.

At recess, I asked him, "What is your name?"

"Harley Davidson," he replied.

That kind of stopped me for a second, "Harley Davidson?"

Yep, he said. "Just like the motorcycle. Our family just moved in to that house right down the road, there where the road forks."

"Oh yes, I know where you are talking about, that big two story house on the right."

"That's the place," he said.

I have been buying a magazine called Country song Round-Up for the last couple of years when I've have a quarter, it has all the lyrics to all the country songs being played on the radio. There are not many stations that play country music in this area. Radio station WOHS in Shelby does, for one hour on Saturday mornings. And a station down in Greenville, S.C. plays country during the week, from four to five o-clock in the evening. I learn a lot of songs from my book, and I sing a lot, I really enjoy singing.

There was a local country band called, "Kermit McSwain, and the Number Three Ramblers". They were on the local radio station, WOHS every Saturday morning for one half hour. They were real good.

This last Christmas Mama gave me a harmonica as a present. I've been trying to learn to play it.

I know the words to a lot of songs that were recorded by Hank Williams, Webb Pierce, Johnnie and Jack, and many other artists.

I am down at Roberts shop.

"Harper," Robert said, "we have to go over to Kings Mountain, and install a transformer on a brick wall, go ahead and put all the tools in the truck that we will need. We will leave as soon as I finish lettering this sign."

"Okay," I said, and I went about putting the tools in the truck we will need.

"Well," I said to Robert, "I have everything in the truck that we will need."

Robert said, "Pliars?"

"They're in the truck."

He said, "Sledge hammer?"

"Yes sir,"

"Star drill?"

"Yep,"

"Lag bolts and shields?"

"Oh yes,"

"Step ladder?"

"I've got it."

He came over and looked in the bed of the truck and said, "Yeah, looks like you got everything we need, let's go."

Off to Kings Mountain we go. Arriving at the job site, Robert marked where the holes were supposed to be drilled in the brick wall, and said, "Harper, how about you start drilling the holes, and I will be getting other stuff around."

"Okay," I said, up the ladder I went with the sledge hammer and star drill, and began hammering the drill into the wall.

"Okay," Robert asked, "Where is the transformer?"

"I don't know!" I told him.

"Don't tell me we came all the way over here to install a transformer, and didn't bring the transformer, son of a b(*+#h, I'll just be G#+ D+%n."

Oh boy, is he having a fit, I'll just keep on hammering, and hopefully, he will settle down pretty soon. My goodness, ranting and raving, ain't gonna help one thing. Where did he go I wonder? Man, this hammer is getting heavy, as I just let it drop, and kinda swing backward behind me, and I hear, "umf unf." I turned around and, ut ohhh, I guess the hammer hit him in the back of his head. He is staggering around, holding the back of his head.

"Oh my god," he said, "What happened?"

I thought he was gonna pass out. I jumped down off the ladder. "Are you alright, Robert?"

"What's going on?" he asked.

I guess he really don't know what happened. "Well Robert, I didn't know you was standing behind me. When I let the hammer drop down, I hit you in the back of the head."

"Well, G—D--- Harper, are you trying to kill me?"

"No, I am so sorry Robert!" I really am.

I don't know what is gonna happen next!

He began to laugh, and I did too, we had us a good laugh.

Robert stood there a few minutes and said, "I think I had better get the hell out of here, before you kill me. I'll go get the transformer!"

A kid by the name of Bobby Van Horn, started to school this week. He is big. He is 6 foot 2 inches tall. It's not easy for him to set down at his desk. He is very outgoing, and friendly, I hope to get to know him, I think, he is the size of a kid that I want him on my side, if trouble breaks out, Know what I mean?

I have been practicing on my harmonica, and I just might be able to learn to play some songs on this thing.

Brodus and I walk home from school each day as you know, and Bobby lives on highway 74, so we walk together, as far as Bobby's house. Of course we talk a lot to each other, he seems to like me, Brodus, No! Brodus decided he would tease him, calling him "ears". Bobby doesn't like that very much. Bobby chases him, and when he catches him, he throws him on the ground, and holds him there until Brodus promises him he won't call him that any more. But, as Brodus gets on ahead of us, to where he thinks Bobby can't catch up to him, he says things like,

"Hey ears, I bet you can't catch up with me now!" Oh yes, Bobby will catch up with him alright, throw him on the ground and rubs his head with his knuckles, and Brodus starts crying. I hear him hollering.

"Harper, help me!"

And I say, "You got yourself into that, and it's up to you to get yourself out. I am not going to help you."

This went on just about every day, as we walked home from school. Brodus could be so aggravating at times.

Bobby came up with this idea one day. He said, "Dad has a charge account up at Blanton's Grocery Store. Let's play hooky from school tomorrow, and I will go up to Blanton's Grocery and get some wieners, buns, mustard, and some drinks, and go way out in the woods and have us a wiener roast.

Mackie said, "Oh yeah, that would be a lot of fun."

So, Bobby, Mackie, Harley and I did just that! It was a lot of fun, unfortunately, that was one of the ways I began my downward spin in my life. We did that a couple of times more, until Bob's Dad got his bill from the grocery store, and that is the end of our wiener roasts. And Bobby is in trouble.

There was a theatre in Shelby called the "Webb Theatre". Among adults it was not very popular, it was more or less aimed at the younger generation, especially on Friday and Saturday.

Admission; children, 12 and under, 9 cents

Adults; 13 and older, 25 cents.

For that admission price, we could see movies like, Roy Rogers, another movie, the Durango Kid, about 5 or more cartoons, selected short subjects, such as the Bowery Boys, with Huntz Hall, or the Three Stooges. Then there was the continued series such as Tarzan, or Superman. Those would end with the star of the show about to get killed. Come back next week to find out if he can escape! They always did. Then previews of coming attractions! And about ten minutes of world news. Not the end of this story.

I have told you that I have always looked older than Brodus. Not good. When we paid admission to get in the Webb Theatre, and I was eleven years old they charged me 25 cents. I cannot convince them that I am only 11 years old, and I argued with them every time. Brodus gets in for 9 cents, because he looks so young. And he is 13 years old. What's a kid supposed to do? People would say, if you are going to the Webb, you had better take your supper!

It is April, and I just had my 13th birthday. No big deal. Maybe I have grown a little bit.

I am still spending a lot of time with Robert.

I stayed out of school yesterday, and we went out on state highway 150, about seven miles out of Shelby. Robert has been painting an advertisement on a billboard for SunDrop Cola. He is painting a picture of a Sun Drop bottle on the billboard. When he outlines the big letters on the sign, I come behind him and fill in the letters, of course with the same color of paint. He says that I help him save time.

"Its four-o-clock," Robert said, "Let's get the ladders and stuff loaded up, and head on home. We have done enough for today."

"Sounds good to me," I said.

Ready to leave, Robert said,

"Harper, you get in on the other side behind the steering wheel."

"Me?"

"Yes you. You are gonna drive!"

"Do you think I can drive this truck?"

Robert replies, "I don't think you can, I know you can, now get in there and drive."

I am pretty nervous as I start the engine, put it in low gear, and accelerate as I let out the clutch real slow, check the traffic and here we go down the highway. I should know how to do this as many times that I've watched Robert do this procedure.

Robert said, "I could not do that any better than you are doing."

"Well, I'm trying, I'll do the best I can." I guess I am nervous and happy at the same time!

"You are doing good, just stay on your side of the road."

We are approaching Robert's house on Cleveland Ave. His driveway is very steep for about 50 feet from the street. And there are high brick standards that are 3 foot square and 7 foot tall with a half gate attached to each standard. These standards are placed about half way up the steep section of the incline. To drive through the gate, it is very close on both sides of the truck. Although I have been with Robert many times when he drove through it, I just did not have enough confidence that I could, no more experience driving that I have.

I pulled the truck to the side of the street and said, "Robert, I think you had better drive this truck up through the gate."

"No," he said, "you can drive through the gate, I know you can, just swing wide to the left lane and turn toward the gate where you will be headed straight through."

"Well, okay, I will try!"

Oh boy, I am so nervous, put it in low gear, swing way to the left turn to the right, perfect, the gate is wide open in front of me.

"Good, good keep going," Robert said, "Give it more gas, go, go!"

I didn't give it enough gas, the engine stalled just past the gate, I put the gear in neutral, and my foot on the brake.

Robert said, "Just hold it right here, I will come around and drive it on in."

When he got out of the truck, he left his door about half way open.

He's coming around the front of the truck, I am so nervous, knowing I've got to get out so he can get in, so I pushed my door open and jumped out. The truck is rolling backward and "crunch". The passenger door that was not closed hit the brick standard. Truck needs a new door.

Another cussing fit set in from Robert.

After he settled down, he said, "Don't worry about it Harper, it was as much my fault as it was yours, I should have driven through the gate like you told me to."

It's almost time for the Cleveland County Fair. There is a group called "Joey Chitwood Daredevils," they put on a big daredevil show every year, they do all kinds of crazy stunts with cars. They are really good at what they do. Their show is one of the main attractions at the fair.

There are four new Dodge cars down at Roberts's shop, he is in the process of lettering them. A couple of weeks before the fair every year, they bring four, or five cars for Robert to letter. He letters, "Joey Chitwood Daredevils," on each side.

Mackie lives within walking distance to the fair. For the last several years, his Dad has allowed Mackie to park cars all around the house, and in a field beside of the house. I help him do that. There is a lot of fair traffic on the road in front of his house. We stand out by the road and bark out; "Park in here, only .25 cents". About every evening, we have cars parked all around the house, and the field is almost full. That is a lot of fun.

I have been driving Robert's truck quite a bit the past couple of months, going to the paint store in Shelby, or the hardware store to pick up anything that he might need. This evening he told me I had to go to Charlotte tomorrow, to pick up some neon.

"All by myself?" I asked him.

"Yep, all by yourself! Do you remember how to get to Ernie's place over there?"

"Oh yes, that would be no problem, I remember exactly how to get there. I know I can drive right to Ernie's shop."

"Okay," Robert said, "I want you to leave here around nine in the morning."

"I'll be here, ready to go!"

I am so excited about driving to Charlotte, that I had a hard time going to sleep.

"Good morning, Robert here I am, all ready to go."

"Okay," he said, as we walked out to the truck. "I want you to be real careful, do not drive over the speed limit, and don't give the police any reason to pull you over."

"You can bet that I won't do that!"

I am on my way to Charlotte, all by myself. I am thirteen years old. Ain't I really something else? Yes I am! I am so happy that I have to set on my hands to keep from waving at everyone I see.

I made it all the way to Charlotte and back today, and I am feeling pretty proud. Robert was glad to see me too.

"How did it go?" Robert asked.

"I didn't have a bit of trouble," I said.

"Sure glad you're back, without any trouble!"

This has been quite a summer, now it's back to school. I still have to walk to Elizabeth elementary school, and get on the bus there, to ride down to Number Three high school. It's about nine miles to Number Three, from Elizabeth grade school.

I began singing on the bus, and playing my harmonica, while riding to and from Number Three. A lot of the kids seem to enjoy the entertainment, at least no one has told me to quit.

One of the kids in the tenth grade works part time up at Blanton's Grocery, Bo Jones is his name, and I know him real well. In North Carolina, kids in high school are allowed to drive the bus routes. He drives a school bus, and he said to me the other day,

"Harper, would you like for me to drive by your place, and pick you up every day, and drop you off after school?"

"Oh lordy," I replied, "I sure would, man, that would be great!"

"Okay, watch for me around seven forty five."

"I'll be waiting," I told him.

He has been picking me up for school now, for the last month or so. This morning he picked me up and continued on his route. We were on business highway 74 and he had picked up about twenty kids on the bus.

I was sitting right behind him on the bus, and I was just a singing, he turned about half way around in his seat, and with a pencil, he was keeping time with me by beating on the cross pipe, that divides the bus driver from the students.

We were just having a good time, and then, all of a sudden, off the road, and down an embankment we went, thankfully it was only about two feet down into someone's front yard, and went a little ways, before he got the bus stopped. Bo opened the front and back door, and told all the kids to get out. We were so lucky the bus didn't turn over. He wanted to find out if there were any injuries. A few of the students were crying, we asked each student if they were hurt, and all of them said no. We assumed that they were just scared. "Thank God".

Bo was afraid he would lose his job, but he didn't. I am glad of that!

Well, another year has passed.

I went down to Robert's shop this evening, and he told me he had rented a place in Shelby, and he was gonna move the shop over there. I was surprised to hear that.

Most of my thoughts about it were, how I will get to Shelby when he wants me to help with something. I guess we will figure out something if he wants me over there.

In the boiler room down at the greenhouses, there is a shower, where a lot of the men employees take a shower after work. This is Friday evening, and I went down there to take a shower, and Howard was there taking a shower. When he finished and came out of the shower he said,

"Hey Harper, what are you up to?"

"Not much," I said, "gonna take me a shower, get cleaned up, after that I don't know what I'm gonna do."

Howard knows that I have been driving Roberts's truck a lot here lately.

Howard said, "I know something you can do!"

"What's that," I asked.

"Drive me down to Blacksburg, S.C., so I can drink a couple beers."

"Oh, Howard, what do you think Cally would say about that?"

"Cally don't have to find out!"

I'm standing there thinking about it, and I know I shouldn't, however it would be pretty cool to be driving his car down there, and it's only about twelve miles.

"Well," he said, "how about it?"

"Alright," I said, "if we can come home pretty early. Can we get back no later than ten thirty?"

"We will be home then," he said.

"I will pick you up at Grandpa's, at seven thirty," he said.

I told Mama a lie and said I was going down to Billy Ray's for a while.

"Okay, don't be too late."

Setting there at Billy Rays, no one is home. Here comes Howard, and here we go to South Carolina. It took a half hour to drive down here.

We arrived at the tavern just across the state line. My goodness, what a run-down, rugged looking building it is. Looks like it should have been condemned many years ago. They must have everything that a drinking person would want, beer and a juke box.

Howard said, "Just set back, turn the radio on, and I will be back pretty soon."

Well, I didn't want to be seen by everyone coming and going, so I pulled the car around to the other side of the building, and backed up into the grass. I don't think I will be too noticeable here.

I have been sitting here now for one hour and a half, he should be coming out in a half hour, for us to be home by ten thirty.

It is ten fifteen and he is not in sight, so I am going in there to see what's going on!

Walking in through the door, I see him setting down at the end of the bar all alone. I walked over and pat him on the shoulder and I said, "Howard, we have got to head on home, man. It's going on ten thirty."

"Yeah, I know. I'll be out as soon as I finish this beer."

I walked back to the car, and waited fifteen minutes, and he didn't show up. So, I went back in to the bar.

He saw me coming in the mirror behind the bar. "Oh, it's you again," he said, grinning.

"Yes, it is me again." I said. "Now Howard, you said we would be home by ten thirty, and we are still here, and it is a quarter to eleven. I am going to take the car and go home now. You can go with me now, or you can find another way home, later. It's up to you," and I turned and walked out the door.

When I got in the car, I saw him coming. I tell myself that I won't do that again.

"Young man," Mama asked, "Just where have you been? Do you know what time it is?"

"Yes Mama, I was up at Mackie's playing monopoly, I guess I just wasn't watching what time it was. I'm sorry!"

Mama said, "You better be watching what time it is, from now on. I will not have you come dragging in here this time of the night."

"I know Mama, it will not happen again!"

I just want to get in the bed. I guess I've lied enough for one night.

"Goodnight Mama. I love you."

"Goodnight," she said.

Chapter Eleven

In school today, they announced that there would be a talent contest in two weeks, for all grades, eighth through the twelfth grade. Anyone interested in entering the contest, should sign up with your homeroom teacher.

Well, Bobby, Harley, Mackie, Bo Jones, and several others, were all over me to enter the talent contest. That's all I've heard for the last three days.

Oh, you could win that they said, I finally said that I would. And I began to get kind of nervous about it, but I signed up for it anyhow.

One day after I had been singing on the bus, a girl by the name of Mary Ellen Gilassphey, (a girl that I liked very much, she was so nice to me, and a couple grades ahead of me) said to me, "I don't know what you have plans to do when you are older and out of school, but I think you should think about being an entertainer."

"Oh, I don't know about that," I replied.

She said, "I'm serious, I think you have a lot of talent."

"Well, thank you very much," I said. "That is awfully nice of you to say that."

Boy, that was a big confidence builder for me, to do the talent show.

I found a pair of overalls that were about two sizes too big for me, and a long sleeve yellow shirt with big red polka dots on it, and someone gave me a man's dress hat, that was popular in the 1920s. I think that will do it for my first public appearance.

All the school students, and most of the teachers were in the auditorium, and it is full. Oh Lord, I don't know if I can do this.

There was a girl, Brenda Sweezy, that played an accordian, and she was very good. She was very pretty, with long blond hair.

I thought to myself, she will be the winner, then I heard someone say, "Now, from the eighth grade, make welcome, Harper Garris". I did receive a very nice round of applause. That helped.

Here I go, walking out across the stage, I acted like I tripped, that got a few laughs.

"Hey ya'll," I said, "I don't know what I'm doing here, but here I am, I guess by popular demand. Some of my buddies, most of you know my buddies, they demanded that I do this, or I would wish I had. What's a kid supposed to do?"

"I am gonna attempt to play a couple of songs on my harmonica for you," (while I am talking I am fumbling in my back pocket like I am trying to find it)

"One of the seniors came up to me one day last week, I won't mention any names, and said, 'let me show you something.' Okay, I said. He said, 'put your hand over your face like this.' And I said, like this? (putting my hand over my face,) 'Yeah, now' he said, 'I am going to try to hit your hand, and you see if you can jerk your hand away before I hit it!' Alright I said, go ahead and try it! He drew back, I saw his fist coming at me, man, I jerked my hand back, and he missed my hand and "splat". Man, that hurt, and my nose is bleeding.

I thought, that was quite a trick, I bet I could pull that on someone else!

The next day, I saw another kid standing out there by himself, beside the school house, and I said to him, hey there buddy, how would you like to learn a good trick? 'What kind of trick?' he asked. Well, I'll tell you, ya see my hand here, (as I placed my hand over my face). 'Yeah,' he said. See if you can hit it with your fist before I jerk it away!"

Boy, everyone really liked that! They just kept on laughing!

I'm standing here, putting my hand way down in my pocket, pretending I'm trying to find my harmonica.

"I'm gonna play ya'll a song on my harp, if I can find it, I know I put it in one of these pockets. Oh, here it is, right under my eyes, in my bib pocket."

I played the song "Under The Double Eagle". They gave me a big applause. I'm about to think I'm a star!

"The next song that I want to offer to you is, I'm lonesome in my saddle since my horse died. Naw, just kidding! I am gonna play, get off the cook stove grandma, you're too old to ride the range". Uh, no, kidding again!" So I played "The Sun Shines Bright On Pretty Red Wings". Oh boy, they seem to like that also.

"Do you know what the cat said when he was standing too close to the buzz saw, and got his tail cut off? This is the end". I left them applauding and laughing.

After all the contestants had finished performing, everyone just sat in their seats.

After about ten minutes or so, one of the judges went out on the stage.

Every one of the contestants did such a good job, it was not easy to declare one winner. We decided we had two winners. That being said, we would like to have Brenda Sweezy, and Harper Garris come up on the stage. We have declared them the winners.

Each one of us was given a fifty cent piece, and a king size Baby Ruth candy bar.

Here it is January, 1953. Everything at home is going real well. Mama has an electric cook stove, and she is very proud of it. And of course a television, and a phone, but we still have an outhouse. Maybe that will change sometime in the future.

Robert's shop is in Shelby now; there is a lot more space in the shop in town, that's good. I have been driving the truck home.

Robert bought a home in Shelby, about a block from the by-pass.

When we stop work each day, I drop Robert off at his house, and I get back on the by—pass, and drive home.

There was a black man came in the shop about a week ago, looking for a job.

Robert told him, "I probably could use some help part time, if you would be interested in that."

"Yes sir," he said, "any work at all would be appreciated."

"What's your name?" Robert asked.

"Everyone calls me DF," he replied.

"Oh really," Robert said. "Would it make you mad if I called you Duck F+#%*r?"

"I don't care what you call me," he said.

It's Friday evening, Robert said, "Ya'll put the big ladder on the truck, we've got to go up to Wendell's department store, and check out their neon sign. They called and said some neon was blinking, probably a piece needs repair.

The store is across the street from the court house. There are a lot of people walking up and down the sidewalk, doing last minute shopping. Stores will be closing at five thirty, and it's about ten after five now.

Robert said, "DF, go inside and find the store manager, and tell him to not turn the power on to the sign when they close, because I will be working on it." We got the ladder set up, Robert is up to the top of the sign, standing on the ladder, he removed the inspection plate, and he has his arm stretched way down inside the sign as far as it will go. I am standing on the bottom rung of the ladder to make sure it don't slip on the concrete.

Robert hollers out, "God D/>#t Duck+#*&r, go inside and tell that son of a B#%+h to shut the G## +%m power off!"

I looked up, just in time to see him pull his arm out of the top of the sign. Looks like he cut it pretty bad, trying to get it out when the power was turned on, it is bleeding pretty badly. He came down to the sidewalk,

Oh brother is he mad, I don't think that manager should come out now! And now a policeman walks up, "Robert," he said, "is that you doing all that cussing we are getting calls about?" That didn't help anything. "I'll be G## D+#n!" Robert said. He knew the officer, and told him what happened. The officer said, "I'm sure I would have done some swearing myself, if it happened to me, but it's my job to tell you to try to keep your volume down, if you can. Do you want the medics to come and check your arm out? I see it's still bleeding."

"No, hell no! I'll be alright," Robert said.

There is a very popular barbeque restaurant out on the 74 by-pass with the name Red Bridges Bar-B-Q. People come from miles around to eat there. Robert's wife, Choc works there as a waitress. A lot of the State Police, as well as the City Police eat there often, so of course Choc knows all of them. Robert told me that his wife sometime gets a hundred dollars in tips during a day's work.

Today after work, I was driving Robert's truck home on the by-pass, and I was about one mile from the restaurant where Choc works. All of a sudden my rear view mirrors lit up with blue lights, and a spot light. I pulled over to the side of the road, and lord was I nervous!

I heard a horn blowing, and blowing, a Cadillac was going the other way, a woman driving the car was just waving, and waving. I think she's waving at the state trooper, and then I realized she was Robert's wife. She went to the cross-over, and came back east. She parked behind the trooper's car. She walked up to the trooper, he was out of his car, and they talked for about five minutes or so. Then he got in his car, and drove away.

Thank God, I felt like a ton had been lifted off of me, and Choc walked up to the truck, and told me that the trooper said there were no tail lights on the truck. "If you can, get them repaired before driving the truck to town in the morning, and be real careful driving on home."

"Oh yes, I sure will." I told her.

I drove on up the road about a mile, to a Gulf filling station, and put bulbs in the lights. They just needed bulbs.

Boy, was I lucky that Choc had just got off work, and was headed home when I got pulled over. She sure saved the day for me.

Mack, Maudie, and their children, Raymond and Linda came for dinner last Sunday. After dinner, Mack and I went in the living room. As I was putting some wood in the heater, I said to Mack, "Mack, what happened when you were in the Navy, that you were injured so seriously?"

Mack said, "Well, there was a ship loaded with explosives, probably some bombs, ammunition, and many kinds of weapons the army uses in battle. There was a ship on either side of that ship, escorting the ammunition ship to Japan.

The ammunition ship was hit by Japanese kamikaze pilots, hitting the ship that I was on, and the ammunition ship. Of course, there were an awfully lot of explosions, and I did not know what happened, until I woke up in a military hospital several weeks later. My work in the Navy, was in the ship's galley, I helped prepare food for the ships personnel."

I said, "Oh man, I guess I could never imagine being in something like that, I guess it was just a miracle that you lived through that. God was with you!"

"No doubt about that," he said.

Going from the elementary school to Number Three high school, there is a road where the bus has to stop at a stop sign, that is state road 226 and it goes in to Shelby, or down past Number Three high school. At that stop sign, Bo would always say, last stop before Number Three. Usually, somebody, one or two boys would get off the bus, and hitchhike to Shelby. I did that too many times. Sometimes Bob Vanhorn and I would get off, and go to the park in Shelby and bowl, or play basketball all day. Other times me and Mackie, or me and Harley would do that. Sometime Bo would go to town with us, and have his assistant drive the bus on to the high school, maybe once or twice a year. I don't know if I was a bad influence on them, or if they were me.

I do know that I failed the eighth grade, I know I missed too many days of school, so I wasn't too surprised about that.

There was a drive-in theatre between Kings Mountain and Gastonia that had just opened up. Robert drew a print of a sign that we could put on the back of the screen that faced the highway. He took it over to the theatre and presented it to the owner of the theatre. The name of the theatre is to be "Diane 29 Drive-In Theatre". The screen was almost like a building, what I mean is that there was a door at the end of the screen that you could enter. There was stairs, that a person could walk up for about thirty five feet. And then a ladder that went just about to the top of the screen, inside.

From the ground, to the top of the screen was eighty five feet tall. At seventy feet, there was a door off the ladder. You can open that door, and there was a ledge to walk out on, that was about six feet wide. From the ledge to the top of the screen was fifteen feet.

Working from the ledge on that fifteen feet space, would be "Diane 29", and the upper case letters and numbers, would be twelve feet high, and the lower case letters will be ten foot tall. We will use sky hooks to hang over the ledge, to print the "theatre" letters below the ledge. We will use safety straps at all times, when we work up there. We will be seventy foot off the ground, all the time we work on the sign.

There will be neon, outlining all the letters on the sign. There will be a large shield around the "29".

The owners of the theatre signed a contract with Robert, that Robert would put the sign that was described, on the back of the theatre screen.

I'll tell you, I just don't think it's gonna be a lot of fun carrying everything we need to work with, up the steps, not to mention carrying the stuff straight up that ladder, that goes up another thirty five feet.

About a week later, we began work on the sign. It was quite a job! We worked for four weeks on that sign. I don't mind heights at all; I made many trips up and down those steps and ladder. When we hooked the sky hooks to the ledge, to lower a walk board down to where we worked on the "theatre" letters, I thought that was pretty cool. The letters were the same size, as the ones up above.

Robert did tell me when we finished the sign, that he had purchased insurance on us, before we began work on the sign.

Brodus turned sixteen on his birthday, and got his driver's license.

He went to Jack Kings car lot and bought a nineteen forty nine Chevrolet. Generally speaking, that's where most people that don't make very much money, buy their cars. A person could get a vehicle there, and make payments of ten dollars a week, until paid off.

Well, there was a reunion coming up, of all of Mama's brothers and sisters, down at Ft. Mill, S.C., about fifty miles from here. She wanted all of us children to go.

Brodus asked Mama, "Can I drive my car down there to the reunion?"

"No son, I don't think you should do that, you haven't been driving enough since you have had your driver's license."

"Mama," Brodus said, "I have driven quite a bit before I turned sixteen that you didn't know about. You think I drove okay when I took you to get groceries?"

"Yes, you did Brodus," she said, "I'll think about it."

Here it is, Saturday, tomorrow is the reunion. Mama said, "Brodus, you can drive your car tomorrow, but you will have to follow Howard. Dallas and I are gonna ride down there with him and Cally."

"O.K.," Brodus said, "Harper is gonna ride with me.

It's Sunday morning now, and here we go. Brodus sitting over there looking as proud as a peacock, you might think that he was king of the roost. Everything is going real well, Howard is up there in front of us, Brodus is not following too close.

Howard is pulling into the horseshoe drive at Uncle Alf's house. There are lots of folks standing around in the front yard visiting.

Brodus has his window open, his arm out the window, waving at everyone, and crunch, Howard had stopped, and we ran right into the rear of Howard's car. Not much damage to either vehicle, Brodus just doesn't have any pride left now, and a lot of laughing going on! We had a really good day at the reunion, good to see Mama's brothers and sisters, we don't see them very often. We took off for home, I think about three thirty. No problems, good trip all the way home.

It's getting late summer, not a lot going on. I don't know whose idea it was, we began talking about going down to Daytona beach for a weekend. We decided, if four of us went, and shared the cost of gas, it would not cost too much for any one of us for the trip, and after all, gas is about twenty one cents a gallon. So it is decided that Brodus, Mackie, Harley, and I will be going. We will drive down there on Friday, as soon as Brodus gets off work, and come home Sunday. Brodus said, "I will drive my car." Not one of us has ever been to the beach before.

Friday is here, we have loaded our bags, towels and stuff, that we thought we will need, and we're off to the beach. We even thought to have a road map. We just didn't really hurry, we didn't need to. We will have all day tomorrow to play on the beach.

Well, Brodus drove until he came to highway seventeen at Myrtle Beach. We went south on that highway, and we were seeing signs saying, "beach", with an arrow pointing to the left, we knew that we were real close to the beach. We kept telling Brodus, turn here, go a little further, turn here Brodus, he finally did turn, but not where there was a sign was pointing "beach, next left". He turned on a road that went down through a patch of trees. You must remember that we had never been to the beach.

So here we go down this road, not knowing that it is sand, and all of us could tell that the car was struggling to keep going, and finally the car just stopped, and the engine died. "What happened?" All of us were asking Brodus. He said, "I don't know!"

All of us got out of the car to survey the situation. All four wheels were marred down in the sand. Someone said, "Brodus, get in the car and see if you can move forward, and we will push." It is just a little ways down to the beach, we can see the water from here. Brodus got in the car, we are at the back of the car ready to push, Brodus hit the starter, and the battery is dead as it can be.

Mackie said, "Well, what are we gonna do now?"

Harley said, "I don't know what ya'll are gonna do, but I am gonna get my blanket and go down there and lie down on the beach and get some sleep, it's two a.m. you know!"

That's what all of us did. And we slept there, with our trunks on, and boy did I sleep! They never woke me up this morning. I slept until ten thirty. Oh, my gosh, I was cooked, from the bottom of my feet, to the top of my neck. I knew I was gonna be hurting for days. I slept on my stomach.

A man walked up to me and asked, "Does that car up there in the woods belong to you boys?"

"Yes," I said, "it belongs to my brother, he is at the beach."

"I can help you get it out, if you want me to."

I said "The battery is dead, and it won't start."

He said, "I can get it started."

"Okay, I will go get my brother, thank you, that will be great! I'll be right back."

I went down to the beach, and found Brodus. I told him there is a man that is gonna help us get the car out of the sand.

"Okay," Brodus said, "I'm coming."

About the time we got to the car, here came the man on a tractor. We thought he was gonna pull the car out.

He got off the tractor, "Have you tried to start the car today?" he asked.

"No," Brodus replied.

"Well, get in there and see if it will start, it's been setting there for a while, it might start."

Brodus got in the car and hit the starter, it started right up.

The man said, "Let it idle, come here and let me show you something." He walked to the back side of the car, and started letting air out of the tire. Of course, as the air left the tire, the tire became wider. He let a lot of air out of the rear tires, and told Brodus to get in, and drive real slow.

Brodus got in the car, put it in gear, and started driving the car on down the little road.

"Now," he said, "If you ever get stuck in the sand again, you will know what to do."

Brodus said, "I will remember that, and I sure do thank you for your help!"

He said, "You boys have a good day, stay out of trouble."

I did not have a good day! I was so burned that I actually hurt, and I tried to stay in the shade the rest of the day. I think the other boys had a good time playing in the water, and in the sand.

It is about five-o-clock, and they are coming to the car. We got something to eat. At the restaurant, Mackie said, "Goodness, I sure didn't know you would get sun burned like that, you are as red as a ripe tomato."

"Yeah, and I feel like it. It sure hurts to set down, especially my back and legs."

Harley suggested that we stay here tonight, and take off for home about noon tomorrow. I'm sure Harper is not enjoying being here at all.

Everyone agreed that would be a good idea.

Brodus drove us back to the beach, and they went back, and played in the water for a while.

I stayed at the car in the shade, I don't hurt quite as bad in the shade, as I do in the sun.

It's getting pretty dark, I suppose the boys will be coming back to the car pretty soon. I got my blanket out of the car, and found a place to spread it out, in a spot I knew would be in the shade when I wake up in the morning. That is, if I get any sleep tonight at all.

Here come the boys, sounds like they had a ball today. They went somewhere to a public bathhouse, and took a shower to wash the salt off.

Brodus said, "Looks like you are turning in for the night, got your bed made up, huh?"

"Yep, I hope I can sleep!"

The other boys are spreading their blankets. I know they are worn out, down there playing on the beach all day.

Sunday morning, I did get some sleep, although I was awake quite a bit. The other boys were still asleep. It is daylight. I'm sure it is still pretty early. I folded my blanket, and put it in the car. I think Mackie began to wake-up and asked me, "What time is it?"

"I don't know," I told him. "Pretty early, I think!"

Mackie said, "I think I've had enough beaches!"

"Well, you had a beach day yesterday for sure," I replied.

Mackie yells out, "Everybody up! I am hungry and I want to go home."

"What?" Harley asked. "Go home?"

"Yeah," Mackie said, "haven't you had enough? I have, I'll tell you that!"

"Alright," Harley said, "I can go along with that, I guess I've had enough salt water and sand. But I want to go somewhere and have a good breakfast before we leave."

We set out to find a restaurant, and we did, I'm telling you, ham, eggs, grits, and pancakes. That should last us, until we get home.

We piled in the car, and away we went, after stopping for gas.

We came about one hundred miles up the road, and came through a very small town, don't even know the name of it , and traveled about three miles past that town. The engine coughed a couple times, backfired and quit running. Well, here we sit in the grass on the side of the road.

Someone asked, "Anyone have any idea what we're gonna do now?" Nobody said a thing.

I guess the first thing that we should do is raise the hood and see if we might find something that we can repair. Looking on both sides of the engine we couldn't see anything that had come loose. None of us are mechanics.

It seems as though we are out in the middle of "no man's land," not a lot of traffic going by.

"Let's get our thumbs out and see if we can get a ride," Harley said, "we're not going anywhere like this." He said, "I think the problem is in the carburetor." We agreed that he was probably right.

It didn't take very long until a fellow stopped and picked us up. "Where are you boys headed?"

Brodus answered, "We are trying to get to Shelby, N.C."

He said, "I'm not going that far but I will take ya'll to Charlotte, been to the beach, huh? Was that your car I saw setting back there beside the road?"

Brodus said, "Yeah it is, it just quit running. We will come back and get it tomorrow, that is, if we get home tonight!"

After getting to Charlotte, I called Howard, my brother-in-law, and asked if he would come and get us. He said yes, that he would be here in about an hour.

We arrived home and boy was I glad. Mama put some stuff on my back. I have no idea what it was, but it did relieve the burning, although it hurts to sit down, or put cover on my back when I go to bed.

Howard gave us permission to use his car to go back the next day and try to bring Brodus' car back. Brodus talked to a couple people at the green house and told them what the engine sounded like when it stopped running. They said it sounds like the carburetor. Brodus got a used one somewhere, we gathered up some tools and took off to see if we could get Brodus' car running and bring it home.

We got back to where the car was, raised the hood, looking to see where to start removing the carburetor, and a very young looking kid walked up and asked, "What seems to be the problem?"

Brodus said, "We were just riding along and the engine backfired and it chugged a couple of times and died, and we could not get it started again."

He looked like he was too young to know anything about mechanics. He asked, "Could I take a look at it?"

Brodus said, "Sure, be alright with me!"

He unscrewed something on the side of the carburetor and pulled it out, held it up and proceeded to wipe it off on his shirt, and screwed it back in. He told Brodus to get in and start it up.

Brodus said, "You think it will start?"

"Yeah," he said, "it will start!"

Brodus got in the car, hit the starter, and it started right up. "What on earth did you do?"

"I removed the needle valve, it was dirty, so I cleaned it off, that's all it took," he said.

"Well, good lord," Brodus said, "that is just wonderful, I am so thankful for that. What do I owe you?"

"You don't owe me anything, I'm glad I could help you boys."

We shook hands with him, and we are on our way home.

We arrived home without any further problem, and man, it is so good to have this last weekend behind us.

School has started, I am back in the eighth grade for the second time. Oh well, maybe it will be easier this time, maybe.

We had been building a very big sign for another department store in Shelby, Robert had traveled to Charlotte, and took the pattern of the sign to have the neon made. We spent a big share of today installing the sign to the building. Robert hired a company to bring a crane and an operator, to lift the sign up, so we could attach the sign to the front of the store. We had already attached the brackets to the wall where we would fasten the sign to, so all we needed was for the crane to pick the sign up two floors, so we could fasten the sign to the brackets that we had previously attached.

He was a very good crane operator; we had the sign attached to the wall in less than an hour. So now we have to stabilize the sign by fastening two steel cables to the far outside of the sign on both sides, back to the brick wall. It took us about four hours to get that completed.

We will bring the neon over here in the morning and install it. Tomorrow is Saturday, so Brodus is gonna come with us to help.

It's Saturday morning, and we are loading the neon on the truck.

Robert says, "Okay now boys, let's be careful, I don't want any neon broken, watch what you're doing! It's a long way to Charlotte, you know!"

If we heard that once, we heard it fifteen times while we were loading it.

We got it all loaded up and on our way. When we arrived there we set the ladder up and pushed the extension to the roof.

Robert said, "Can you boys get the neon up on the roof without breaking any of it?"

"I'm sure we can," I replied. "Brodus can bring one piece of neon at a time, about half way up the ladder and I will take it on up and put it on the roof."

Robert said, "I'm gonna go on up on the roof, there are a few things I want to check out on the sign before we start attaching the neon."

Brodus and I began taking the neon up to the roof, a lot of trips up and down the ladder.

O.K. now, watch out, can you guess what's coming next?

Brodus was standing at the back of the truck where the tool box was setting, and Robert yelled down to Brodus, "Brodus, throw the pliers up here on the roof," and before he could think about what he said, the pliers were on the way, "NO! NO!" Robert screamed.

But it was too late, pieces of neon went every which way.

All hell broke loose. "G++ D3+7t Brodus, didn't you know you just brought all that neon up here?"

Brodus said, "I was just doing what you told me to do."

Robert sputtered, "I know that, good G## almighty, son of a b+%#h, what in hell am I supposed to do, I only wanted to finish this sign today, now everything is all f(+?#d up. Well, let's sort this s++t out and see if there is any neon that is still good and see what we have to reorder."

As it turned out, there are six pieces of neon that are destroyed. I'm glad he didn't tell Brodus to throw the hammer up here! Robert marked on the pattern the neon he needed Eddie to make. He sent it to Eddie's shop in Charlotte. When he finishes, someone will have to make the trip to Charlotte.

Embarking on another year, I can't help but wonder what it will bring. I hope it's not another year like last year! I guess it's up to me for the most part, to make it good.

Chapter Twelve

Back in school, in the ninth grade, and I absolutely do not understand math at all. Our teacher, Mr. Hamrick, was very strict and firm. When I asked a question, he would usually say, if you would have been paying attention you would not have to ask! That pretty much told me to not ask, and no one at home could help me with math.

Mr. Hamrick was also the basketball coach. Most of the students called him "Babe Hamrick," I don't know where that name came from. Maybe they thought he had somewhat of a baby face. One thing we all knew about him was that he had the smoking habit. Between classes there was about a five minute break, the boys that smoked would head for the bathroom in the basement for a quick puff. As we went down the stairs we would always meet Mr. Hamrick coming up the stairs, and there would be heavy cigarette smoke in the bathroom!

I am not really encouraged to go to school by anyone at home, and I guess I was too embarrassed to ask any of the other students for help with math or any other subject.

Maybe Robert was somewhat of a father figure, I have certainly learned a lot being with him, that is, as far as electrical and metal work, and of course neon, and I did get to where I could do some sign lettering. On the other hand, he was definitely a bad influence on me. He was not honest, he cheated and lied. His language was not good at all with a young boy hanging around with him. But, for some reason I kept spending a lot of my time with him.

He never mentioned sex, that never ever came up except for the four letter word he used quite often. Maybe being young like I am,

I liked the attention he gives me. I just don't know any other way to describe him.

It's April, and I just had my fifteenth birthday.

I'll be glad when school is out, I don't know what I will do this summer, maybe a part time job where I can get paid for what I do.

I struggled on through until school is out; it is the first of June and we just heard that Jack and Cecile are coming down to visit in a couple of weeks, it will be nice to see them.

Within three weeks I pretty much knew what I was going to do for the summer.

Jack and Cecile arrived, Jack was driving a brand new nineteen fifty four Ford.

After a few days Cecile asked me, "How would you like to go back to Indiana with us? I'll bet you could find a job for the summer, and we will bring you back before school starts."

I replied, "I guess that would be up to Mama, I would like to do that."

Cecile talked to Mama, Mama said it would be okay, if she was sure that they would bring me back before school starts in September, and make sure that I didn't get in any trouble.

"Oh," Cecile said, "he won't be getting into any trouble!"

In a few days we were on our way to Indiana. I was glad to be getting away for the summer. I'm hoping I can get a job up there. I had been to Indiana once before when Howard and Cally took Mama, Brodus, and me up there on their vacation.

We made the trip in one long day; we left early and arrived here very late. We came to Akron, IN where Jack's Mother lives. Jack said we will go up to New Paris in the morning, that's where they work. It's about an hour north of here.

It's Sunday morning, we are on our way to New Paris. Jack and Cecile live in a basement, it sure ain't fancy, and there are curtains between the rooms where we will live, and the furnace and other parts of a regular basement.

A man and woman by the name of Millers own the house, I never knew their first names. They are very nice people, we use their bathroom up stairs, that is not very handy, but I don't think they charge too much to rent the basement.

Jack works in a factory here in town called Smokercraft. They make boat oars and campers. Cecile works just down the road at a chicken processing plant. I will go looking for a job in the morning. I am looking forward to that.

Ceicle woke me up at seven thirty this morning. "Breakfast is ready, get up, we have to go find you a job."

"Okay, I'm on my way, be there in a minute."

Goshen is the nearest big town, about twenty thousand I would say. We were all over the place looking for someone that might hire a fifteen year old boy, I didn't find a job until we started home. There is a nursery where they grow evergreen plants and young trees, and they do a lot of landscaping and lawn mowing and things like that. Kimes Nursery is the name of the place. They told me I would be doing a little bit of everything.

Jay Kime was my boss, he was very nice. "Can you start tomorrow?" he asked.

"Sure can!" I told him.

"Alright," he said, "I'll see you at seven in the morning."

"Thank you very much, and see you in the morning!"

We left the nursery early this morning and went to a house that they just finished building, there were five of us. We did a lot of raking, getting the small rocks and dirt clods raked out, and trying to smooth it out, and get it ready to fertilize and plant grass.

We left there and came back to the nursery about two-o-clock. Then I had to go out in the trees and hoe the weeds out until time to quit.

Jack was here to pick me up after work. "How did your first day go? Jack asked me.

"Very good," I told him, "it wasn't a bad day at all. I'm sure I can handle it."

Cecile was cooking supper when we arrived home, pork chops and mashed potatoes. She sure makes pork chops proud, very good.

Today we went to a house right beside a big lake, we had to repair a sea wall at the back of their house and repair their pier. We were working on that just about all day. We got back to the nursery just in time to go home.

On Thursday and Fridays all the employees mowed grass, I usually worked with a push mower, and another man used a riding mower. I did the trimming. There were a lot of houses where we had to mow, especially when we got a lot of rain. Most of the houses were very large, I supposed they were very wealthy home owners.

Every Wednesday Jack takes me to work, and hauls the bicycle, one of his old bicycles, so I can ride it home from work because they get off work before I do. They go to Akron to check on his Mother, and they drive back up here early Thursday morning.

It's about four miles from where I work to where we live. About half way, there, is an old grocery store, and a lot of homes and it is called Waterford Mills. I usually stop there and get me something cold to drink.

I go with them to Akron on Friday evening, and we spend the weekend there and come back early Monday morning. Akron is a very small town, population around thirty five hundred.

Actually, that was my summer this year, same thing over and over, day after day, and week after week.

About the middle of August, we left to go back to Shelby, N.C. I was really glad to get back home, to see Mama, Brodus and my sisters and all my friends. As they say there's "no place like home".

It will be time to start back to school pretty soon. I failed the ninth grade, so I will repeat the ninth grade this school year. I am going to do my best.

I guess I am paying more attention to girls than I ever did before. I sure don't know anything about them, but I am sure I will learn. A girl in my class seems to like me very well, and I like her with one exception, she has very bad teeth. We write notes back and forth in school, I guess one might say that we were very fond of each other; we talk to each other between classes. Her first name is Dixie, that's all I will say about her right now.

Thanksgiving is just around the corner. I see Jack Cogsdale often, he comes by and picks me up and we go to the show or something like that. I'll be glad when I get my license and a car.

But that will be a while yet.

Today is Christmas day. Harley picked me up after we had dinner, he had a girl with him and I had called Dixie. She said she could go riding with us. We picked Dixie up and we were just riding around, we went to the Carolina Drive-In and got something to drink. I asked Harley to go back by my house, that I needed to get something. When we got to our house I asked Dixie if she would like to go in and meet my family, she said sure. I introduced her to all my family, they were all setting in the living room, the little "Warm Morning" heater was keeping the house warm.

Standing there in our living room looking around would pretty much tell anyone what our life style was like. The honest truth was that we are not wealthy, and that is easy for anyone to see.

At any rate she doesn't talk to me at all any more, I found out later that her parents owned a grocery store. I had never known that, maybe her parents were wealthy. Whatever the reason, our little affair is over with!

Life will get better, a lot better. I know it will.

I'm not doing much better as far as school goes, I started this school year with hope that I could do a lot better than I have done. Things just don't seem to come together for me, and I know for the most part I cannot blame anyone but me.

I guess my first big mistake was that I should have been a little bolder in school and got the help I needed with my school work. I'm sure I could have done so much better if only I had put my mind to it. I wish someone would have given me more encouragement than I had.

I suppose I will probably drop out of school in April when I turn sixteen, and go to work at the greenhouses like the rest of my family have done.

I sure would like to have a better life in the future than some other people I know.

Bobby Van Horn has a steady girlfriend now and I don't see much of him. Harley and I see each other a lot. He picks me up and we go hang out at the local burger drive inns, lots of girls go to them places. Harley has a 1949 Hudson Hornet, it is really cool.

I haven't been writing much for a while. There really hasn't been much to write about. As you probably suspected I've had my sixteenth birthday and yes, I quit school.

Mama did not tell me to not quit school, but she told me if I did that I would have to pay her ten dollars a week to live here. So, just like I said earlier, I am working at Patterson's Greenhouses.

I make twenty two dollars and ninety cents a week. I will work here until I find a better job; it's not easy to find a decent job when you are only sixteen.

I did go over to Jack King's Car Sales and junk yard, and bought a 1949 Ford. I had to pay $10.00 down, and I have to pay $10.00 a week. At least I have my own vehicle.

Mackie was telling me about a street in Shelby where several girls get together about every evening at one or the others home and dance, sing, or just whatever. He has been seeing a girl over there by the name of Yvonne. He said that I should come over with him sometime, that I might like one of the girls that I would meet. "Okay" I said, "come by and pick me up the next time you go, and I will go over there with you."

Mackie came by this evening and picked me up and we went over to Yvonne's house.

He parked along side the street in front of her house.

"See what I told you," he said, "just take your pick, but don't pick Yvonne."

"Well," I said, "maybe you should introduce me to them."

"I will, come on get out."

"Ya'll gonna just set out there in the car?" one of the girls asked.

Mackie said, "No," as he opened the car door, "we're gonna come and get ya!"

"All of us?" one of them asked.

Mackie said, "Probably couldn't handle more than one."

Walking up on the porch Mackie said, "This is a friend of mine, his name is Harper Garris."

I think all of them said, "hey, Harper," at the same time.

"This one right here is Yvonne," as he put his hand on her shoulder, "remember what I said about her!"

"Okay, okay, I do remember."

"Over there in that rocking chair is Betty, the other girl on the swing is Annette, and I guess I haven't met the one standing by the door there."

Betty said, "Her name is Amelia, she lives around the corner down there," pointing to the next street down the block.

All of us just sit around talking about first one thing then another, teasing each other, just having fun. As the evening went along

I worked up enough nerve to ask; "Betty, would you give me your telephone number?"

"Sure, I will write it down for you, call me any time!"

"I sure will, I will give you a call tomorrow."

"I'll be waiting," she said.

Betty seemed a little shy, she spoke softly, and not so fast, like she was choosing her words. I liked that about her, and of course I thought she was very pretty.

I called Betty the next evening. "Hey Betty, could I pick you up and the two of us go to the drive-in and get a milk shake or something to drink?"

"Sure, that sounds great to me," she said.

I was a little nervous driving over there, thinking if she liked me, maybe I can get a little more relaxed with her today. I arrived at her house and she was waiting for me.

"Hey there," I said, as she was getting in to the car. "And just how are you this evening?"

"Oh," she said, "I am just fine. What have you been doing all day?"

"Working," I said, "I work every day from seven a.m. 'til five."

"Really, where do you work?"

"Patterson's Greenhouses," I replied, "do you know where that is?"

"Yeah, I think it is out on seventy four, toward Kings Mountain."

"Yep, that's where I work, they don't pay very well, but I'm hoping to find a better job."

"What about you, what did you do all day?"

With a silly smile she said, "nothing!"

"Oh my," I said, "anybody can do that, but it doesn't pay very well either."

She said, "I have been out of school for a year, and jobs aren't easy to find."

"Wow, did you graduate already?"

"I knew you were gonna ask me that question, I quit school last year, and I am sure that's why I can't find a job. What do you think of me now?" she asked.

"I don't feel any different now than before you told me that."

"I quit school back in April, myself. How do you feel about me now?"

As she was sliding across the seat closer to me, she said, "I don't feel any different at all!"

"Okay," I said, "I'm glad we got that talked about."

Our feelings for each other seemed to grow as each day goes by. We began seeing each other almost every night of the week.

There was one night last week when we were out together, and we came back and I parked in the yard, pretty close to the front porch. We were all wrapped up in each other's arms kissing and making out, we had no idea what time it was. All of a sudden the porch light came on and her Dad stomped out on the porch.

"You get your G=# D+#n ass out of that car and in this house right now. Just who in hell do you think you are, young lady?"

"Good night," she said, "hope I see you tomorrow, love ya."

I said, "Good night, love you, you will."

And I did, I am back at Betty's tonight!

"Did you get in big trouble last night? I asked.

"No," she said, "Dad's bark is much scarier than his bite. He is really a puss and a sweet man, and he loves me to death. And I love him. He does get in moods sometime! He tries to protect me."

The summer is quickly passing by, and I hate it. I love the summertime.

Working down at Patterson's has been an experience for me. They have an old Ford pick-up truck, it's all beat up, and no one has tried to take care of it at all. There are no doors on it, one rear fender is missing. Patterson owns a farm about eight miles out in the country, and there is a lake on the farm.

When the pots of flowers in the green houses get too old and the leaves start falling off, and they just don't look very good. They will get rid of them. We have to knock the plants out of the pots, and fill up a flat with the flowers and carry them out to the truck. We throw them in the pick-up until the truck is loaded, and haul them down to the farm, and unload them there. It was no big problem to get it unloaded. There was a very steep hill that went down to the lake. We back the truck down that hill as fast as we thought we could go, and then slam on the brakes as hard as we could, and guess what? The truck is unloaded. Heaven help us if the truck doesn't stop!

We have a dog, just a mutt, but he is a good dog. His name is

Ring. He stays outside all the time. We came home for lunch today, and when we headed back to work after lunch, Ring decided he would follow me back to work at the greenhouse. I ran him back to the house a couple of times, and I didn't see him again.

There was a large fan, about four foot square, at each end of every greenhouse, that was used during the summer months.

I went back to work when I arrived at the greenhouses. I was working between two flower beds, when I looked up, there was Ring standing about ten foot from me between the two flower beds. I hollered "Ring" about as loud as I could, and he turned and started running.

I guess he thought that was a window where the fan was, and he jumped through it, man, what a noise it made. I went out the door thinking I would see a dog that was all sliced up. No, there he stood, wagging his tail. He was okay, except he was missing one ear. I could not believe that. I felt so sorry for him. Then he went home and stayed there.

Brodus has been taking the roses and carnations to Vaughn's green houses, a place in Charlotte that buys them from Patterson's, and they ship them all around the world.

Well, since Brodus is eighteen now, they made him a salesman. So they called me in the office and asked, "Have you ever driven in Charlotte?"

"Many, many times," I told her.

"How would you like to take the roses and carnations to Charlotte every Monday, Wednesday and Friday?"

"Yeah, I would like that very much," I told her.

"Alright, starting Monday, that will be your job."

Now, back to Betty, I like to get back to Betty. I am gonna take her to the county fair this evening. We have a very big fair here every year.

I know we will have fun, I did win her a teddy bear, cost me six dollars and twenty five cents, and she is worth every bit of that.

We didn't stay very late, we came home and parked in front of her house, not in front of the porch, for sure.

We began to neck, like we did so many times, and somehow here I am on the passenger's side. We are getting really warmed up to say the least. I mean she was all over me. She was straddling my leg like I have never known before, and rubbing all over me. What am I supposed to do? She is two years older than me, probably more knowledgeable about sex.

I wrote earlier what I knew about sex, which was nothing! Oh, I heard my buddies talk about sex. But we were never allowed to even say the word in our home. At sixteen, I had never even seen a real photo of a nude female.

In my mind, I thought if a man really cared and had strong feelings about a girl, he should respect her enough to not want to have sex with her. Many guys would think that I am crazy I suppose, but that is how I feel!

Perhaps I am very embarrassed about my situation here in the front seat, not to mention how nervous I was. Oh yes, at the same time my body was very excited. So, I was too naïve to know what to do.

I'm sure she could have given me some lessons about sex tonight, that I never knew and probably would not know for a long time to come.

I brought it to an end when I said, "I guess I had better be going home."

She straightened up in the seat and said, "Okay, I better go in the house."

I do not want to know how she feels about me now, and I hope she doesn't think I have bad feelings about her, my feelings are still the same.

Cecile called our house and told Mama that she and Jack would be coming down on vacation, and they would arrive in one week.

Jack and Cecile arrived here today. They were here when I came home from work. It's good to see them again. Mama cooked a big meal for them this evening. At the supper table Cecile looked at Jack and said, "Well honey, go ahead and tell him what you have been waiting to tell him."

Jack said to me, "I am the assistant manager at a gas station in Goshen, and one of the full time workers is working a notice, he is quitting in a week, and the manager is looking to hire someone. We are wondering if you would be interested in the job."

"Oh, my goodness Jack, I don't know, I guess I would have to think about that a little bit. What kind of station is it? Would it be changing oil, washing cars, and stuff like that?"

"No, no," Jack said, "we don't do anything like that at all. All we do is pump gas, check their oil if they want us to, clean windshields. And we do some cleaning around the station, like washing the windows, cleaning the gas pumps and such stuff as that. It is owned by one person, and he owns another station in Warsaw, about twenty miles away. It is what they call "independently owned and operated" by one person. It is called Kaufman Oil Company. The position that is open is that you work from six a.m. until three thirty p.m. Monday through Friday, on Saturday six a.m. until one p.m. and off on Sunday. The job pays sixty five dollars a week."

"That sure is something to think about," I said. "That is three times what I make at the greenhouse. Let me think about that for a day or two."

"Well," Jack said, "we will be leaving to go back to Indiana Sunday, which will give you six days to make up your mind!"

I got cleaned up after supper, and I am on my way to see Betty, boy oh boy, what a decision I need to make! What in the world am I gonna do?

I cannot imagine what Betty will say about it, I sure care an awful lot about her, and she will be the reason if I don't go. I don't think she will like this at all. I will find out when I talk to her about this

"Betty," I said, "I have something very important to talk to you about."

"Okay," she said, "go ahead."

"I told you my sister and brother-in-law was coming from Indiana on vacation."

"Yes, you told me," she said.

"Well, they have a good job offer for me out there, and they want me to go back to Indiana with them."

"Did you decide if you were going to go?"

"I haven't yet. I wanted to talk to you first, before I made up my mind. What would you do if I went? Would you say it is over between you and me if I went, or could we remain as we are now as far as our feelings are concerned? If I went, I would continue to love you and feel the same about you, how would you feel about me?"

"I don't know what to say," she said, as the tears welled up in her eyes. "I have never had anything like this happen. I don't know how

I would feel if you left. I don't know if the feelings would be the same if we were not seeing each other like we do now, I can't promise you that. I don't know, I just don't know!"

We continued seeing each other every evening through Saturday night. I had made my mind up reluctantly, that I was going, maybe against my better judgment.

We promised each other we would write often, and that I would be coming back soon. At sixteen, do you know in your heart that you can really love someone? Or do you just think you do? I guess time will tell.

Jack, Cecile, and their daughter Brenda, and I left the next morning for Indiana.

As we traveled along, my emotions are just running wild; my stomach seems to be churning like never before! Is this a mistake, I ask myself? I wanna go back home, no I wanna keep going. My mind is so messed up!

I guess Cecile sensed something was bothering me.

"Are you alright, Harper?" she asked.

"I don't know," I replied, "I sure do have a lot of thoughts going through my mind, thinking about home, and Betty and everything."

"Well you are gonna be alright," she said, "we will do everything possible to make you feel at home, and be happy in Indiana. You will get used to it, you will have friends up there, and we think you will like Indiana."

I sure do hope I will!

Jack said, "I'll bet you will like your job, probably meet so many girls that you can't take care of them all."

I'm thinking, I don't want to meet many girls. I just want to be with Betty. I know that they don't know how deep my feelings are for Betty right now.

Well, we talked and traveled through the day and half the night, and arrived in New Paris, IN at about one thirty in the morning, and so tired.

Chapter Thirteen

Jack has a nineteen fifty five Mercury, but the trip was still tiring.

Neither Jack nor Cecile went to work today, they stayed home to get rested up from the trip.

Cecile works at a factory in Goshen where they make clocks. The name is Time, Inc.

They are hoping to buy a small house just south of town here in New Paris. We live in this basement apartment now, where they lived last year when I was out here.

Jack said, "Harper, are you ready to go meet your future boss man?"

"As ready as I will ever be, I guess."

"We will go over to the station this morning and see Carl, you will find out that he is really a nice man."

After we drink some coffee we did go over to the station in Goshen.

Getting out of the car Jack said, "I sure hope you will like your job here, I'm sure Carl will hire you. I told him all about you. That's Carl walking this way now," Jack said.

"How was your trip, Jack?" he asked.

"We had a real good trip," Jack told him. "Carl, this is my brother-in-law that I have been telling you about, this is Harper Garris. Harper, this is Carl Holcomb, the manager of the station here."

We shook hands with each other and said our hello's,

Carl asked, "So, do you think you will like this part of the country?"

"Oh," I replied, "I'm sure I will, I guess Jack told you I spent the summer here last year."

Carl said, "Yes, he did mention that, you worked out at Kimes Nursery. Come on inside the station, it's not quite as hot in there."

We walked inside and Carl began to ask me some questions.

"Jack tells me you would like a job working here, he told me that you would be a good worker, and that you were a good kid!"

"I try hard to be as good a worker as I can possibly be. And I have never been in any serious trouble, and I am trying my level best to stay out of trouble. My Mama taught me well!"

Carl said, "I am glad to hear you say that, and I believe what you tell me, and I will give you the job, and let's see how you do, I'm sure you will do well."

"We furnish the uniforms," he said, as he pulled a piece of paper out of his pocket. What size pants do you wear?"

"I wear thirty, thirty pants, and size fifteen and a half shirts," I said.

"Okay, good," as he wrote that down. "I want to have your uniforms here before you start. How would you like to start on Monday?" That would be great!" I said.

Carl said, "I will be working Monday morning when you get here, and I will show you around."

I said, "Ok, I'll see you then!"

Carl came out the door behind us and said, "Oh Harper, I forgot to tell you your hours, start at six a.m. and get off at three thirty every day except Sunday, you'll be off on Sundays," he said.

I said, "See you Monday morning at six."

We went home, Cecile had dinner waiting for us. After dinner Cecile took Jack to work, he has to be there and ready to go to work by one thirty. She has to take him to work so she will have the car to take his supper to him in the evening. Brenda and I went with Cecile.

Tomorrow Cecile will go back to work on her job, so Jack will have to take sandwiches for supper.

The hours that Jack and Carl works is as following;

Jack works from one thirty until ten-o-clock p.m.

The night shift worker comes in at ten and works from ten p.m. until six a.m.

Jack comes back to work at six a.m. and works until one thirty p.m. That makes up a twenty four hour day!

Carl works the opposite hours, it's kinda like on twenty four and off twenty four.

The third shift person works seven nights a week.

Cecile said they would be working on the process of buying that house when Jack has time off before and after work.

Cecile rides to and from work with her friend that works where she works, her name is Norita, I don't know her last name.

Well, it sounds like they are gonna be buying that house, we'll be moving in within a couple weeks.

This is Friday morning; Jack is off work until one thirty today, he said to me, "Harper, let's go to town, there's something I want to show you."

"Okay," I said.

Jack drove us to a car lot, we got out and walked over to a nineteen forty nine Packard. He said, "You are going to need a car to drive to work, this one is in pretty good shape, and it don't look bad. We could get it with no down payment, and the payments are thirty eight dollars a month. I will have to have it in my name because you are too young to sign a contract. Would you like to have this car?"

"Oh yes, I would love to have this car!"

He said, "You've got it, it's all yours. I'll go in and sign the papers, and get you a temporary plate, I will try to hurry. You will have to get some insurance on it you know."

"Yes, I'll do that," I said.

Jack came back out of the office and I said, "Thank you so much for getting this car for me, I sure do appreciate this."

"That's o.k.," he said, "just be real careful driving it."

"You can bet I will!"

We went home and Jack got ready and went to work at about one-o-clock.

My car is big, it's very comfortable and easy to drive, and it is black. It rides so good. It has a straight eight engine in it. Most guys would not say it was cool, but I sure like it!

Jack went to work, I got my paper and pen and set down here at the table, and I am writing a letter to Betty. I've got a lot to tell her, my address and about my job, and that I have got a car. I try to write her a letter every day. I'll be glad when I get a letter from her, I am so anxious to hear from her, I think of her all the time.

Cecile came home from work, and she was all excited, she said we can move in our house next weekend.

She asked me, "Do you know who owns that big black car in the drive way?"

"Yep," I proudly said, "it is my car."

She asked, "Where and how did you get it?"

"Jack and I went to town this morning, and he helped me get it, and I sure do like it. We can take Jack his supper tonight, I will take you."

"Well good, he will like that," she said.

Cecile cooked up a good supper, pork chops, mashed potatoes, and green beans, man was that good, mmmmmm, good!

Off to Goshen we go with Jacks supper. "What do you think of my car?" I asked her.

"It sure rides good, and it is very comfortable. I like it a lot. Maybe I will drive this to work, and you can ride with Norita!"

"Maybe you won't, no, no, and no. I guess I will drive this to work myself. Thank you."

Well, we got moved in to Jack and Cecile's house this weekend. It's kind of small, but it's very nice, I like it. Cecile has been busy all weekend putting up curtains and getting everything arranged in the house. It has certainly been a busy weekend for sure.

It is five thirty Monday morning, and I am on my way to work. It is the first week of October, and it is pretty nice out as far as the weather goes.

I arrived at the station about five forty five and Carl is just getting to work.

I parked my car back behind the station and went inside. Carl said, "Come on back to the back room. Here is a uniform for you, put this on," he said.

"Okay" I said, and he went into the front of the station and closed the door.

I got undressed and put the uniform on, (it is totally white) and went out front.

"How does that fit you?" he asked.

"Seems to fit pretty good," I told him.

"Looks pretty good," he said. "At the end of each day you should take one uniform home to put on the next morning, and bring the dirty one back and put it in the barrel in the back room."

"That sounds good," I told him, "I will do that."

Carl said, "After work today, I want you to go down the street here to Adams store and buy a cap like I have on, and we will pay for it. They know what caps we wear.

A white cap with a hard bill, like a boat captain or a policeman would wear.

Carl said the company where he rents our uniforms did not have the name "Harper" to put on my shirts, so he had them put "Sam" on mine, which was fine with me.

After I was dressed in my uniform, I went out front where Carl was, he said, "I will show you around, and tell you what your clean-up chores will be each morning when you come to work, when you are not taking care of customers. No matter what you are doing, when a car pulls on to the drive, drop everything and take care of the customer, the customer comes first, always.

The first thing you do is clean all the gas pumps with Bon-ami, get your sponge wet and rub some Bon-ami on the pump and after it has dried, wipe it off with a clean dry rag. They will shine up pretty nice.

And then, get the bucket from the back room and put some soap and water in it and the long handled brush and wash the islands around the pumps real good, and rinse them off with the water hose. Another job you will be doing is to wash all the big windows in the front room inside and out every other day. In the meantime just take care of the customers. Do you think you can handle all of that?"

"I'll bet I can," I told him.

After I finished all of my chores, I asked him if there was anything else he needed me to do.

"No," Carl said, "just watch for customers entering the driveway, I will be helping with the customers when they come in. I will go to the driver's window to find out what they want, regular, or ethyl, and you stand at the back where you put the gas in, and I will relay their order back to you. And you can help me clean the windows of the car after you set the nozzle to automatic, if they only want one or two dollars worth, just stay with the nozzle until you have finished pumping the amount they want. If you pump more than they ordered, then you have to pay the difference."

It's going real good today, I am learning as I go along. Carl pointed out that all we sell is gas and oil, and we sell anti-freeze in the winter months. He was telling me that the first time they forecast the temperature to be below freezing, we will get a big rush on anti-freeze sales. He said most people drain their radiators in the spring and put water in it and drain their radiators again in the fall, and fill it up with anti-freeze. That's good for business!

Carl said, "Most of all we sell service, that's what most people want, when they come in, give them a big smile, pump their gas, check the oil, if needed and get them out as fast as we can. Oh yes, we also sell cigarettes. And, we have a Coke machine. Cokes are six cents a bottle in the machine.

Oil prices range from fifteen cents a quart to fifty five cents per quart."

Trying to figure out how to find all of the hood latches can be a little tricky, if they can't open them from the inside. As far as that goes, sometimes finding the gas cap could also be a little tricky!

My first day went very good, Carl and I talked a lot to each other, and Jack came to work at one thirty, Carl had to check out before he left, that took him about forty five minutes, and I worked with Jack until three thirty. That's when the part time help comes in every day, they are school kids.

Betty is on my mind just about all the time, I'm driving home hoping I get a letter from her, and of course the job is on my mind.

I stopped and got the mail at the post office, no letter today, I'm disappointed, I wish she would write more often.

A car pulled in the driveway, oh that's Cecile and Norita I guess, I haven't met Norita, she is coming in too.

"Harper, this is my friend that I ride to work with, her name is Norita Dooley. This is my brother, Harper," she told Norita.

"Well, my goodness Cecile, you never told me he was so good looking."

"I'm not," I said, "but thank you." I'm sure my face is red.

"Well you sure are," Norita said. "I'm gonna tell my little sister about you, you just might like her, and, I have an idea that she will like you."

"I hope she would, I would like to meet her."

Well, Norita was a pretty girl, but she was very big, should I say plump, maybe very overweight. I don't mean to say something bad about her, she is so nice and I like Norita.

I am just thinking, I have never been attracted to big girls, and if her sister is big like her, I may not be interested in her, anyhow, I do have a girlfriend, but she is in North Carolina. Perhaps maybe, I would feel a little better about living here if I could meet and make friends with some girls and boys about the same age as me.

My first week working at the station went real well, I think I am beginning to get used to what I am supposed to do. The work certainly is not hard, and so far, I like it. Carl has been very nice to me. He is a very firm and serious kind of a man.

Tomorrow I am going down to North Manchester and visit my sister Anne, and her husband Bill. You have met them before. It is about fifty miles down there to where they live. I haven't seen them since I got here, over a week ago.

I have received a couple of letters from Betty this week; it's so good to hear from her. I sure would love to see her, but I can't for a while. I don't know when I will see her again.

I arrived here at Annie's about one-o-clock this afternoon, Bill came out to the car as soon as I pulled in to the driveway.

"Hey Bill, how are you doing?"

"We are fine," Bill said, "how are you doing?"

"I'm doing real good, I guess," as we shook hands. "Is Annie home?"

"She's got dinner just about ready, you got here just in time, come on in."

"Whose car is that?" Bill asked.

"It's mine," I said.

"How do you like it?"

"I like it a lot, it runs good," I told him.

Walking in the door, Annie said, "Hello stranger, it's about time you coming down here to see us!"

"That's for sure," I replied, "but you know I've been pretty busy since I got here."

"I'm sure you have been, It's good to see you."

"Well, it's so good to see you also."

"Well," Annie said, "sit down there at the table and let's eat dinner.

I had a real nice visit with Annie, Bill, Neva and Barbara this afternoon, and I got home about five thirty this evening.

Jack and Cecile were here when I arrived home.

"How was Annie and family?" Cecile asked.

"They all seemed to be just fine. I was happy to see them, and they seemed to be glad to see me."

Cecile has supper on the stove, I guess we will be eating soon. After supper I'm gonna write Betty a letter, let her know what I have been up to. I like not having to work on Sunday.

But it's back to work tomorrow. I'll be working with Carl in the morning, it really doesn't matter who I'm working with, I just like my job. I sure don't have to work hard, and I like Carl, and he seems to like me so far. He is married and has two children, a boy and a girl.

I stopped at the post office on my way home from work, wow, two letters from Betty, she must have a lot to say, I hope it ain't something that I don't want to hear.

I read the letters when I arrived home, everything is alright, she says she loves me.

There's a little dairy bar up town, they have burgers, drinks, milkshakes and a pinball machine, I like playing that. I come up here sometimes in the evenings for something to do. The lady that owns the dairy bar is very nice, her name is Lillian Lehman.

I keep hoping that I will meet someone to be friends with, either boy or girl.

Another week is behind me, and I haven't met anyone new, I guess I will go up to the dairy bar again tonight for a while. I look forward to the letters that I receive from Betty, but that's not like having someone to visit with or hang around with. Surely I will meet someone soon, I think I would be a good friend for someone, ha, ha, I'm just thinking out loud.

I went up to the dairy bar tonight for a while and played the juke box and the pin ball machine, that would be a lot more fun, if someone was with me.

Sunday morning, Cecile made a big breakfast for us, it wasn't eggs, grits and biscuits, but it was good. We had some ham, eggs and potatoes. We never had potatoes for breakfast back home. I had never eaten potatoes for breakfast until I came to Indiana. It sure is different.

October, 1955 This is a wonderful day!

Maybe the best day of my life, time will tell, I don't remember when I have been more excited, or feel so good. Suddenly, I like Indiana, let me tell you about it.

After dinner, I was setting at the kitchen table, and a car is pulling in to the driveway, I said, "Norita just pulled in to the drive," and I looked away, Cecile went to the door.

"Come on in," she said, "who is this little sweetie with you?"

"This is my sister that I have been telling Harper about, I want to introduce them."

There is a step down to the living room from the dining room.

"You come down here," Norita said to me.

I saw her, oh did I see her.

"Harper, this is my sister Miriam."

"Miriam, this is Harper, the guy I have been telling you about."

I didn't hear everything she said; my mind was going a mile a minute. She is so beautiful, well, I'm thinking, she won't care about me, she's too pretty for me.

"How are you?" I asked her.

"I am good," she said.

I think she is a little shy, but I am too, when It comes to meeting girls.

All of us just set and talked for a while, Cecile said, "Jack will be getting home from work soon, and maybe we can do something when he gets here."

I am thinking, I sure wished that girl would like me. She sure is pretty.

Jack arrived home, and Cecile fixed him his dinner and put it on the table for him. Norita introduced Miriam to him.

Cecile asked Jack if he had thought of anything that he wanted to do this afternoon.

Jack said, "I was thinking about driving over to South Bend to visit my brother Kenneth, what do you think, Cil?" That's what he called Cecile!

"That's sounds good," she said, "maybe Norita could ride over there with us."

At that point, they were all talking but I couldn't hear what they were talking about.

Cecile came over to me and asked if I could take Miriam Home. "Sure," I said, "I will be glad to."

Now, let me tell you where Miriam lives. If you were to go out in the back yard at this house and look across the field, and it was a pretty big field, maybe eight or nine hundred yards across, you could see her house. To get to her house, you have to drive north up the road about a quarter of a mile, turn left and drive two blocks, and back to the left again, drive down a long lane to her house.

Cecile said to Miriam, "You will have to show him how to get to your house."

"I will," she said.

We got in the car, and I really wanted to spend a little more time with her than what I had spent, so I asked her if she would like to ride out to the drive-in and get a root beer?

She said, "I don't have any money."

"Oh," I said, "don't worry about that, I'm buying."

She said, "Root beer sounds good."

I ordered two small root beers, nickel each.

We talked a little bit and I said, guess we better get going, so she directed me to her house, she got out of the car, and I turned the car around and went back to our house. It didn't take very long to drive back to the house and when I got there and went in the house, my goodness was I surprised. Miriam was standing there in the front room.

Cecile said, "You was supposed to take her home so she could ask her dad if she could ride to South Bend with us."

I was so embarrassed and so happy at the same time. I said, "I sure did not know that, but I am glad that you are going with us. What I want to know is, how did you get back over here so fast?"

"I ran across the field," she said.

I just want to pick her up and squeeze her; I think she is so sweet, but I guess I had better not do that.

It was so much fun, having her ride with us to South Bend and back. She told me about some of her friends, Trula, Shirley, and Trula's boyfriend, Steve. "I will introduce you to Steve, I think you guys will get along fine." It sure will be good to meet other people more my age.

When we returned home, Norita said, "Miriam, I had better be getting you back home, before Dad comes looking for you."

"When will I see you again, Miriam?"

"I hope soon," she said.

"Yeah, me to!"

This day was the best day I've had since I've been in Indiana, and I'm hoping and looking forward to many more. I sure do like that girl!

But, there's Betty, I sure haven't forgotten her, in fact, I guess I had better write her a letter tonight, if I can get Miriam off my mind long enough.

Jack and Cecile's daughter, Brenda, is in the first grade at the same elementary school Miriam goes to. Miriam wrote me a note, telling me how she enjoyed being with me yesterday, and gave the note to Brenda to bring home to me. That was a really nice surprise! I found out that Miriam is in the eighth grade and thirteen years old. But she looks and acts older.

Chapter Forteen

Work at the station is going real well, I am liking it more and more. To me, it's really not work, nothing like when I was working at Patterson's green houses in the dirt. Sometime this job is kind of boring, but I am making three times what I was making back home.

The weather is beginning to cool off here, and I have been hearing all kinds of horror stories about how bad the winters can be around here, I am not looking forward to that at all. Carl said we would be getting in a half of a semi-trailer load of anti-freeze any time, and the rest of the load would be going to the station down at Warsaw. He said we would probably sell all of it.

It's the end of October, and it's getting colder every day, Carl ordered coveralls for all the employees to wear, and we wear them over our other clothes at work.

They forecast the temperature tonight to get down to twenty five degrees, that's cold! Carl said I might have to work later today on account of the anti-freeze sales would keep us all very busy all day and in to the evening. What a day this was, I mean we did sell some anti-freeze today; I didn't get off work until eight-o-clock tonight. Our anti-freeze sold for a dollar and seventy nine cents a gallon. People were buying from two to five gallons. The customers kept all of us on the run like you would not believe. I earned my pay today!

I have been getting a note from Miriam almost every day, I am sure glad of that, but I don't know when I will see her again.

Miriam said in a note that she was going to see If her Mom would let her spend the afternoon with Shirley this Sunday, no one would be home but her, and she was gonna ask Steve and Trula to be there too.

And that she would introduce me to all of them. I sure hope that works out, she said she would let me know for sure by Friday.

As it turned out, she went to town today, Friday, with Norita and they came back here before they went home, what a surprise! She told me that Sunday afternoon was all set up, and I sure am looking forward to that. Man, what a sweetheart!

Sunday is here already, I am on my way to Shirley's house, a little nervous, but looking forward to it.

Pulling in to the drive, Miriam is coming out to meet me.

"Everyone is here" she said, "it's so good to see you."

"Oh it's so good to see you too. It seems like forever since I've seen you!"

"It sure does," she said.

Walking in the door, I see three people setting on the couch in the living room.

Miriam said, "I want you to meet the guy that I have been talking about all week, this is Harper."

All of them said, "Hi, Harper."

That is a word that I am not used to saying, "hi", we didn't say "hi" back in North Carolina. When we greeted someone, we said "hey" or "hey there". But that was alright.

I replied, "Hey ya'll, good to meet you, I've been looking forward to it, Miriam talks about ya'll a lot," they had a grin on their faces, I guess because of my accent.

Miriam said, pointing at each one of them, That is Steve, and Trula, and at the end there, is Shirley."

We didn't do anything to speak of this afternoon, except just talking and getting acquainted with each other, I sure enjoyed meeting all of them.

Steve works at a place called the "Farmers Exchange," an area farmer's newspaper that is published once a week, he works part time running the printing press after school. He seems to be a really good kid, and I like him. I told him where I live, and asked him to come by and visit me. He said he would!

The day ended much too soon, Miriam and her friends had to go home and get ready for church, and Steve took Miriam home. I have not met Miriam's Mom and Dad yet.

Miriam's family are members of the "Church Of The Brethren" here in town. Sounds like they are avid church goers, and that is good.

As the weeks come and go, I have met Miriam's parents, I go to their house to see Miriam sometimes. I don't know what they think of me, with my southern accent and all, and the fact that I left school early. They seem a little apprehensive of me, but of course they don't know me, and I understand that.

Miriam has another sister named Ruth, and a brother, his name is Jim, he is about my age.

Most people call Miriam's Dad "Pappy", and her Mom's name is Mildred.

They will allow Miriam to go out with me sometimes, if Ruth can go along, which is just fine, as long as we can see each other. I like Ruth a lot. I, of course am sixteen, three years difference in our age, seems like a lot now, but as we get older, it won't seem so much different.

Steve and I have become very good friends, we see each other often when we are off work at the same time. We spend a lot of time at the dairy bar playing the pinball machine, or we go out to the truck stop about three miles south of town and play the pinball machine out there.

Tomorrow is Thanksgiving, I think we will all be going to Annie's for dinner, I'm sure there will be a house full of people.

When we arrived home last night from Annie's, Jack said to me, "Harper, come in here to the table and sit down, we would like to make a proposal to you."

"Okay," I said.

Jack said, "Since we are trying to buy this house, we have a lot of financial obligations with the light bill, insurance and other bills to pay, we need to get rid of a payment if we can. So here is our proposal to you. You take our car and take over payments, and we will take your car and take over your payments, your payments are a lot less than ours, and that would help us a lot. What do you think of that?"

I'm sitting here thinking, wow, that would be so cool driving around in a nineteen fifty five Mercury hard top, red with a cream colored top. I could hardly believe that!

I asked, "Are you serious, Jack?"

"Yes, very serious," he said.

I said, "You have got a deal." We did a hand shake and the deal was made.

I hope this was not a big mistake, I'm thinking to myself. I should be able to afford it, the payments are sixty dollars a month, and I make sixty five dollars a week.

Time flies, and here it is Christmas Eve. Everyone is busy shopping and picking up their last minute gifts. I bought Miriam a jewelry box, I hope she will like it.

The families will be gathering here for Christmas dinner tomorrow, I'm hoping Miriam can come over so I can introduce her to all of my family. I want them to meet her.

The house is full of people, and food is everywhere you look, enough to feed an Army.

After dinner, Cecile said, "Harper, why don't you go over to Parson's and see if Miriam could come over here for a while."

"Okay," I said, "I will."

Well, they have a crowd of people here at their house also.

I asked Miriam, "Do you think your Mom would let you come over to our house for a while and meet my relatives?"

"I"ll ask her," she said. She went to the living room where everyone was visiting and asked her Mom to come out to the kitchen.

When her Mom came to the kitchen, Miriam said to me, "You ask her!"

I said to her, "Would you let Miriam come over to our house for a little while? I would like to introduce her to my sister's families."

She thought for a minute, and said, "Yeah, o.k. I don't want you to be gone very long." We promised not to be.

We had a great Christmas day, Miriam enjoyed meeting all my relatives that were here.

What a wonderful year this last year has been, I hope this year will be as good.

I haven't heard from Betty for a long time, I guess she just gave up on me, perhaps its best, as I am seeing Miriam more and more often. Ruth, Miriam and I get together three or four times a week, and go to the drive-in theatre, or just go riding around. We enjoy being together.

It's February, Miriam just celebrated her fourteenth birthday, and maybe her parents will let her go on dates with me without a chaperone now. That would be great, guess we will find out.

We have been going to church regularly, in fact I joined the Brethren Church here in town, I got baptized, and I am a very good boy.

There's not just a whole lot going on these days besides work and seeing Miriam. Steve and I spend time together when we are not with our girlfriends. Summer is here and we go down to the lake at Milford and go swimming about once a week, that's fun, it is so hot here now, the temperature has been in the upper nineties the last few days, and it is really hot on the drive at the station

Miriam's parents are allowing Miriam to go on dates with me now without a chaperone, a couple of times a week, and we are enjoying the freedom of being alone.

We have our favorite places to go out in the country on a county road and turn off on a small farm road and drive into some woods and park. I have my radio tuned to WLAC out of Gallatin, TN, and listen to rhythm and blues. That is one of our favorite past times while we are making out, necking, or whatever you want to call it. Steve and Trula know where we park, sometimes they come and park beside us, and we just visit, and listen to the radio. When we are alone we might get a little carried away, but we know when to stop. For now we will just call it discovery.

I have had my seventeenth birthday, and I am older and seriously have a desire to learn about the opposite sex, that's all. You remember Betty, I guess I was embarrassed more than anything back then, because I was so naive. This is different in the sense that Miriam is so young, and I am too, for that matter, but we do talk freely about sex a lot. Oh, we get excited often, can't deny that. We talk about other things too.

I love her so very much, and I know she loves me too. We even talk about when she finishes school, and we get married, a house and such things as that.

You may think that we are young, and it's just puppy love. Well, keep reading.

Miriam rides with me to North Manchester once or twice a month to visit with Annie and Bill. Of course Annie thinks we are too young, especially Miriam, to be seeing each other as much as we do. She has told me that a couple of times, and I know she cares about me, and she is trying to keep me in the right direction, and I love her for that.

For some time now, we have experienced sexual satisfaction together, without actually having sex, there are many ways of course.

Tonight it was different. We were parked, and both of us were so involved. I had been pressuring her for some time for us to make love together. She never thought we should do that, she was so much stronger than I was. She always asked me if Betty and I made love together, and I lied and told her, yes we did.

We went beyond our control and we just couldn't stop, for me it was heaven on earth, when it was over Miriam cried, and I felt so bad, I hardly knew what to say. I felt so guilty, and I know she did too. That was the first for both of us! We just hugged each other so tight, like we had never held each other before, we couldn't seem to let go. I love her so much and I want to spend the rest of my life with her. I will never forget this day, ever!

We got through our annual anti-freeze rush this last week, I'm sure glad that's all over with, that's a very busy time and a lot of work!

Miriam and I and Ruth were up town at the dairy bar this afternoon, just talking and hanging out, and I got this crazy idea. I said to Miriam.

"Do you think your folks would allow you to go to Florida with me, during your Christmas vacation from school? Oh yes, and Ruth, perhaps you could go with us also."

"Oh, that would be so much fun," she replied.

"That sure would, we could just have a ball. Driving down there and visiting my folks, and ya'll meeting my relatives. I guess it would be a miracle for your parents agree to let ya'll go with me."

Ruth said, "If we start begging Mom and Dad now to let us go, maybe by then they would be ready to give in, and let us go."

I said, "Well, ya'll better get started now, you only have about six weeks to talk them in to letting you go."

December eleventh, I went over to see Miriam, just as I got the car stopped, she came running out the door to the car, hollering, "We can go, we can go. I am so happy."

She was so excited and so was I. "They really said ya'll could go, huh?"

"Yes," she said, "I can hardly believe it."

"Me either, I cannot hardly wait to go."

"Ruth is so very excited too," she said.

Brodus is working at the station now, and he has been, for about a year. Carl is giving him time off so he can go with us also.

We even talked Steve in to going with us, that's five now. We have a car load.

We left on the evening of December twenty first. Miriam's folks gave us enough food to eat on the way, sandwiches and cake, and more cake. Enough food to get us there. The temperature is eight degrees. I had a 1951 Oldsmobile convertible. There was a slit about two inches long in the top, right above the passengers head. As crazy as it sounds, it never has leaked a drop, no matter how hard it has rained.

As we traveled south, one of us would stick our finger through the hole to see if it was warming up outside.

Just ride, guide, talk, and eat. Nothing exciting, until we got down in Kentucky.

We got pulled over by the police. It was about one-o-clock in the morning. He wanted to know where we were going this time of the night.

I said, "We are on our way to Florida to spend Christmas with our Mother."

"Okay, I saw your Indiana plates and I was hoping you were not run-aways.

Ya'll have a good trip and be careful, Merry Christmas," he said.

The finger through the hole thermometer told us it was warming up a little bit, until we got out of the car, it is cold....out here.

We arrived in Florida about twenty eight hours later. Oh yes, it sure is warmer here, like sixty degrees warmer, than when we left Indiana.

We had such a great time spending a week in Florida with my family. Now, it's back to the frozen north.

We had a ton of fun on our trip, and it was just wonderful seeing Mama and the rest of my family, but it sure is good to be back home in Indiana. We were very blessed with a safe trip going and coming.

We have a Coca- cola machine at the station, and a Coke cost six cents each. On the bottom of each bottle is the name of the town or city where the bottles were made, such as South Bend, maybe Ft. Wayne, or cities such as New Orleans, or Miami, Fl. We play a game with the names on the bottom of the bottles; someone will ask another person if they wanna go out of town for a Coke. If the other person agrees to play, then both of you buy a Coke from the machine. The person that has the bottle closest to Goshen has to pay for both Cokes.

A customer came in to the station today. As I was pumping his gas and cleaning his windshield, I noticed a guitar laying on the back seat of his car, I asked him, "Do you play that guitar?"

"Well," he said, "I bought it to try to see if I could learn to play it, but I pretty much give up on it."

"Would you sell it?" I asked.

"Oh, I probably would," he said.

"How much would you be asking for it?"

He said, "I'll sell it for twenty five dollars."

"I'll give you five dollars now, and twenty dollars when I get paid on Friday."

He said, "I will keep it 'til Friday and you can have it when you pay me the rest."

"Alright!" I said. "Sounds like a deal."

I am finally gonna have me a guitar, I'm excited about that.

Another Christmas and New Year has come and gone, and it's work, and seeing Miriam now. Miriam is helping me with the guitar, she has a very good ear for music, and she had piano lessons for four years.

I take that guitar with me everywhere I go. I am getting some pretty good callouses on the end of my fingers from playing it. I have got to where I can play and sing a few songs in the key of "G". I think Miriam is getting tired of me playing it so much, she doesn't complain about it, but I can tell. I know that I have an awful lot to learn, just to be able to play the songs that I want to play and sing.

Miriam will be fifteen next month, and I will be eighteen in April. She will have three more years of school after this year. That seems like such a long time. Oh, but I will wait! I could just hang around, working at the station, and possibly get drafted in to the army when I am twenty one or twenty two, and I would not want to get married and then get drafted, and if a war broke out, anything could happen.

As you know, when a man turns eighteen he has to go to the selective service office and register. The way it is, when a man gets drafted, he has to serve two years of active duty. And I learned that a person could ask the clerk to draft a person and he could tell her when he wanted to leave and go into the army, and they would allow you to do that. That is called volunteering for the draft. When you do that, you spend two years in the army just like you were drafted.

So, I have got a plan. When I go to register, I will volunteer for the draft and tell them that I want to be drafted, and go in to the army in October, that way I will be able to spend this summer with Miriam.

The lady said, "That sounds good to me, you will get your draft notice in the mail about two weeks prior to going to Chicago for your physical."

And, that is just what I did.

I have a strong feeling that Miriam will not like this decision at all, but I feel it is a good decision, considering the situation as it is. Knowing that Miriam's Mom thinks we are seeing too much of each other anyhow. I also know that some other boy could steal her away from me, I don't know what I would do if that would happen. Two years is an awful long time. I will have to hope and pray that that doesn't happen.

After I left the Selective Service office I went to Miriam's house, no one was there except her. I said to her, "Hey baby, come in here and set on the couch with me."

"Is something wrong?" she asked.

"I sure hope not," I replied.

"I am so hoping that you will not get too upset with me, or mad at me, but I made a decision today that I am pretty sure that you will not agree with. I hope you will hear me out and understand my decision. Today I went and registered for the draft. And I will be going in to the army in October for two years."

She asked, "What do you think I am supposed to do for two years while you are gone?" She began to cry.

"Oh baby, you have so many friends to spend your time with, the time will pass real fast, and we will be back together before you know it. I just want to ask you if you will wait for me?"

"Of course, I will wait for you." she said. "Will you wait for me?"

"Oh, you have to know that I will wait for you. I love you so much!"

I went on to explain my decision about her having three more years of school and we could be married after she graduated from school, and that it could be a test of our love for each other.

"That's true," she said, "that sure will be a test."

"We can do it," I said, "I know we can. It will be a test to prove our true love for each other."

"Well hey," I said, "we have all summer and part of October to be together, so let's have a ball."

"Yes, let's do."

And we are having fun, going to the drive-in-theatre, parking in the woods, and driving down to Manchester to visit with Annie's family.

Miriam's folks invite me over to eat with them sometimes, I like that, and they eat a lot of greens which I never cared about, growing up. But I never left their table being hungry.

I have talked to Carl a lot about my brother Brodus. I told him, when I leave for the Army that he should contact him and see if he would come up and work here at the station.

He said if Brodus is as good of a worker as I am, he just might do that.

I said, "Oh, he's every bit as good a worker as I am, and I know you would like him."

"That's something to think about I guess," he said.

We went to the drive-in-theatre last night; Miriam said they were showing a movie that she would like to see.

It finally got dark enough there and we got involved with each other, I mean we moved close to each other, the touching began, the kissing was serious and there was no stopping, no stopping, until:

The interior of my car lit up like someone turned on a five hundred watt light bulb, shinning directly on us. We stopped, cooled off instantly, we're caught, zipper pulled up quick, he turned his head for that.

"How old are you?" he asked me.

"I'm twenty."

"How about the girl, how old is she?"

"Eighteen," I replied. Of course that was a lie, but it worked.

"Okay, you guys set up there in your seat and watch the movie or you will have to leave."

"Okay," I told him.

"Ain't that just our luck," I said to Miriam, "Here we are on the back row, nothing behind us but darkness, and he has to show up and totally destroy our wonderful moment."

Miriam said, "Well, it's not very wonderful now, that scared me half to death, I don't even care about the movie now, let's go home."

"Okay!"

This has been such a wonderful spring and summer, until now. This is the last week of June, on my way home from work I stopped at the post office and got the mail; one letter was addressed to me, from the selective service office. I opened the envelope,

Be in front of the Olympia Candy Kitchen in Goshen on July the first at five-o-clock a.m. to board the bus to go to Chicago and take your physical for the Army.

This is a terrible surprise, so much for spending the summer with Miriam.

Miriam and Cecile took me to catch the bus, and there were about twenty other guys there waiting to board the bus. It was not a happy scene. I hated so much leaving Miriam standing there as we pulled away, no idea when I would see her again, oh, what a feeling.

We were in Chicago all day, all the guys taking physicals. All the guys that passed physicals, including me, boarded a train for Ft. Leonard Wood, Missouri. We arrived there in the middle of the night and were put on buses to go to the base. Everything was moving so fast. We didn't have to think about what we were gonna do next, they tell us.

Five thirty this morning I hear someone blowing a whistle and yelling, get your lazy asses out of that sack, this is not your Mama's house. Get dressed, make your bed, and be in formation outside the barracks at six-o-clock.

We managed to be in formation like he told us to be at six-o-clock.

There was a stand outside about eight ft. square, and about eight foot tall, where a person could go up steps to the platform and it had a roof over it. A Sergeant came walking across the yard, went up the steps and picked up a microphone and began cussing us.

Okay all you G## D+#% dog faced girls, my name is Sergeant Ellis, I am in charge of everything you do while you are under my command. You WILL do everything I tell you to do. You will eat, sleep, get dressed and if you cuss me I better not hear it. Do not come to me with any questions, we will tell you everything you need to know. This Army will do your thinking. The corporal standing to your right over there will lead you to the mess hall for breakfast, and you will be back here in formation at seven-o-clock.

Arriving at the mess hall, one single line through the cafeteria, get our food, set down at a table, all the guys are talking, not for long. There's a man big enough to kill a bear with his bare hands and my gosh, is he ugly! He has the biggest long handle spoon that I have ever seen, shaking it at everyone. I think he is the mess hall Sergeant, over and over he is saying, do not talk, in my dining room, don't say a G*d D$+# word, or I will bust your f%%ing head, eat and get out of here. I have two thousand more pusses to feed breakfast to, shut up and eat, and you had better eat what's in your tray, or you will be sorry. When we left through the back door, there was a PFC standing there watching us empty our tray in the big garbage barrel. If he decided you left too much food on your tray, he would put you on KP.

Back at the barracks we did have about fifteen minutes to relax before the next formation.

The horn blows for formation, everyone runs outside, Sergeant Ellis is climbing the steps to his kingdom.

"I noticed," he said, "there are rocks, big and small just lying all around on the ground and I don't like it. You little girls will pick up every G## D+m# one of them and place them beside that tree over there behind where you are standing. That includes all the rocks around these three barrack buildings to my right and left, and you better have that done by eleven hundred this morning, so you had better get busy!" Another NCO, I think a Sergeant Price was his name dismissed us, and told us to get them rocks picked up. Everyone was picking up the rocks and putting them on a pile.

By eleven hundred, as far as we could tell, all the rocks were piled up by the tree. SGT. Price told us to go in the barracks and get ready to go eat dinner, so we did.

In a single file we went through the cafeteria and got our meal, behind each pot of food there was a person there to serve us what we wanted. The old ugly SGT. was behind them yelling, take what you want but G—D--- it you better eat it, do you hear me, get your food, sit down and eat and get the hell out of here.

That's what we experienced every time we had a meal, after a while it began to get kind of amusing, but I didn't laugh, nobody did, at least until we were back in our barracks.

We were called out for formation, and Sgt. Ellis was on the stand waiting for us.

He said "I'm mad as hell! Someone has picked up all my rocks and put them in a pile. So girls, you will take the rocks from that pile and scatter them out all around the barracks where they are supposed to be."

We did this over and over for the Sgt., because we assumed there was nothing else for us to do.

The next morning we began processing in, what I mean by that is we would be receiving our military clothing. So we get in a line, and enter a building where we went up steps to a long narrow platform. The first thing we received was our duffle bag. As we walked along that platform there were guys standing below us.

The first person said, "Small, medium or large?"

I replied, "Medium," he handed me three pair fatigue pants.

The next person said, "You look like medium," and handed me three shirts.

And the next person set a boot in front of me, and said, "Try this on, how does that feel?"

I replied, "It feels kind of tight."

And he said, "Who the hell do you think you are, some kind of shoe specialist? Maybe you should be down here where I am, fitting everyone with boots, if you are so G**D#+% smart!"

"Oh, no, no, that feels real good, these are fine." As we moved on down the ramp, we received our underwear, gloves, caps, socks, and our dress uniforms. I am glad this day is over!

After a nights rest, at formation we were told we would be in classes all day today, and we were. We just had tests all day long. I guess the tests would tell them which base we would be sent to for further training.

After a week of hell at Ft. Leonard Wood, Mo, we loaded on several busses, no idea where we were going. In the wee hours of the morning we were informed that we were at our new home. No one knew where we were.

A sergeant came walking out of a building and ordered us to "fall in", which means get in to a formation. And he made his speech:

"I am 1st Sergeant Edward Steel. Welcome to Ft. Hood, Texas. Listen real well to what I have to say, you will hear many rumors, but the fact is you will do your basic training at Ft. Hood, and your advanced training here, unless you go TDY for special training at another Army base. When you finish that training, you will return back here to Ft. Hood. Everyone here will be together until you finish your tour of duty. You will finish all of your training by the first of December, at which time there will be an Inspecting General here to inspect you and all of your equipment. Then you will be given a fourteen day leave, and report to Ft. Dix, NJ, at which time you will board a ship bound for Germany. The personal that are enlisted for two years will spend eighteen months in Germany, and be returned back to the states. Disregard anything else you may hear, unless there is a war or national emergency. That is all I have to say for now, other personnel will show you to your barracks and rooms."

This morning they allowed us to sleep in. Sergeant Powell came into our rooms and introduced himself, and informed us that he is our platoon Sergeant. He told us where we would be eating our meals and where the PX was located if we needed tooth paste, shaving items and such as that.

For the last six weeks we have done a lot of training. We have marched and marched until everyone knew how to count and keep in step, we have had any number of classes, setting out in the middle of a field in the hot Texas sun. And watched many training films in a hot dark building, air conditioning is unheard of at Ft. Hood.

We qualified with a M-1 rifle, and they taught us to take it apart totally, and put it back together with a blindfold covering our eyes.

The infiltration course was the practice that scared the living hell out of all of us. If you do not know what that is, I will tell you.

Picture a field fifty yards wide and eighty yards long, with a fence on each side, Rows of barbed wire running back and forth across the field about eighteen inches off the ground and telephone poles placed left to right every fifteen feet through the course. To add to the craziness as you crawled, with your field pack on your back and your rifle cradled in your arms, there were five thirty caliber machine guns being continuously fired about two foot over your head as they fanned the guns back and forth across the field. That's not all. There were small charges of explosives underground all through the field that would be set off here and there as you crawled through the course. That will scare any person half to death the first time you experienced it. No, that's not all!

You have to do it again at night, everything is the same except the machine guns firing, every tenth round is a tracer, meaning that round is lit up and you can see it as it goes over your head. That was by far, the worse part of basic training.

A week or so after basic training we were in formation and the Sergeant asked if anyone is familiar with an air compressor. I raised my hand.

He said, "Come to my office after formation."

In his office he said, "Garris, pack all your things, go to the finance office and get a check for your traveling expense. My secretary will give you all the paper work that you will need. You are going to Ft. Belvoir, VA to school."

I received enough money at the finance office to be able to fly to Chicago, and then catch a train to Elkhart, IN where Miriam, Mama and my brother Brodus was waiting for me as I walked off the train, What a thrill for me! Oh, so good to see them, especially Miriam.

They gave me seven days to go from Ft. Hood to Ft. Belvoir, so I had five days at home. That was just great!

I spent eight weeks at Ft. Belvoir taking classes to be a Heavy Equipment Mechanic.

I returned to Ft. Hood the middle of November, and they gave everyone a thirty day leave before we had to report to Ft. Dix, NJ to begin our voyage to Germany on January the first.

I left Temple, Texas on my way to Sanford, FL on a Greyhound bus. I rode that dog for thirty six hours and finally arrived there, what a trip! After I left home in nineteen fifty five all of my family moved from Shelby, to Florida. I am going there to visit them before I travel to Indiana, and on to Germany.

After spending a week in Florida with my family, I decided that I would try to hitchhike to Indiana, and save as much money as I could. I hitchhiked from Sanford, FL to Goshen, IN in Thirty hours.

Brodus is living in an apartment in Goshen, so I went to his apartment for the night. I guessed that I had better not go to Miriam's and wake their family up at midnight, I will see Miriam tomorrow, and I can hardly wait.

This morning I walked up to the station where Brodus was working and visited with him for a while, he had a lot of questions about the Army. He let me use his car while he was working, although I will have to pick him up from work at three thirty. I really don't have anywhere to go until Brodus gets off work at three thirty, and that's the same time Miriam gets out of school, so I will just stay at the apartment for a while.

The rest of the time that I was home on leave I was with Miriam a lot, of course it was just wonderful to be with her. But the time goes by so fast.

Miriam and Brodus took me to the bus station in Ft. Wayne to catch the bus to Ft. Dix, NJ. God, I hated to leave, especially not having any idea when I would see Miriam again, or Brodus either for that matter. Knowing that Miriam had dated a few other guys, just tore me up, she told me she had, and at the same time she said that I was the only one for her. Over and over, she told me that she was waiting for me, and when I was out of the Army, she would be all mine. That I prayed for.

I arrived at the base in Ft. Dix, and as I was reporting in, I was told that we would board the ship the next morning. Our company commander volunteered our company to board the ship two days early to do cleaning before the other troops got on board.

It would take forever for me to tell you all about this ship, so I will just say, lordy, its big!

Three days later we are leaving the United States, we passed the Statue of Liberty and within a few hours all I can see is water.

I remember years ago when I was growing up, I asked a lot of men that I knew who traveled overseas on a ship, did you get sea sick? Everyone I asked said, oh, I didn't, but just about everyone else did. That sure caused me to wonder!

The first night out, there were guys throwing up everywhere I went. On every stairway, and the bathroom floor, guys with their heads against urinals, over stools, oh my goodness, what an awful mess.

The third day out the ocean got rough, I mean real rough, and you would just have to be there, but be glad you weren't. Ships have "heads", in other words bathrooms on the bow end of the ship, and near the stern, which of course is the back area of the ship.

Example; the waves are so high it pushes the bow of the ship very high, and if I am walking up steps when the ship is going up, it is so hard to do, it feels like your leg will not raise to the next step, however, if the bow is going down, you find yourself running down the steps, it goes down so fast. I almost find my body in the air, like it went out from under me. Think about this; I am trying to set on the throne in the "head", when the bow goes up, I am pressured so tight against the seat that there is no way that I can stand up, and then the ship goes down so fast that my butt leaves the seat, and when I'm coming down the seat is coming back up, "smack". Just try to get something done with that going on! The sea continued to be that rough for three days.

Every morning after breakfast, (that was fun also) all the troops were ordered to the top deck, so the area where we spent most of our time could be cleaned, and that took them until noon to do that. Now, in addition to it being so cold outside, and the wind blowing so hard, the ship is rocking so far over side ways that water is splashing up on top of the deck, and we are getting all wet, this happens every morning. Lordy, what am I doing here?

Am I sea sick? No, believe it or not, I am not sick, but we are not there yet!

There is a store on the ship, movie, and barber shop. In fact I think you can get about anything you want on this ship. Many of the troops are playing cards, poker and blackjack. Not me, I don't gamble, if I did, I know I would lose.

The last two days on the ship I had to work in the bakery where we made bread. The smell of the hot yeast almost got to me. I did not throw up though, I am a survivor.

We docked at the port of Bremerhaven, Germany at noon today, right off the ship into buses to go board a train, and we traveled to Nurnberg. Upon arrival in Nurnberg we boarded buses to Johnson Barracks, located about six miles west of Furth, Germany. And this is where I will live for the next eighteen months.

The next several days will be getting to know this area, what company is in each barracks, I am in Headquarter platoon "A" company, and there are "B" "C" "D" and "E" companies on our base here. Our base has a very high security fence surrounding the entire base, and there are guards at the gate twenty four hours every day.

The barracks where I live is close to the fence, when I look out the window, and through the fence, I see the street and a Gasthaus on the other side of the street. And fortunately our platoon is on the ground floor, of four floors.

As I go out the door , I see a full empty block of grass, a statue and the flagpole in the center, there is a street all around the block, and barracks that house the troops of the other companies, and the EM club and the NCO club, plus the Service Club that all the troops use. The coffee shop is in the Service Club. They will allow you to check out a guitar to take to the music room to play, I will probably do that sometime.

I have been here three months now. I work in the motor pool during the day. They assigned me a truck mounted air compressor to operate and take care of, do all the maintenance, and keep it clean. We go to the motor pool at eight a.m. until twelve, we take an hour for dinner, and back to the motor pool until five p.m. That is how we usually spend our day up to now. In the evenings we shoot pool in the day room, there are four tables. Sometime we play ping pong.

In the service club there is an EM club, meaning "Enlisted Men's Club", kind of like a tavern for all the guys that are ranked up to a sergeant, (they are not allowed). Beer costs twenty five cents a glass, so you can imagine that is a busy place during the evening hours.

A friend of mine is a pretty good guitar player, the two of us go over there often and sign out a guitar, and he has taught me a lot on the guitar. I am learning a lot more than when I first came in the Army.

I have been receiving about three or four letters a week from Miriam, she keeps me up to date with what's going on at home. It makes my day so much better when I get a letter from her, especially when she sends me a few photos.

This morning they announced that we would be leaving to go on bivouac at o: eight hundred in the morning. We will be gone for three weeks, I'll bet that will be interesting, it's the first time for me. It will be the first time that I will drive my truck anywhere off base.

Well, we are preparing to leave, they are getting all our vehicles lined up in the order that we will be traveling. When we ask where we are going, they tell us to follow the vehicle in front of us. I guess that means that we don't need to know where we are going. Okay, whatever!

We have been driving for about four hours now, we came through a few towns, it is interesting to see some of the houses and the store fronts. The streets in the towns are very narrow. I see ox pulling what they call "Honey Wagons", liquid manure tanks that they spray on their crops. Some are hauling manure.

We finally arrived at somewhere. We drove off the highway into some woods where they are telling everyone where to park, and telling everyone to set up our pup tents near our vehicles. After our tents were set up and our sleeping bags were in place in the tents, it was time for our evening meal.

After we ate, most of us went back to our vehicles, checking oil in the engines and performing some light maintenance.

There were eight or ten of us, including the company cooks, just setting around and talking about things we were doing before we came into the Army, and two young boys walked up. After attempting to talk to them, we got the idea that they had been around some Army bivouac areas before. They were asking for food. One of the cooks went to the mess truck and brought back a gallon can of peaches. In Germany a lot of beer is bottled in large bottles, and the cap on them are made with very stiff wire attached to the cap, and to open a bottle you just flipped the wire holding the cap on it, and the cap remained attached to the bottle. The bottles were refilled at the breweries and sold over and over.

When the kids saw the can of peaches, of course they wanted it, so the cook made some motions and tried to act like he was opening a flip top bottle. The boys got the idea, and in their own way of asking, how many do you want?

The cook held up six fingers, and the boys took off running. Well we wondered, are they gonna bring some beer, or did they think we were asking too much for the peaches.

We got our answer about one half hour later. Here they came, each one of them carrying six bottles. They were so happy to get the peaches. We were camped there for five days. We loaded up and left that neck of the woods. After we traveled close to a hundred and twenty five miles, we left the road and set up camping again, I do not have any idea where we are, however, they have told us that they will do our thinking, we will do the working.

There was food of some sort traded for beer here, also. This place is about the same as the last place.

We were out in the field almost four weeks and we arrived home this evening about five p.m.

Here it is June, and we have been on bivouac three times since we have arrived here in Germany. I don't mind being on bivouac so much, but I sure do miss taking a shower every day. I take my steel helmet, better known as "steel pot" to the mess truck and get hot water to shave with. That helps a little bit.

They told us at formation this morning that we will leave early in the morning and travel to the Danube river and construct a bridge across it, of course you know we are in an engineer battalion, and the entire battalion will be going. I'm looking forward to that, I think.

Chapter Fifteen

This morning when we arrived at the sight by the river, I was told where to park my truck so my air hoses would be accessible, all the sergeants were yelling out orders telling everyone to move it, move it, move it, they told me to stay on the truck and make sure my air compressor was keeping good pressure. The troops from Bridge Company were dragging the big floats off their trucks and inflating them with air, as soon as they had two floats filled with air they began attaching the eight by eight inch by twelve foot long square aluminum tubes to the floats. Everything is assembled together using steel pins. It took seven hours and thirty seven minutes to have the bridge across the Danube finished and a tank driven across it. After about an hour of rest, they called a formation.

Okay, the battalion commander Lieutenant Colonel Fishback tells the troops to disassemble the bridge, and load it on the truck, and you will began building this bridge again, one hour after you have it loaded on the trucks.

The bridge was taken all apart and loaded on the trucks and they took their one hour break.

There they go again unloading the trucks, all the men are more familiar with what they have to do now, even as tired as they must be, they are working faster than ever. The officers are hollering at the men to move it, move it, we have to be faster than this.

It is beginning to get dark now, and it is cooling off some, but most of the guys are sweating and beginning to slow down. They have it finished, and they were told that it took six hours and twenty two minutes. Faster than the last time anyhow.

The bridge was disassembled and loaded on the trucks, and at one thirty this morning we are getting back to our barracks.

Very short night; we are up at six hundred hours this morning. We had our breakfast and were called out for formation at seven hundred hours. We were informed that the record for building that bridge was five hours and twelve minutes, by the last engineer battalion that were stationed here.

Colonel Fishback announced, "You men will build that bridge in less time than they did. We are going back to that river today and we are not leaving until you have broken that record. I know you can do it, and you will do it, and it's up to you as to how many times you build that bridge today. Take over Sergeant," he said.

"Men, you heard the Colonel. We will be pulling out in half an hour, so if you are able to grab some snacks to take with you today, you had better get them, and be in your trucks and ready to pull out in thirty minutes."

The bridge was assembled three times and torn down three times today. God, what a rough day and night it was. On the third time of building that bridge, a new record was set. We beat the old record by seventeen minutes. Man, what a happy and tired bunch of soldiers we were. It took all day and all night. We arrived back here at the barracks at seven hundred hours this morning, and they called a formation.

They told us to go eat a good breakfast and go to bed. We will see you in the morning.

The calandar tells me it is the first of November, time sure does fly, on the other hand it seems like I have been here three years.

One of the guys was saying that one of the airlines was having special price for troops that were interested in flying back to the states for the Christmas holidays.

I could buy a round trip ticket to fly to New York City for three hundred and ninety dollars. When I came in the Army I signed up to have an allotment taken out of my pay to send to Mama, so I wrote her and asked if she could send me four hundred dollars so I could come home for Christmas. And she said yes. I found out that another guy in my platoon was going home for Christmas, and he was going to Ohio. He said his wife was meeting him at the airport in New York, and that he would bring me home to Indiana. I bought my ticket and I am ready to go home, leaving December the ninth. I was so thrilled that I was going home for Christmas, I can hardly wait.

We flew to Shannon, Ireland, fueled there, and we flew on to Newfoundland, fueled there and flew to New York. David Hinkle's wife was there waiting for us when we landed at the New York International Idlewild Airport. We were so glad to see her, and I didn't even know her.

We left New York and the two of them drove all night, and we arrived in Goshen, Indiana the next morning about nine thirty. Of course Miriam was in school. Brodus had bought a new English Ford, it is a very small car. I waited until Miriam was out of school, and Brodus got off work and he took me out to Miriam's house, and I was waiting there when she walked in from school, oh boy, was she ever surprised. She knew I was coming home but she wasn't sure when I would get here. Needless to say, I am so thrilled to see her, it has been a year. We talked and talked, Brodus came about seven-o-clock and we went to town, the three of us, and got a sandwich. She asked me what I was gonna do about seeing the relatives in Florida. "I don't know," I told her.

"Brodus, do you think you could get off a week over Christmas?" I asked.

"I'll find out," he said, "I will talk to Carl tomorrow, I think he will let me off."

"Honey, do you think your folks would let you go with us, let's see, say, if Ceicle was going along?"

"Well, I'm not gonna let you go without me," she said.

"I guess I will have to talk to Cecile and see what she says, I'm sure she will want to go, and I'm sure she will have to get Jack's approval."

Brodus said, I "know me and Jack could never take off work at the same time."

"Okay," I said, "we have got work to do to get this plan finalized."

Today I talked to Cecile. "How would you like to go to Florida over Christmas with me and Brodus?"

"I would love to go to Florida with ya'll."

"What do you think Jack would have to say about it?"

"I will talk to him and find out, I think he will be alright with it," she said.

"I sure hope he will," I said.

Brodus came home from work this afternoon and he had asked Carl if he could be off about eight days over Christmas, and told him the reason. Carl told him that it could be worked out.

"Hey Babe, how did things go, did you ask your Mom about Florida?"

"Yes I did," she answered. "Mom said it will be okay with her but, she said she would have to do some talking to get Dad to agree to it."

Miriam and I have been in deep conversation about a guy in school that she has been dating for the last year. I knew him, his name is John, and she tells me that she has to do something while I'm gone.

"Do you think that I should set home every night and never do anything?" she asks.

"There are many things you could do besides dating while I'm gone. You tell me how much you love me and that you always will, but how do you think I feel, being so far away and knowing that you are out with someone else. It just tears my heart out."

We talked about that a lot while I was home and she never told me that she would not date.

I told her that I may as well date one of those German girls when I go back over there, hoping that she would say I wish you would not do that. But, she said, "Well, I think you should do that."

That didn't make me feel any better. I really didn't want to date anyone else. I will just keep hoping and praying that she will still love me when I return home.

Miriam's Dad gave permission for her to go with us to Florida, of course I am so excited about that. I know we will have so much fun on the trip, and we are looking forward to visiting with our folks there also.

It's December nineteenth, we are leaving as soon as Miriam gets home from school and gets her clothes packed. I sure hope everything goes well, after all, Cecile's baby boy, Jackie, is only about nine months old. He seems to be a good baby.

Brodus has been talking a lot about how good the gas mileage is with his new English Ford. He says it won't cost us much for the trip. I sure hope so, because I ain't got much.

We drove into the night, south bound on state highway 9, that way we could bypass the larger towns, especially Indianapolis. We were talking, and keeping everyone awake, it's after midnight. Jackie was sleeping when Brodus said, "Oh my goodness, we are almost out of gas. I saw a sign back there that said Hope, five miles, we can get some gas there if we make it that far."

The town of Hope was just a wide spot on the side of the road, with not even a gas station. We kept going and about five miles south we ran out of gas.

"Well brother," I asked, "what do we do now?"

He replied, "Well brother, you tell me. We can pray, and we had better." We had talked earlier about there not being very much traffic on this road.

Thirty minutes later Brodus said, "I see head lights in the rear view mirror. Maybe he will stop, we have to get help soon, because it's gonna be too cold for Jackie pretty soon."

The car is getting closer and Brodus got out of the car and put his thumb out. The car pulled up and stopped right beside Brodus. Brodus spoke to him a couple of minutes, and opened the car door and said, "The man said he will take me to a gas station about five miles up the road and get some gas, and bring me back. I will be back soon, ya'll just hang on!"

They were back with gas in about a half hour, and we were on our way to that gas station to return the can and fill the tank with gas. Now I'm telling you, Brodus stopped about every hundred miles and filled the tank.

"We ain't gonna run out of gas again on this trip!" he said.

We continued our trip, and never had any problems at all. We enjoyed ourselves so much, with our families there. My oldest brother Boyd lives in Mt. Dora, Florida. He served in the Army during World War II, and I haven't seen him for several years. I thought he would be glad to see me, especially since I am in the Army now, so we went to his home to visit. He is living in an upstairs apartment now, with steps on the outside to climb up to enter his apartment. His wife came out on their porch when we pulled into the drive. We spoke to each other for just a short while and she said, "Let me go get Boyd, I'm sure he will be glad to see you all." After about fifteen minutes he came out on the porch and said.

"Hello Harper, how are you?"

"I'm just fine, how about you?"

"Well Harper, I would like to visit with you for a while, but I just don't have time now. Perhaps you could come back to visit us again sometime."

"Okay," I replied, and got back in the car and left. I was hurt so much, but that wasn't the first time that my feelings were hurt by him, but he is my brother and I love him.

Our time in Florida went so fast, seemed like we just got here and it is time to leave. I have to get back to Indiana to prepare for my flight back to Germany, and I hate to think about that. Miriam and I have had some wonderful time together these last few days. God only knows how much I hate to leave. Brodus and Miriam took me to the bus station in Ft. Wayne for my trip back to New York City.

Leaving the airport in New York, looking over the city, climbing higher and higher, any other time it might be very exciting, but it wasn't, my heart was so heavy thinking about the six more months that I have to spend in Germany. Lord, I sure hope the time goes fast.

Back in Germany nothing has changed. Of course I didn't think it would. I'm thinking the best thing to do is just try to make the best of it. Miriam sent me a big coffee can of cookies that she baked. That was so sweet of her. She packed them in lots of cellophane paper. But, when I received the package and opened it, it had a strong smell of coffee. They were good, even if they did have a little taste of coffee. My friends called them coffee cookies.

It's March and we have been on bivouac two times since I've been back. One time I caught crabs when we were gone. When we go on bivouac there has to be a deep long ditch dug out called a slit trench to use as a potty. I am sure I caught the crabs when I used that trench, because I didn't have them when I left the barracks.

After we returned to the barracks, I asked different guys if they knew the best way to get rid of them.

One guy told me the best way that he knew of was to soak a rag with the stuff they use in the motor pool to clean parts with, and rub it real good in your crotch and in your hair down there! And I guarantee you will get rid of them. Here I go to the motor pool, and I soaked this rag with that solution and went to the bathroom in the barracks, dropped my fatigues and shorts and began to saturate my crotch: Oh my God, someone must have built a fire down there, but I don't see any smoke, I cannot stand this, I believe my legs will burn off if I don't do something about this! Off comes the rest of my clothes and I am in the shower, I am scrubbing and scrubbing with soap and my wash rag, Lord, more soap, I thought I might have to call the fire department. The burn seemed to simmer down quite a bit, so I put my clothes on. Perhaps it would not have been so bad if I hadn't scratched my crotch raw before I tried that.

As I was preparing for bed tonight, I checked myself and yes, I still had my crabs.

I worked on my truck in the motor pool today. I did a little touch up painting in the wheel wells, and under the hood.

After work I went over to the medic's office where guys go when they are ill, as I went in the door I found that it was kind of a hangout for a lot of the guys. There were eight or ten guys setting around just talking. I didn't want to ask for anything that would get rid of crabs in front of all those people. I stood around for a while and one of the medics walked in to the back room, so I walked back there where he was and I asked, "Do you guys have anything in here that will get rid of crabs?"

He said, "Yeah, I will get you something that will get rid of crabs, I'll be right back." He went on toward the back of the room, when he came back, he walked toward the door where everyone was and hollered loud, "Hey Martin, what did you do with that box of crab powder?" Well. So much for trying to be discrete about it! Anyhow, Martin went into the back room and came back with a small box and handed it to me and said,

"That'll take care of 'em critters!" And it did! After three days I was free of 'em critters.

Two weeks ago I managed to get an overnight pass on a Saturday night. So I left around six-o-clock and headed out to Nurnberg. I went to a Gasthaus and had me some supper, and then I went to a popular bar where a lot of the soldiers go to drink, or maybe find a girl to go home with for the night. I guess I am no exception.

There I sat all evening, couldn't get up enough nerve to talk to any of the girls that were in the place. I just sat there drinking beer and Cognac.

It's two in the morning and I am seeing things that ain't things. Oh, there is a girl setting over there at a table all alone. I think I will move in on her, she looks pretty good. Now I am brave, as I tell myself. "Could I buy you a drink?" I asked.

She replied, "We will have to hurry, they are about to close."

"Okay," I said, "order us a drink, beer for me."

While we were waiting, she asked, "Where are you staying tonight?"

I replied, "I don't know!"

"Would you like to come to my house for the night?"

I guess I said yes, we walked for many blocks and finally she said, "Here we are."

I stayed the night with her, actually, I do not remember very much after we arrived at her home, but when I awoke this morning, I did not have any clothes on.

She came into the bedroom when she realized I was awake. First time I saw her since I sobered up.

No, No, No, I'm thinking to myself, surely I didn't sleep with that, ugly just ain't the word. She is awful, must be at least twenty years older than me, and oh, so ugly, so wrinkled she needs to be ironed. I give her one thing. She is so nice, so very nice. And she said to me.

"Now you just stay in bed, I am going down to the store real quick and pick up a few things and when I return, I am gonna cook you the best breakfast that you have ever had. You stay right there now, I'll be right back."

Before she closed the door I was putting my clothes, on as fast as I could. I know what you are thinking as you read this book, but you aren't here! I'm leaving this house as fast as I can, and I hope I don't meet her coming back.

I am safely back to the barracks and I am not talking about last night to anybody.

It is the last of April, and I just turned twenty years old. I think I need a letter from Miriam. It has been a few days since I have heard from her. I will probably get a couple in one day, which happens sometimes.

We were leaving the motor pool today, just getting to the gate when we heard an explosion. We began to hear a lot of hollering and goings on, so we went back down to where we could see a lot of guys in a big circle, and smoke coming up from the middle of all of them. When we got to where we could see what was going on, I'm not sure I wanted to see. A soldier was laying there on the blacktop, and he had been on fire, all his clothes were burned off of him except his boots. His entire body was burned. He was laying there saying,

"Can someone help me, please help me."

Someone said, "There is help coming, they will be here soon. Help is on the way."

There was an Armored Personal Carrier setting close by, and someone said he was welding in that "APC" and a spark must have ignited the fuel tank. I hope I never see anything like that again. I never did hear if he lived or not.

We should be leaving Germany in five weeks or so. Oh boy, a lot of guys will be so happy to leave here, including me. Not that we don't care for Germany, we had just rather be back home in the USA. Americans are so blessed to be born and raised in America. America is not perfect, that's true, but with all of its imperfections, it is a wonderful place to be.

Just to celebrate leaving Germany I got an overnight pass. I went to Furth to a nice, quiet, Gasthaus and had me a Veiner Schnitzel with hash brown potatoes. The place seemed to fill up with customers, mostly German, a few Americans. They were drinking and before long it wasn't a very quiet place. I drink a few beers. I was just enjoying the atmosphere and a young girl came to my table and asked,

"Would you buy me a drink?"

I replied, "Sure, have a seat."

We exchanged names and had some conversation, she seems very nice. I could not say she was nice, because most nice girls don't ask a guy in a bar to buy her a drink! I thought she was pretty, OK, OK, I know what you are thinking. I am not drunk, and she is pretty.

We spent the entire evening there, well until around midnight.

She asked, "Are you coming home with me?"

I asked, "Is that an invitation?"

"Yes," she said, "I hope you will."

"Okay, let's go." We did not walk too far, several blocks I guess, we stopped on the side walk in front of her place.

She says to me, "When we go in there is a big room, and chances are there will be a lot of couples lying on blankets on the floor. Lots of girls bring their dates here for the night. It is very dark in there, so hold on to me, I will lead the way. Okay?"

When we entered the front door it was so dark I could not see anything. I began to feel rather apprehensive about this! We went through a door, and I could vaguely see that we were in a bathroom.

And she said, "Okay, let's get undressed."

After we undressed, she pulled me into the bath tub. First time for everything!

It has been two weeks since the bath tub episode, today was pay day. A guard from the guard house came to my room and said,

"Garris, there is a girl at the front gate wanting to see you."

"Okay, I'll be right there."

When I arrived at the gate, there she was, the bath tub girl. I was surprised.

"Hi," I said, "what's going on?"

"Hello," she said, "I came out to see you because I need some money to pay my rent. You got paid today, didn't you?"

"Yes I did," I said, "but I don't have any money to give to you."

"Wouldn't you like to come to see me every week at my apartment?" she asked.

"No, because I don't get a pass every week and I sure will not pay your rent." With that being said, I turned and went back to my room. I guess I had better stay here for a while, maybe I can stay out of trouble!

We will be leaving here in the morning, on our way home. I do not believe there is one soul in this country that is as happy as I am!

What a wonderful feeling it is on this big 'ole ship, it is the last of June and the ocean is so calm, we are thankful for this.

The fifth day out, our ship hit a huge whale, I'm telling you it was large! The sharp nose of the ship hit the whale right in the middle of its body. They stopped the ship, and backed up to remove the whale from the bow. The next morning there was a picture of it in the ship's newspaper. I do not know why I didn't save that newspaper. I know some people will not believe that.

At Fort Dix, NJ they put us on an old worn out troop plane to Chicago. I am sure glad that plane made the trip. It was so hot and it had no air conditioning, and sometime it felt like it was wobbling. God, I was thankful to get out of that thing!

We received our release papers and final pay, and I was not sure how I was gonna get to the train station. I began walking toward the gate and I saw them. I can hardly believe my eyes. There stands Miriam, Norita, and Norita's husband, Harry. What an awesome surprise, I could just go over there and kiss all of them. I was so happy.

We talked and laughed all the way back to Goshen, I could not tell you the thrill it is for me to be back home to stay, and be with all my loved ones. I just thank you, God.

I went back to work for Carl at Kaufman Oil Company. He said he was glad to have me back, and I am glad to have a job. I think we have the same customers that we had before I went in the Army.

I don't have a car, I have to find a way to get out to New Paris, I usually find a way. I have only been seeing Miriam about three or four times a week. She has been telling me that she is not seeing John any more, I am glad of that. She had been seeing him the last six months that I was in Germany, and she had told me at Christmas that she would not see him anymore, that hurts.

It has been about a month since I got out of the Army, Carl and I was talking this morning at the station, and the subject got around to Miriam, as to whether she has been seeing John.

Carl said, "Oh I bet she is seeing John on the nights that she don't see you."

"Oh no," I said, "I don't believe she is. I don't believe she would lie to me like that! Anyhow, I don't know how I could find out, not having a car and all."

"Are you supposed to see her tonight?" Carl asked.

"Yes, I am."

Carl said, "Do you want to find out? If you do we could find out tonight."

"How?" I asked.

"Well, is she still working there at the New Paris Drive-In?"

"Yes," I told him.

"I'm sure you know what time she gets off work, we could ride out there and park across the street in that used car lot and see if she leaves with John, when she gets off work. I bet she will. You will have to call her and tell her that you have to work here, and you can't come out tonight."

I did that, now the stage is set. We will find out for sure. I will show Carl that he is wrong!

Miriam gets off work usually around nine-o-clock. We arrived here at about eight forty five.

John and Miriam walked out of the restaurant together, and got in John's car. I think my heart stopped beating. I am so torn apart, I believed her.

"Do you want me to follow them?" Carl asked.

"I guess so," I replied. After we drove a little ways, Miriam slid over against John in the seat, and John put his arm around her neck. When we were entering Goshen, I guess the street lights made enough light that he could recognize that we were following them. Miriam slid back across the seat. I don't know why, the damage was done. They drove on up to Main Street and pulled over and we pulled over behind them. I got out of the car and stood there for a few moments, and John walked back to where I was standing. I said to him,

"Well John, I just hope to hell you have better luck with her than I did!"

He did not say a word, just turned and walked back to his car. Carl took me to my apartment.

I did not sleep at all, I did go to bed, just lying there thinking all night long. I guess she loves him more than me. That's all I could think about. I can't blame John. I know if I was him I would want to be with her also.

I cannot understand why she was always telling me how much she loved me and cared for me and that I was the only one for her and then, there she was with him! My God, what a night!

I did come to work today, but my mind was not on work. Miriam was all I could think about. Maybe I should just let her go. But I don't think I can without talking to her just one more time.

I called her when I got off work and asked if I could talk to her. She said I could. So I went out there tonight.

"Why have you been lying to me?" I asked her.

"I didn't want to tell you I was seeing him because I was afraid I would lose you, I guess you don't understand."

"I guess you were afraid you would lose John too," I said.

"Well," she said crying, "I don't know what to do. I care so much for both of you."

"Would you date me again? I was so afraid this would happen when I went in the Army, and my worst nightmare has come true. You will never know how I feel about you, I guess."

She asked, "Would you be willing to allow me to date John and you too, you know, alternate, I know that would help me to make up my mind which one I cared about the most."

Hopefully I will have a car pretty soon and I know it will be a lot better for me, because I will be able to ask some other girl out. Yes, I told her we can do that. As bad as I wanted to, I did not kiss her when I left.

I finally did purchase a car, a nineteen fifty Desoto, It is a very nice car, very clean, rides good, and it is black. It's a four door, which is not very "cool" in today's youth standards, but it is very comfortable and roomy, and it's mine!

I have told Carl about working with Robert Sullivan, the sign painter.

He asked me, "Could you letter the big billboard beside the station here?"

"Sure," I told him, "that would be easy."

"Tomorrow morning after your usual chores are finished, you can start painting the billboard."

"I'll do that," I told him.

Well, this morning I put a coat of white paint on the big billboard. It should be dry tomorrow and I can letter it.

There is a girl that walks by here every day, if I ever get up enough nerve I'm gonna go out there and see if she will talk to me when she is walking by. She looks like she is about my age, and she is very cute.

It's August and school will be starting pretty soon. Miriam will be a senior this year, her last year of school, and I wonder if I will take her to the prom, or if John will. I guess it's too early to think about that now.

I did talk to the girl that walks by the station every morning. She sure seems nice. I would really like to date her.

I began lettering the sign today, it is big. It reads, "YOU CAN

PAY MORE, BUT YOU CAN'T BUY BETTER". Each letter is about fifteen inches high and each stroke is about four inches wide. After I painted a few letters, Carl walked out here and said,

"Well you are doing a very good job, maybe you can paint all of our signs."

"I will do it," I replied.

As I was painting the sign, I had two other people come to me, asking about signs that they needed. I had high school boys ask me about painting names on the rear fender of their car like, "The Rebel" "Kon Tiki", "Bad Jose", it has become a fad around the area, and I am making a little extra money, this is good.

I got a date with the girl that walks by the station, her name is Bonnie, we went to a movie, and went out to the drive in and got a root beer. She was supposed to be home by eleven-o-clock. We didn't get there until eleven thirty. I was nervous, I turned the headlights off before pulling into the drive, she said,

"Just pull over there in the grass, a train will be coming by soon, then I can get in the house, and they won't hear me come in." There was a railroad track behind her house.

She was right, the train is coming, she got out of the car very quick, I put that old DeSoto in reverse and here I go. NO, I am not moving, it had rained all evening and I just sit here with my tires spinning. Oh boy, I've got to get going before the train has passed. I was digging my tires into the dirt. I began to move just a little bit, forward, backward, forward, backward and the train is gone, and finally the car began to move backwards, and I backed out into the street, and I left two deep tire tracks across their lawn. I guess I am in trouble again! I'll find out in the morning.

Tomorrow night is one of my date nights with Miriam, of course I am looking forward to seeing her.

While I was in the army, Jack and Cecile moved down to Akron, IN. That's where Jack's Mother lived until she passed away, they live in the house where she lived, so on Sundays I make my rounds, going to visit them in Akron, and when I leave there, I usually go over to N. Manchester and visit with Annie's family.

I have dated a few different girls since Miriam told me she wanted to date Jack and me, until she made up her mind which one of us she loved the most. There was a man that came into the station on a regular basis, and he had a daughter that was very cute, very outgoing blonde that acted like she knew she was cute. I think she is eighteen years old.

She drove into the station last Saturday morning and I asked her, "What are you doing tomorrow afternoon?"

She said, "I don't have any plans, why?"

I said, "Would you like to just go out riding around with me?"

"I would love it," she said.

"Great, I will pick you up around two."

"I'll be waiting," she said.

And I picked her up like I said I would, she was ready like she said she would be, she was pretty and I could have really fell for her if she wasn't so silly. She slid across the seat against me when she got in the car, like we were going steady. I drove out to New Paris, driving down the street there, just who do you think was walking along the sidewalk? It was Miriam! I thought to myself well, I am in trouble again. I pointed her out to Marie,

"That's the girl I have been dating."

"Really," she said, "she is very pretty!"

"Yeah, I think so too," I said.

Actually, as much as I love Miriam, I just don't like to be with her the night after she was with John, I guess I am a little weird that way.

I called Miriam and asked her If I could see her Saturday night, today is Thursday. She said,

"I'm glad you decided to call me, do you have a date tomorrow night?"

I replied, "No, why, do you?"

"No," she said, "I thought maybe you were going to see that girl that was with you Sunday afternoon, looked like she was all over you."

I asked, "Was you with John last night?"

"No," she said, "I haven't been with John since I saw you on Sunday. Why don't you come out here tomorrow night, I want to talk to you!"

"Is it about something bad, that I don't know about?"

"No, I don't think it's something bad, and I hope you don't think it is either."

"Okay, I will be out tomorrow night, I'll see you then."

I have no idea what she wants to talk to me about, if it concerns John, or if she has met someone else, or what. I am a little anxious to find out!

We are deep into the fall, the leaves have turned colors and it is beautiful outside, cooler of course, but I always liked the fall weather, and it is comfortable at work. We will be selling a lot of anti-freeze soon. The boss likes that a lot. A lot of people are traveling up into northern Michigan to see the fall colors. Most of the farmers have finished their fall harvest. Lots of corn and soy beans are grown here in Indiana. When the corn is planted in the spring, it takes no time at all for it to be peeking through the earth, especially if we have been blessed with a lot of rain. By the end of August, driving along the county roads, the corn is so high on both sides of the road, it looks like there are high green walls closing in on you. If you have never been in northern Indiana in the late summer, it would be worth the trip to plan a vacation here, see the large farms, and get a good idea how the Amish live, there are so many Amish shops in and around Elkhart County. We know you would be happy to see our part of the country. In this age of such sophisticated farming equipment, the Amish men still plow their fields with horses, big horses. There's a lot to see, come and visit.

Oh, I guess I just got distracted there for a moment. It is Friday, and I just pulled into Miriam's yard, looks like she is coming out to the car, and she got in!

"Hi there," I said to her. "Hi to you," she said, "I haven't seen you in forever it seems like."

"I assumed you were busy."

"Okay," she said, "I want to get right down to what I wanted to talk to you about. I want to ask you if you seriously still love me."

"Oh Miriam, I have loved you so much, ever since the day I met you, you should know that. Why do you ask me that?"

"I know that you have been hurt about me seeing John, and other guys that I dated while you were away in the Army. I know now that I had rather be with you than any other guy that I have been with, no matter where I'm at, or who I am with, you are on my mind, and I love you so much."

And her tears began to fill her eyes, I am stunned I guess, for a moment, I am just speechless.

I told her, "I hardly know what to say, baby, you don't have to cry. What you just said makes this the happiest day of my life! I want to ask you though, did you and John have a big argument or something?"

"No," she said, "when I saw you with that girl last Sunday, it hurt me so bad, it made me think that I could lose you, and I don't want to lose you. I went by John's house and told him that I would not date him any longer."

"Does this mean that you will go steady with me?"

"Yes," she said, "will you go steady with me?"

"I'll go steady with you for the rest of my life, I am so happy, and I feel better than I have for a long, long time."

The days and weeks have passed us by. Where do they go, just slip away right before your very eyes. Thanksgiving has passed, and I sure have many things to be thankful for, and I am. Christmas has passed. February is here, and so is Miriam's birthday, she turned eighteen years old today. I have permission from her Mom and Dad----

I said, "Darling, you know that I have loved you so much for so many years, and I will love you forever, I have this question to ask you."

I am on my knees and I took hold of her hand and as I placed the ring on her finger I asked, "Will you marry me?"

She replied, "Yes, yes, I will marry you," as the tears began to flow.

We chose September the fourth for our wedding day. Miriam is so happy.

"Oh," she said, "there is so much to do between now and then. We are gonna be so busy."

Chapter Sixteen

What a wonderful day in my life, I have been hoping and praying for so long that this day would come, and it has.

I went to the senior prom with Miriam in June, which was very exciting for both of us, especially for her. Her graduation was such a special day. Such an accomplishment for her, and I am so proud of her.

It is time to go get our marriage license so we went to the county clerk's office in Goshen.

"Do both of you have your birth certificates?" she asked. Miriam showed hers to the clerk, and I told her I was twenty one.

She said, "Anyone getting married must have their birth certificate."

"I was born in North Carolina, and I never obtained one. Our wedding is this coming Sunday, and I'm not sure I will be able to get it by Friday."

She said, "Well you are gonna have to get it if you want to get married."

I called the courthouse in Shelby, NC and told them my situation and the lady told me if I wired them the money today, they would get it in the mail to me today, airmail. So, we went to the Western Union and mailed them twenty dollars, the cost of the birth certificate would be five dollars, so I thought I would send a little more to cover everything. It did not come by Wednesday, so I called Robert, the sign painter, and asked if he would get my birth certificate and send it "Western Union". He told me he would. And by Friday I still did not have it, we went back to the clerk's office in Goshen and I told her what all I did trying to get my birth certificate, and she said,

"Oh my goodness, if you did all of that and still did not get it, I will go ahead and give you kids your marriage license."

"We just thank you so very much," we said.

Our wedding took place at the Church of the Brethren in New Paris, with the Reverend Kenneth Hollinger officiating. Steve and Carl stood up with me. Oh, it was so hot, about ninety degrees!

We had a beautiful wedding, the church was full, oh what a ceremony. Annie and Cecile and their families were here, and of course all of Miriam's family, and it looked like all the church members.

As we were departing the church, there was the car all decorated up with "Just Married" written all over it and tin cans tied to the back bumper, and we were driven all over town with many of our friends following us and blowing horns. What excitement!

When we returned to the church, I asked Miriam, "Are you ready to travel?"

"I cannot wait to get going," she replied.

We left on our honeymoon around six-o-clock, our plans are to go to Shelby, NC, and over to the east coast, and from there, drive on down to Florida.

Miriam asked me, "When are you planning on stopping, and getting a room for the night?"

"I am not sure yet," I replied. "I really wanted to get on down the road, and get some miles behind us before we stop."

She said, "Better not wait too long, or we won't be able to get a room."

I don't know what in the world I am thinking. I guess I am just trying to get to North Carolina as quick as I can, I am anxious to show off my wife.

I began to get sleepy around one A.M. Miriam said,

"If you are so determined that we drive all night, just stop and let me drive before you kill us." I stopped and she got behind the steering wheel. She woke me at four thirty saying,

"I cannot stay awake another mile. We are at a motel, would you go in and see if they have a room available?" I went in and got a room.

We carried our suitcases into the room and began getting ready for bed. Needless to say, Miriam is not in a very happy mood with me at this point.

I asked, "Honey, are we--" she interrupted,

"No," she said, "I just want to go to bed and get some sleep, goodnight!"

We are almost to Shelby, NC. We stopped at a restaurant and ate dinner, after we finished she went to the restroom. When she returned she announced, "monthly time". See, you were in such a big hurry last night to get here, and now, do you see, you missed out on a great opportunity! That's what, "get some more miles behind us", has cost you!

"Too late I know, I do regret it very much, and baby, I apologize. Will you forgive me? Stupid gets a hold of me sometimes."

We got a room in Shelby, (yes we did), stayed here overnight and here we are on the road again. We did not get an early start this morning but that's alright, we have plenty of time. Miriam seems to be in a good mood today and I am happy about that.

We just rode along and talked about the future, had a lot of laughs.

"How far do you think we will get today?" she asked.

"I really don't know, we are just about to Charleston, SC, after we get through there, we will find a motel."

"That sounds good to me," she said.

Driving through Charleston she said,

"This sure is a beautiful city, the stores and homes are so old, must have been here for many, many years. And the tree limbs hanging over the streets makes it look like we are driving through a tunnel, it is so pretty."

"It sure is a beautiful city," I echoed what she said, "could be a great place to live."

We finally got to the south side of the city and I said,

"I guess we could start looking for a nice motel."

Miriam asked me, "Are you tired now?"

I replied, "No, I'm not tired."

"Just keep driving if you want to and if I get sleepy, I will just lay my head in your lap, if I won't bother you."

"Well, that will not bother me at all, I like that you know. I don't know how long I can stay awake tonight, but, we'll see." Around eleven thirty she gave up and laid her head in my lap and said,

"Wake me if you need me."

"Okay," I replied.

I think I am on U.S. Highway 17. It sure is a lonesome road, four lane divided highway with crossovers here and there, the only thing you could see was pine trees on both sides of the road, reminded me of a forest. I don't know how close to the ocean we are, but I think we are pretty close. I will not go looking for it.

I haven't seen anything, gas station, car or house for many miles, am I in the twilight zone? This road feels like it. Anyhow I am totally awake; the man on the radio is saying a hurricane is approaching the south Florida coast. They are not sure if it is gonna go up the east coast or go around into the gulf.

Driving with my bright lights on I caught a glimpse of something moving into my side of the road from the grass. There are curbs on both sides of the highway and they are just at the edge of the driving portion of the highway, about six inches high. I guess it would be difficult to pull a car off the road even if it was necessary. I am thinking whatever was crossing the road ahead of me would be across the road by the time I got there, so I did not pay any attention to it.

I am driving seventy miles per hour, and all of a sudden I see what it is, it's an alligator, and it is huge. By the time I realize what it is, it is half way across the road, half of it was on my lane and his other half was in the left lane. God, what am I gonna do? My quick decision was to get as far to the right of the road as I could and maybe, I would hit him on the smaller side of his tail. Oh boy, it was like hitting a log.

Miriam jumped up, scared half to death.

"What happened?" she asked.

"I just ran over an alligator!"

"An alligator? Where was it?"

"It was crossing the highway, and I could not go around him with these curbs beside the road."

"Can we go back? I would like to see it. Is it dead?"

"I don't know if it is dead, but yes, I am gonna go back when I come to a crossover to turn around."

We turned around and made it back to where it was, and he was just lying there, flapping his tail back and forth. He wasn't dead. I must have hit him in the belly because he is bleeding really bad.

The only thing I know to do is to keep driving on south and when we come to a gas station or some place that has a telephone, I will stop and call the state police and let them know what happened. That alligator could cause a bad accident.

We drove at least a hundred miles and did not see one place where we could make a phone call. I did not see any signs directing traffic to any towns.

We were getting very low on gas and we came into an area where there was some sign of life. All the gas stations we have seen are not open until six or seven a.m.. So to avoid running out of gas alongside the road out in the boondocks, we decided to pull into a gas station and sleep in the car until they opened the station.

Sleep? I thought we could sleep in the car. It is not gonna happen! Oh, it was so darn hot, and when we rolled the windows down, you would think we sent invitations out to all of the mosquitoes in Georgia to come and eat free!

A man came and opened the station at seven-o-clock. I filled the tank with gas and we were on our way, we were only about three miles from the Florida state line, and we arrived at Mama's house about twelve thirty today. Oh man, what a trip we have had coming to Florida.

Everyone here is talking about the hurricane, it is coming up the west coast of Florida, and the meteorologist are saying that it could turn and go east at any time. You know what? That's all we need now! That would top off our honeymoon trip!

Overnight the hurricane that was named "Donna" turned east and it is heading directly toward Sanford, FL and that is exactly where we are.

The flower farm in Shelby, NC where all my family was employed, purchased a small flower farm outside of town here, and my brother-in-law, Howard and his family live here and Howard works here. And my brother, Brodus works here.

Brodus' boss asked if he knew anyone that could come and work today as they try to tie moving parts down so "Donna" would not blow everything away. Brodus called the house here where I am and asked me if I wanted to work a few hours at the greenhouse today. I told him I would. I went out there to work and I got back to Mama's house at seven thirty this evening. Weather people on TV are saying that "Donna" would probably pass over Sanford around two a.m.

Mama cooked us up a real good supper and after we ate, Miriam, Brodus and I settled in at the dining room table with a deck of cards, playing rummy. By then the power had went out, so we were playing by candlelight. We had decided that we would stay awake until the eye of the hurricane passed over. We had our snacks and drinks and we were ready to stay up for a while.

We could hear the wind getting stronger and man, the rain was coming down! About eleven thirty a screen was blown out of the window and landed against Miriam's back, she was setting in front of the window until then.

The house was built of cement blocks with no dry wall on the interior at all. The wind was blowing so hard that water began to come through the walls in the rooms facing the west. We were trying to keep the floors dry with towels and whatever we could find to soak up the water. I think it was about one thirty when Miriam and I was setting on the couch, and just could not stay awake, so we went to sleep. Mama stayed awake.

She told us this morning that the eye of the hurricane passed over the house about three-o-clock this morning, electricity was out all over town. The streets were all flooded; the drive-in theatre screen was blown down, and a lot of minor damage everywhere you looked. I know it could have been a lot worse. We are very fortunate, and thankful.

Miriam and I went over to New Smyrna Beach and spent most of the day. We were there long enough to get a good sun burn. Miriam just loves the beach, I am not crazy about it myself.

We are on our way home, and we are anxious to get all of our wedding gifts put away and get our apartment arranged the way we want it. We will remember our honeymoon trip for a long time, it sure was exciting, to say the least.

Back to work we go.

The time goes by so fast, all of a sudden it is springtime, nineteen sixty one, and we are working every day. We do not like our apartment at all, so we began looking for another place. Someone told us about a man living alone and he was hoping to find a couple to move in with him. The price wasn't bad, so we did.

A month after we moved in there, Miriam found out that she was pregnant, we were so happy. We started talking about names, boys and girls names, we thought Angela would be good for a girl and Jeffrey for a boy.

Well, two months later, Miriam began having problems with her pregnancy, she was really having pains.

She was at work one morning and she began spotting, and throwing up. She came home and called the doctor, and he told her, that it probably wasn't anything serious, but she should call back later if the pain didn't let up. Late in the evening, she called him back, and couldn't talk to him because he was at the hospital. So at two in the morning, I called him.

"Doctor, something has to be done, I don't know how long she can suffer like she is!" The doctor said,

"I haven't slept since I got up yesterday morning and I have to lie down for a few hours, have her at the hospital emergency room at six-o-clock and I will meet you there."

We were up the rest of the night, and I had her at the hospital at six and the nurses took over trying to help her until seven a.m., when the doctor came in.

He was with her for a while and he came to where I was waiting, and told me she had a miscarriage.

I asked him if he could tell if it was a boy or a girl.

He said, "I could not really tell because the pregnancy was only three months."

"Would you like to see it?" he asked.

"Yes I would," I told him. So he showed it to me. He had put it in a glass, it looked like a glass jar. I could not really make out the features of it, myself. We were very saddened about that, But God knows best.

We're not too happy living in the house with Charley Edwards, and we have been looking for other options and we came across a home on Wilkerson St. about two blocks from where I work. The house needed repairs, work that I could do, and we could afford it, so we purchased it on a land contract for five thousand dollars. I went to work on that old house in my spare time. With Miriam's help we put hardwood flooring down in the living room, bedroom and dining room. Then I undertook the job of building and installing kitchen cabinets.

Well, what do you know? Miriam went to the doctor today, when she came home she said to me,

"The doctor told me that I am pregnant, and I am worried about it, as I remember what happened the last time."

"Oh honey, you are gonna be just fine, I know you will, we will have our first child, and I am very excited about it, and I want you to be also."

On August twenty fifth, nineteen sixty three, our little Jeffrey Alan was born. His weight is Eight pounds, fourteen ounces. We are so proud.

The summer of nineteen sixty four, Brodus called me from Florida and asked me if I wanted the job at Patterson's greenhouses hauling dish gardens up to Shelby, NC every week. Miriam and I talked it over and decided we would go down there and I would take the job. Living in Florida seemed inviting.

So, we relocated to Florida. The weather just might be too hot, but we will try it for a while. Maybe we will get used to it. Perhaps this is a mistake moving down here. Time will tell.

On some trips to North Carolina I have a drop in Savannah, Georgia. It is a beautiful town, and then I will deliver the rest of the load to Shelby.

Last week I delivered in Shelby, and Knighton Patterson, Mr. Patterson's son, who is in charge of the green houses here in Sanford, FL had me drive on up to Randleman, NC to pick up some parts for his new car, which is a Plymouth.

The garage where I went to, is none other than NASCAR's great driver Richard Petty's. Richard is driving Plymouths now. I guess that's why Knighton wanted parts for his Plymouth. He is probably attempting to soup his car up.

Our relationship with my relatives down here is not going very well. I am not sure if we are gonna be here very long.

It has been three months since we moved down here. I received word that I am supposed to call Ethan Kaufman in Warsaw, IN.

"Hello, this is Harper Garris, are you Mr. Kaufman?"

"Yes I am, and I have a question for you."

I said, "What can I do for you?"

He said, "I think you probably know the station manager here at the Warsaw station."

"Oh yes, Max Fribley, I do know him."

"He is leaving his management position here in Warsaw, and I am wondering if you might be interested in being the manager at this station?"

"I should talk this over with my wife and see what she thinks about the offer, I will be back in touch with you within twenty four hours."

"That will be just fine," he said. "I will look forward to hearing from you, thank you for calling."

I told Miriam what happened and she was just short of jumping up and down.

"Are we gonna leave here today?" she asked.

"No, maybe in a week we will be leaving, I have to call Mr. Kaufman back and tell him I will accept the job, and get everything taken care of here."

Here we are back in Indiana, and I am managing the station here. This is not a hard job. I am responsible for everything that is in this station. I hire and fire all the employees. I have to keep a correct inventory of everything we sell every day. Each person that carries money for change to the customer, has to fill out a work sheet at the end of his "on duty" hours and it goes to the accountant in his office next door.

We have oil and anti- freeze in the storage room, and if a certain kind of oil on the shelf is sold out, we go to the storage room and get another case and replace it on the display shelf in the station.

There is an inventory card that we use to subtract a case of oil, when we bring a case of oil to the front. That way, we always know how many quarts of oil or gallons of anti-freeze we have in the back room by looking at the inventory.

Let's say a customer comes into the station and buys a full case, 24 quarts of oil, and the station employee gets a case out of the back room for him, and that employee is dishonest and does not mark it off of the inventory card, and puts the money in his pocket. Someone will have to pay for it when the inventory in the back room is counted. We kept a lot of inventory in the back room.

Only one person carries money for change. If one of our part time employees waits on a customer, and the sale is $5.40 and the customer gives him a $10.00 bill he has to take the $10.00 bill to the shift manager and tell him $5.40 cents out of $10.00 and he takes the change back to the customer. At the end of each shift the shift manager has to account for everything that was sold on his shift. Keep this in mind as you read on.

When I took over management of this station, I'll just say that it had not been kept up very well at all, it was very dirty, and it was going to take a lot of work to get it in the shape I thought it should be in. So I went to work, cleaning the bathrooms, painting the walls and floors, and I had them looking very good. Every time someone would use one of the restrooms, one of us would check it when they left to make sure it didn't need any attention. I have the night shift man to wash the drive down every night with soap. Every morning the shift manager has to clean the pumps with Bon-ami. We cleaned and painted everything that needed it, and that was almost everything.

Mr. Kaufman's office was in the room next door where the accountant's office was. He came over a couple times a day to use the restroom, and he told me,

"I don't remember when this place looked so good, you sure are doing a fine job."

I am painting and lettering all the signs on days when I am off duty, he pays me extra for that.

A fellow by the name of Junior Shoemaker works opposite of me on the day shift. He comes in at one thirty and works until ten P.M., when the night shift man comes in. Then he goes home and comes back at six a.m. and works until one thirty. Then I come to work and he goes home for twenty four hours. And I come in and work the same hours as he did. It's kinda like I'm on twenty four and off twenty four.

Junior was employed here for years before I came here, and so far he seems to be okay. I believe he is around fifty four years old. I found out that if he gets upset with a customer he will tell them off. I do not like that at all, no way to do business. I believe Junior is honest. He hasn't done anything to make me think he isn't.

We have a Seminary about four miles, east of here at Winona Lake, a lot of the local people in Warsaw call it a "preacher factory", but the men that work the night shift here are enrolled in college out there. There are two of them working here, and they alternate the nights they work. They are very good men and they do a very good job.

We found a house that we could buy on land contract, so we will be moving in there within a week. It's about five blocks from the station. The man we are buying it from has been transferred to a plant in Canada.

We went up to New Paris last Saturday evening to visit some friends, Bob Wineland, and his wife Shirley, Miriam went to school with Shirley.

Bob said, "There is a country band playing over at the Sportsman bar in Syracuse, (a small town about twelve miles away,) you want to go over there for a while this evening?"

"Sounds good to me, I'll see what Miriam says about it."

Miriam said it's o.k. with her, so we are on our way to Syracuse. Bob said he's never heard the band before, but someone told him that they were pretty good. I guess we will find out!

When we arrived, the band was playing. I noticed right away that the man singing was a customer at Kaufman's in Goshen, when I worked there. Tom Smith is his name.

When they took a break, Bob went over to the table where they were setting and talked to them a little bit.

The band returned to the stage and played two or three songs and said,

"I guess we have another person in the house that sings, let's get him up here to sing a couple songs. Let's all make him welcome, Harper Garris, come on up here and sing."

Man, I looked at Bob and said, "I'm gonna kill you when I get a chance!"

Well, I did go on stage and sang a couple Buck Owens songs. Buck is my hero. I sang "Under Your Spell Again", and "Excuse me, I Think I've Got A Heartache". The band seemed to like how I sang, and I received a big hand from the bar patrons. I sure did appreciate that. When the band took their next break, the bass player, Harry, stopped at our table, and asked me if I was in another band. I told him no.

Then he asked me to come outside with the band. All of the band members were outside, except Tom.

Harry asked me, "How would you like to be the singer in our band?"

I said I would, but I would not want to do that to Tom.

Then he said, "You would not be doing that to Tom. We were gonna fire him tonight when we finished up here."

I told him to give me a phone number and I will call and let him know tomorrow, I will have to see what my wife will say about it.

On Sunday, Miriam said, "I'm not really crazy about it, but I won't stop you from playing in the band, I know how you like to sing and play your guitar, so if you want to do it, it will be alright with me."

I am happy about that, and glad that she thinks it will be okay.

On Sunday I called Harry and told him that I would join their band.

He asked me when I could practice with the band.

I told him I could practice Wednesday evening.

On Monday, I talked to Mr. Kaufman and asked him if my job would be in jeopardy if I joined a band.

"No," he told me, "I think everyone should have a hobby or something to do in their spare time, as long as it did not interfere with their employment."

This makes me wonder if playing in a band will be a part of my future, and where it will take me. I love to play my guitar and sing, and I love country music.

I went to practice with the band tonight, and found out the drummer quit the band when the band fired Tom. Oh well, now I guess Harry, me, and Lefty can play together. Lefty plays lead guitar, and he is pretty good.

I told Harry and Lefty about a guy I knew that might like to play with us. His name is Ollie Henderson and he plays a little lead guitar and sings pretty well. The guys seemed to like that idea.

So the next day, I called Ollie and asked him if he would be interested in playing with us. He said he would try it for a while, and see how it would go.

There is a restaurant with a bar here in Warsaw that serves very good meals, and there is a large dining room. After nine p.m. they close the dining room.

I went down there last evening and talked with the owner, she told me everyone called her Vi. I asked her if she ever thought about having a band play on Friday and Saturday nights, to keep the supper guests in here longer. There is plenty of room for dancing also.

She said, "I have thought about it, but I'm not sure how it would go over with the people that come in here."

I told her that I thought we could keep the crowd if she would give us a chance for a couple week ends. I told her our price and she booked us for the coming week-end. This is the third month that we have played there every week-end. And the place was full every night.

Things come around and things go around. Lefty quit the band. That gave us a chance to try to find a drummer, and we did. Terry Harrell began playing drums for us, and he was a good drummer, and a very fun guy to have in the band.

I guess perhaps I knew it would be difficult to keep all the band members together. Now Ollie has left the band. I decided that I would play lead guitar, and we would try to find someone to be the front man and be the lead vocalist.

Terry knew a fellow that would fill the vacant spot. A man named Jerry and he was a good singer, so now we had a four piece band, I am the first to admit that I was not a very good lead guitar player, but we got by very well.

We began playing other venues for miles around, Moose Clubs, Eagles clubs and private parties.

The four of us have been playing together for about three years. It has been fun for sure.

Chapter Seventeen

Miriam received word from the doctor that she is pregnant.

"I bet we will probably get our little girl now," I told her.

"Oh, that would be nice," she said.

This summer has pretty much just flown by, just working at the station, and the band has been playing about every weekend.

The next thing you know it is December the eleventh. I am working, Miriam called me at the station around ten thirty and said,

"Honey, I think you had better come home, I am having some serious pains, my water broke earlier this morning."

"Okay, I will call Junior and have him come in and I will be home shortly." When I arrived home, she was waiting with her suitcase packed, and we headed to the hospital. The nurses were attending her and I was by her side for about twenty minutes, and she said she was feeling a little better, so I told her I was gonna step outside and smoke.

I came back in the hospital about five minutes later, and they were taking her down the hall to the delivery room. Our second boy was born, how wonderful. The nurse told me I could come and see my new son. What a beautiful baby boy!

"It sure didn't take long did it honey?"

"No it didn't, I guess he was ready," she said, "I sure was ready."

A nurse asked me to come to her office to answer some questions, like they normally do. She asked if we had agreed on a name for him and I said,

"Jesse Joe Garris," I don't remember Miriam and I discussing that name. There was a man who worked at the greenhouses in NC whose name was Jesse Fitch, I really liked him, so I named Jesse after him. Miriam told me later that she liked the name.

Another couple of years have passed with nothing really exciting happening until someone told me about a show called the "Indiana Jubilee" that was broadcast on a local radio station at Peru, IN, and a lot of bands played there. Miriam and I went down there one Saturday to check it out. We found it to be very interesting. We found the person who was in charge of the show, and asked him how we could get our band on the show.

He said, "We don't pay the bands, they come because they want to get the show up and going, but later we do want to be able to pay the bands." The man we talked to was the stepfather of Loretta Lynn and her sisters, Peggy Sue, and Brenda Gail. He told us to bring the band down any time and we could get a thirty minute slot on the show.

I told the rest of the band about what I found out, and agreed that would be fun to do. Of course it doesn't pay anything, I told them, and they said that would be okay.

Our band went down there yesterday and we played two, one half hour shows, one show at eight and another show at ten-o-clock. The building was full of people, and they seemed to enjoy us very much. The band and I sure did enjoy playing there. We met a lot of other musicians. We all agreed that we will go back and play there again.

We have been playing at the "Jubilee" now for about a year. Not every Saturday night, but very often. If we tell them that we have a booking in a club later in the evening, they will let us play at seven or seven thirty, and we still have time to get to the club and play.

Work at the station is going well. I think we have some good employees. I have two high school boys working part time, and they are very good workers.

I hope I haven't got too involved with the band, I believe I have been successful playing in the band and managing the station, it has been rough getting my financial obligations taken care of. One hundred and ten dollars a week is not enough, considering the hours I work and trying to purchase our home and a vehicle, now with another child coming along. Maybe I am in line for a raise, I hope.

Well Miriam is pregnant again, Miriam really wants a girl. So we are trying, and praying that this pregnancy will go well.

I'm sure a lot of people are not aware that Loretta Lynn's Mother and Step-father, Tommy Butcher, moved from Kentucky to Wabash, IN.

Loretta was married in Kentucky, and she and her husband, Mooney, moved to Washington state and lived there a long time before she ever had a hit song.

Peggy Sue and Brenda Gail sing at the Indiana Jubilee every Saturday night. Brenda Gail will later become "Crystal Gail" after she graduates high school and goes to Nashville.

I met a fellow at the Jubilee by the name of Bill Cullough. He is an outstanding lead guitar player. Also the drummer in his band is a very good drummer, his name is Jerry.

Bill approached me with an idea he had. "Harper, you have a good bass player, but your ability to play lead guitar sure leaves a lot to be desired. I like the way you sing.

Now, he said, I wonder if you and Harry would be interested in leaving your band and coming in with me and Jerry? Perhaps then we could be Brenda and Peggy Sue's back-up band."

"Well Bill," I answered, "that sounds really good to me. However, I will have to talk to Harry…" "Hold on," He interrupted me. "I have already talked to Harry and he thinks it will be a good idea."

The other two guys in my band, Jerry and Terry was not very happy about it, in fact they were very upset. But, that's life, I did what I thought was best for me.

Life was going so good until today. We are one month behind on our house payment.

Phil did not like being in Canada, so I'm sure he was just waiting for a chance to take his house from us. We received a notice today that we will have to vacate the house within thirty days.

I think, perhaps Mr. Kaufman received word that we are having our house repossessed. Is that why he decided to audit the gas station?

He came into the station while I was on duty and said,

"Harper, give me all of the company money that you have, and I will call you when I want you to come back to the station later today."

I am worried because I haven't done an inventory in the back room for a very long time. I suppose there could be a shortage in there if the employees have not been subtracting the items that they brought to the front room on the inventory card.

Mr. Kaufman called and asked me to return to the station at five-o-clock. Driving into the station, I saw Warsaw's chief of police, and then I thought that I was in trouble.

I asked Mr. Kaufman if the audit revealed a shortage, he would not tell me.

Officer Young said "I need you to drive down to the police station."

Entering the police station, a detective escorted me to a back room.

"Have a seat," he said, "I will be right back."

He came back and said to me,

"Harper, the audit today showed that there is over twelve hundred dollars missing in the stations' operation funds. What I want you to do is write on this pad, why did you steal money from the company."

"I did not steal any money from the company!"

"Well, money is missing from the station and you are the manager, and you are responsible for it, aren't you?"

"Yes, I am."

He told me, "If you do not write a confession on this yellow pad here, you will go to jail tonight! I know God d#%+ well you are guilty, and if you want to go home tonight, you had better admit that you are guilty."

I am so scared and nervous, I don't know what to do, Miriam is home, seven months pregnant and sick. So I told him I would admit taking the money but I did not have any idea what to write down.

He said, "I will tell you what to write."

So I wrote down what he told me to write, then he told me to drive over to the jail. So I did, and they arrested me.

"Can you make bail?" they asked me.

"Can I make a phone call?" I asked.

"Yes you can," he said.

I called Miriam, and she called her Mother, and her Mom and Dad came and posted bail, and we went home. My God what a day!

As it turned out, after further investigation of the station's funds, I was only short three hundred and twenty seven dollars. I appeared in court later, the judge charged me with a misdemeanor, and fined me thirty five dollars.

I wrote a song entitled, "Baby Sitting with the Blues", and another song, "I should Have Kicked Myself in the Bottom". We recorded it in a local studio, it did not really do much for the band. Those songs were fun to play in clubs, but that was about as far as it went.

We moved back to New Paris, and rented a house that belonged to a close friend of Miriam's parents. It is a very nice house, and he charges us eighty dollars a month rent. Now I need to find a job!

Miriam's brother, Jim got me a job where he works for a trucking company hauling sand to Gary, Indiana and delivering to a ready-mix company. Then going to the steel mill in Gary and getting a load of slag and hauling it to Ft. Wayne, IN and delivering there. From there, going to an aggregates yard and getting a load of gravel, and hauling it back to the company's yard in Goshen. The name of this company is Zook Inc. They own nine semi dump trucks.

I really like my job here, especially with only nine drivers it is easy getting to know everyone.

July the twenty third, one more time, Mr. Zook contacted me and told me to come to the yard, that I was about to become a father again. I got home as fast as I could and got Miriam and we headed to the hospital in Warsaw. Another boy was born. We are so happy with our new little boy. We sure do love our boys. Miriam named this one, she named him after her brother, and me. His name is James Harper Garris

I have been employed for about six months. Seven of us drivers went down to Leesburg, a small town about eight miles south of New Paris, about two a.m. and loaded our trucks with sand and we are on our way to Gary, IN to dump our sand at a redi-mix yard. But on our way, five of us stopped at a restaurant in Westville, IN to have breakfast and just "shoot the bull" for a while. We finished our stories and got in our trucks and headed out, three of them pulled out before Butch and I pulled out of the parking lot. Butch pulled out before me, I got on the road and before long I was on the Tri-States parkway which is also I-80 and I-94. I thought to myself, my, traffic is really heavy this morning, but it was moving along. I noticed smoke rising up in the air a long way ahead of me which was not unusual for the area, probably someone burning trash or something. Now I am in a construction zone, looks like they are making preparation to resurface the berm of the road, they had it scraped down about a foot beside the road, of course they had those orange traffic cones along the edge of the road.

I began to get very close to the smoke I had been looking at. The Cline Ave. exit is coming up and there is a bridge over Cline Ave. I am not going to exit there.

Do you remember me making a remark quite a while back when I said, 'I hope I never see anything like that again'.

This is by far the worst accident that I have ever seen in my life. Just before I approached the bridge I looked over to the right and saw a truck that had turned over and the cab of the truck was totally engulfed in flames and I just got a glimpse of the printing on the tailgate that read "Zook". Oh my God in Heaven, that is the truck that Butch was driving. I slowed down very fast, and pulled over on the berm after I crossed the bridge, as I am walking back across the bridge, I am thinking that Butch did not even have a chance, and wondering what could have happened, and all of a sudden I saw Butch as he climbed to the top of the embankment.

He got down on his knees and began pounding the ground. I finally got to him, obviously he was devastated. I just did not know what to say to him, but I said,

"Man, what in the world happened?"

He said, "I got two of them out!"

"What?" I asked him.

He said, "I got two of them out," as he pointed down the embankment behind him. Then I saw what he was talking about. There was what was left of a Ford Mustang convertible that had burned. I see the remains of two people in the car. Then I saw two people setting on the ground a little ways from the car, and they were burned very badly. That's all I will say about that.

I stayed there with Butch until Mr. Zook, the owner of Zook, Inc. arrived, along with his brother, to talk to the State Troopers.

I asked Mr. Zook if I could make my delivery in Gary and go back home, I was a bundle of nerves, myself.

"No Harper, I believe it would be the best for you to go ahead and finish your usual run." So I did.

I know this is one day that I will never forget as long as I live. Every time I drove past the accident area, I could still smell the burnt flesh.

I told you earlier that there was construction going on, there were the orange cones beside the road for a couple of miles. As you would expect, the morning rush hour was in full swing, it's five forty five in the morning. The highway is three lanes. There are cars and trucks as far as I can see. Traffic is like this every morning, except Sunday.

I talked to Butch a couple of weeks after the accident, and I asked him if he would tell me what caused the accident.

"You know how heavy traffic is on the Tri-States Expressway that time of the morning?"

"Oh yes, I sure do," I answered.

He said, "I might have been following a little close to the truck in front of me, you know if you don't, other cars and trucks will change lanes, and squeeze into your lane right in front of you.

I did see trucks and cars ahead of me going into the center lane, but I didn't know why. Then, all of a sudden the truck in front of me moved over into the center lane, I could not change lanes because there was a truck beside of me, and in front of me was a Mustang convertible traveling about twenty miles an hour. I tried to drive my truck off the right side of the road behind it, but I could not do that. Everything was happening too fast. So, I ran over the rear of the car, and somehow the truck dragged the car down the twenty foot embankment. The car's gas tank was ruptured and caught fire, and burned up the car and truck."

From what we learned later, the Mustang had a flat tire and they were trying to make their way to an exit.

I would like to tell you this, about my getting arrested, and fired, at Kaufman's gas station A month after I left my employment with Mr. Kaufman, the book keeper, Gerald, came to our house. I answered the door; I thought that I would never see him again. He said to me,

"Harper, did you know that Mr. Kaufman sold the station at Warsaw to some friends who live in Indianapolis?"

"No, I did not know that!"

"Well, Mr. Kaufman has highly recommended you to them for the station manager. And they asked me to come up here and talk to you personally. Do you think that you would be interested in taking that job back?"

"Gerald, considering what I went through down there, as hard as I have worked at that station to clean it up when I first went to work there, the hours I worked, for the pay I received, not to mention accusing me of stealing money from him that I did not do and getting arrested and having a criminal record the rest of my life, I would not ever think of working at that station, never!"

"Thank you Harper," Gerald said. "I will tell Mr. Kaufman and the new owners what you told me. It is good to see you again, and I wish you the very best."

That was not the end of it, a week later the new owners of the station came to our house and told me they came with strong recommendations of my ability to manage the station. He told me,

"We know the complete history of the time you were employed there, but we will promise you much better employment, with a better wage, and we will not be there looking over your shoulder every day."

"I believe you folks are very kind," I said. "I don't know you, but I guess that does not matter. But what I told Gerald last week is the same answer I have for you. I am not interested what so ever, but I do appreciate your offer, and kind remarks."

And that was the end of that!

Tommy Butcher decided that he would book Loretta on some shows. Loretta has not been recording very long, the radio stations are playing a couple of songs now, but she hasn't received enough publicity yet to warrant putting her own band together. When someone books her for a concert, they have to book a band to back her up.

Tommy Butcher booked her and her brother, Jay Lee Webb, and Brenda and Peggy Sue, and our band to play back-up for the entire show.

The concert will be in Tipton, IN in a month. We have a lot of work to do to learn all the songs they will perform. I am convinced we are capable of it. Peggy and Brenda sing just about all of Loretta's songs at the "Jubilee" and at the clubs where we play.

The day of the concert is here, and I am nervous as we stand back stage and prepare for the concert. I haven't even looked around the curtain to see if there was a big crowd, I was afraid to!

It's show time, and we began playing rhythm as the curtains were opened. I don't think I have ever seen so many people in a building, all of them applauding and whistling. Lord, I know my knees are knocking, and I have to sing, I have to now, I began singing a Buck Owens song, "Act Naturally", as I sing I begin to calm down a little bit. And soon I was feeling pretty good. We performed for thirty minutes, and I introduced Jay Lee, he came out and sang four songs and introduced Brenda and Peggy. While they were singing, Jay Lee walked over close to me and said,

"Your fly is open!" Oh God, I'm thinking, I turned around and walked toward the back of the stage to "zip it" and discovered it was not open at all, I looked over at him and he was laughing.

Of course when Loretta was introduced out to the stage, the crowd almost went wild. She performed for an hour, she really put on a good show.

As it turned out, we were booked to play four more shows with Loretta.

We provided back-up for many artists from Nashville, Bobby Helms who wrote and recorded "Jingle Bell Rock" and "You Are My Special Angel", also "Frauline". And we worked a lot with Kenny Price of the TV show, "Hee Haw".

I terminated my employment at Zook, Inc. in July, 1968, and I took a job with Starcraft Marine as a truck driver, delivering boats all over the U.S. and Canada, I like this job very much. I sure see a lot of the country.

For the first six months driving for Starcraft, I was dispatched on trips that were anywhere from six hundred to a thousand miles, then I started making trips to Denver, Phoenix, and Salt Lake City.

I am dispatched to Westfield, Massachusetts with a load of boats, I left the yard about six p.m. and I drove until two a.m. and slept four hours and began driving again, and I arrived in Westfield at noon. There was another Starcraft driver there unloading his boats and he said to me,

"When are you expecting to get back to Goshen?"

I replied, "Oh I would like to get back tonight, but I didn't get very much sleep last night, so I don't know if I can make it all the way there tonight."

"Okay," he said, "we should run together and maybe we could make it."

I said, "Sounds good to me."

We drove into the night, and when we arrived at the New York, Pennsylvania state line we stopped for coffee.

"I'm gonna have to stop and sleep pretty soon, I can hardly keep my eyes open."

Randy pulled a little box of pills out of his pocket,

"Here" he said, "take a couple of these," as he laid them on the table, "they will keep you awake."

"What kind of pills are they?" I asked.

"They are Bennies, haven't you heard of Bennies before, that's what most truck drivers use to stay awake."

"No, I have never heard of Bennies, but I will take them, if they will keep me awake." So I did.

We left there and those pills did not help me at all. But we did make it down to the first service plaza on the Ohio turnpike. I did not get out of the truck.

Randy came over and asked, "Are you ready for some coffee?"

"No," I replied, "I am gonna go to bed. I'll see you back at the yard."

So, he left!

I got laid off at Starcraft for the summer, and I'm not sure what I am gonna do for a job.

Chapter Eighteen

There is a farmer's newspaper, "The Farmers Exchange", printed here in New Paris, published and sold once a week. Miriam works there one day a week; she inserts one section of the paper inside the other section of the newspaper and prepares the paper to be mailed out to the subscribers.

She came home for her lunch break today, and told me that they changed their linotype method of printing to a different method of printing called offset printing, and that they are getting rid of all their old printing equipment. She said she asked Lawrence Yeater, the owner, what he was gonna do with the old equipment, and he said he would probably have to give it away, because it is so out dated. She told me that I should go down there this afternoon and see if there is anything you think you want.

I went in to the office and saw Lawrence, and he asked,

"What can I do for you?"

I said, "Miriam told me you had some old printing equipment you was gonna have to get rid of. So I was just wondering if I could take a look at some of it?"

"Of course you can, come on back here with me."

There was a lot of it, but I didn't see anything I could use, or wanted, and then I saw an old mounted router with a foot pedal that I could raise the router up and down just by stepping on the pedal. I had an idea when I saw that. I asked,

"Are you gonna give that away?" pointing to the router.

"Oh no," he said, "but I will sell it to you for thirty five dollars."

I said, "I will give you twenty five!"

And he said, "Sold."

Now, Miriam was not very happy that I bought the router!

She asked why did I think we could afford that with me being laid off, we need all the money we have, and can get.

I said, "Well I will take it back if you want me to."

"No," she said, "we will make it somehow."

I went to the lumber company and bought some lumber, and started practicing routing names in the redwood with a v-shaped router bit.

I did get a job delivering snowmobile trailers.

When I was home I just worked and worked with the router, and I began selling yard signs that I carved in redwood. In a year or so I was making all the signs for Elkhart County Parks and Recreation. I had bought some other tools that I needed, an air compressor, shop vac, and heavy duty sander. I even started making and selling signs at the county fair. I enjoy that so much! I had to make a sign shop on wheels that I could pull with the car to some other fairs and town festivals. I have made quite a bit of money with that twenty five dollar investment.

When I began driving for Starcraft Boat Co., the trucks they had were International, about one size larger than a pick-up truck. There was a boat loaded on top of the cab, and at least eight boats on the trailer, which made a pretty big load for the truck. Driving west into a head wind was pretty rough.

Of course there was no air conditioning in the trucks, and that made it almost unbearable driving across the Mojave desert when it is 110 degrees in the summer time at night. From Needles, CA to Barstow, CA is 150 miles, all desert.

There is a sleeper bunk behind the seat that I can crawl into through the back window of the cab. But in the winter months the truck heaters did not blow any heat through that back window opening to the sleeper bunk to speak of, so I always keep plenty of blankets to roll up in. But it is a place to stretch out and get some rest.

I am continuing to play with my band, "The Country Travelers", and driving for Starcraft, but it is taking a toll on me. Someone told me a while back that diet pills were the best thing to take to stay awake. There is one, it is black, a capsule that would keep me awake for thirty six hours if I wanted to stay awake that long. I wanted to drive a truck because I could make pretty good money to support my family.

And I wanted to play music because I love it so much, now here I am taking trips to California and Oregon and using a lot of diet pills to stay awake so I could get back home to play music on Friday and Saturday Nights. No, I am not proud to admit that, but that is my situation that I am in now.

When I began driving long distance in 1968, many of the interstate highways were not completed, such as route 66 from Chicago to California and of course many of the east-west interstates had not been completed, and I tell you I'm learning more and more every day about this truck driving business.

Last week they dispatched me to Woodville WA, just north of Seattle, my first trip across the north-west. Pipestone pass in Montana was snow covered, but I managed to get across it in pretty good shape. Traveling on west, to the top of Lookout Pass, leaving Montana and entering Idaho, was in good shape. It is not a good highway but they are working on the interstate across there. It is slow going with so much heavy equipment working.

In Washington state the interstate was finished until I reached Snoqualmie pass, it is just a four lane highway that is not divided at all. As I am beginning to climb, it is raining, telling me that at least there is no ice on the roadway. I am almost to the summit and here comes a Ford station wagon passing me. There were several children in the back, I assume a family on vacation.

We are going down the pass and it is very steep, up ahead I see that station wagon going sideways, and I realized that we are on solid ice, my trailer began to come around to my left side when I applied the brakes to attempt to slow down, then I began fighting the steering wheel to try to get the truck straightened out, so the trailer began coming back around and just kept going around and this truck did a complete circle on this four lane highway. If I can't get this thing stopped somehow there is gonna be a terrible accident. I think I will just lay down on the floor, maybe I won't be hurt so bad, as I began to lay down my shirt sleeve got caught on the trailer brake lever. Oh, what on earth am I doing, I set back in my seat and started pulling on the trailer brake lever just a little bit at a time. The truck did began to get straight and started to slow down. The truck stopped just before I came to a very sharp curve. I just sat there, my entire body shaking. Thank you God, and thank you for a lesson I have learned.

Just as I got the truck stopped, there went that station wagon real slow, that passed me earlier. How and when did I get in front of him? WOW!

I have been teaching Jeff some chords on the guitar since he was five years old, and he is getting pretty good playing chords.

We were gonna play a show over at Topeka a while back, the venue was called Sycamore Hall, a really nice place to play a concert. Jeff is six years old and he asked me if he could sing a song on the show.

"Do you think you can do that, I asked him?"

"I know I can do that!" he said.

"What song will you sing?"

"I want to sing "Hey Good Looking"."

"Get your guitar, I would like to hear you sing it."

He got his guitar and sang it for me, and he did it very good! And he did it very good on the show at Topeka. Topeka is a small Amish town, and the Amish just love country music, and the place was full of young Amish boys and girls. I did not think they were gonna stop applauding after Jeff sang. That was his big debut in music. We are so proud of him.

Well, it is nineteen seventy three, and I am gonna have to give up on driving or playing music before I kill myself in an accident or the pills will kill me.

I made up my mind last week, and told the other band members that I was leaving the band. They seemed to be okay with my decision.

The deciding factor as to my decision to leave the band was this;

I am returning home from a trip to California, and I have been taking a lot of diet pills to keep me awake. I don't think I have slept five hours since I left California.

I remember driving through Indianapolis and heading north and driving through Elwood and getting on highway thirteen, the next town is Wabash, about forty miles north.

The next thing I remember was seeing a sign that read, "Welcome To Warsaw". I do not have any recollection of driving through Wabash at all, and there are four turns driving through that town. I drove at least seventy five miles that I do not remember. The only thing I do know is that God is with me. He cares for me and keeps me safe.

I will tell you the truth, when I am at home now, the upstairs is alive with two young boys listening to records and Jeff playing his guitar with it, and Jesse has taken up boxes and cans and some of Miriam's pots and pans from the kitchen, and he tells me he is gonna be a drummer.

I said, "Well, that's good, just keep on practicing." He had an old cymbal that the drummer in my band gave him a long time ago. I cut the broom off of its handle and made him a cymbal stand.

About a year ago we bought Jeff an electric guitar and amplifier.

I am pretty sure Jesse will be deserving of a set of drums for Christmas.

I got very upset with the dispatcher at Starcraft, and I left my job there.

I was able to get a driving job at Smokercraft Marine here in New Paris.

I came home from a trip today and Miriam said to me,

"Honey, get your guitar and play a couple songs with Jeff, he is really getting good on his guitar." So we played a couple songs and I was really impressed, I said,

"Son, you must be playing that guitar all the time. Do you ever do anything else?"

"Sometimes," he said, "but I want to get as good as I can. Do you think I'm doing pretty good?"

"I know you are doing very good, I don't know how you have learned so much so fast! Just keep it up."

We didn't wait until Christmas to get Jesse a set of drums, his birthday is December eleventh, so now he has a set of beginner drums. We told him, as you get better playing the drums, we will get you a better set of drums, so you had better practice a lot.

"Oh I will," he said.

And he does, with records, and with Jeff. I'm telling you, sometime we think the ceiling is coming down.

Santa Claus brought Jesse a highhat with the cymbals for Christmas, and he can use the broom handle stand that I made for the big cymbal.

Not far into January, Jeff and Jesse told Miriam,

"You know Mom, if you would learn to play bass guitar we could have us a four piece band, with Dad playing rhythm and singing."

Well, I'm thinking, oh boy, here I go again, I am still driving a truck, and gone a lot, and the boys were wanting to play music. I agreed we could get Miriam a bass guitar and amplifier, and she could start taking lessons. She is taking lessons at the music store, and Jeff was kinda teaching her at home. I will have to admit that she is beginning to play pretty good, and Jeff is playing guitar now, better than I ever did, and I cannot say enough about how well Jesse was playing the drums.

I have a buddy truck driving friend, he and his family go to the camp ground every weekend during the summer. They came to our house one evening when we had our music equipment set up in the living room and kitchen and we were practicing. They listened to us for a while and Jerry said,

"Why don't ya'll come up to the campground on Saturday and practice up there?"

"Oh Jerry, I don't think we are good enough yet to go somewhere else and play."

"Well, I think you are," Jerry replied. "You guys could set up your equipment in front of our camper, and practice there. I bet your band would draw a big crowd."

Jeff and Jesse thought that would be a great idea.

"Oh Dad, that would be so much fun, let's do that dad," Jesse said.

"Alright," I said, "I guess we could."

We enjoyed going up there last night and playing some music and yes, we did draw a pretty big crowd, the boys really enjoyed it.

During the early spring of 1976 I was in Wyoming on a trip to the west coast, and a truck passed me that had a bumper sticker that read "Happy Birthday America", I guess because of America's bicentennial. And I could not get that phrase off my mind, and I thought that would be an excellent song title. Well, I thought, I had better get busy.

Then as I thought of a verse, I would stop and write it down, think, stop and write it down, think, stop and write it down. I wrote that song in about one hundred and fifty miles.

Miriam and I decided it would be a good idea to record it.

There is a good recording studio in Goshen and our band recorded "Happy Birthday America" and on the flip side we recorded another song that I had written entitled, "This Must Be Heaven".

Miriam's sister, Norita sent the record to the Bicentennial committee in Indianapolis, and she told me later that she did that.

About three weeks later I received a letter from that committee, asking me if we could take our band to Washington, D.C. and perform the song on the Capitol steps. And we did that on Indiana day In Washington, D.C. and we also performed at the Lincoln Memorial.

Julie Dooley, our niece was with us on the trip, and she sang with our band there. It was very exciting, and we had so much fun and it made all of us feel so very patriotic. Quite an experience!

We named our band, "The American Travelers". For the last year we have been playing in alot of clubs such as the Elks Club, Moose Club, and Eagles Club, on the weekends.

When our family band first started playing, Jeff was eleven and Jesse was eight years old. Everywhere we played, the people just could not believe their ages. We are getting booked in clubs for miles around in northern Indiana and southern Michigan.

Bill, the guy that used to be my lead guitar player in the band that I left a couple of years ago, told a show promoter about our band. His name is Kurt and he works with police departments all throughout the state of Indiana. He promotes shows to raise funds for the F.O.P. "Fraternal Order of Police".

He called today, and said, "Is this Harper Garris?"

"Yes it is," I told him.

"Someone told me that you have a hot lead guitar player in your band. Is that true?"

"Very true!" I told him.

"I am looking for a band to play a show for me on October the fourth. Can you do that?"

"Yes we can," I told him.

He said, "The show will be in Peru, IN at the Circus City Festival building, and I want your band to open the show at six-o-clock p.m. I will need your band to provide backup for two guests that will perform on the show.

Your band will play twenty minutes, and each guest will perform for twenty minutes, then there will be an intermission for twenty minutes, and then Jennie Pruitt, the lady that recorded "Satin Sheets" will be introduced for a one hour show.

"Okay, that sounds good to me," I said.

"Looking forward to seeing you then," he said.

The show went well, there were some nervous kids on that stage, Jeff and Jesse I'm talking about!

After the show, Kurt asked me if we would be interested in working more shows for him.

"Oh sure," I told him.

He said, "I will be in contact with you on some upcoming shows."

We began to work a lot of shows for him, we provided backup for Ferlin Husky, we opened many shows for Carl Perkins, he is such a nice guy, he wrote the songs, "Daddy Sang Bass" and "Blue Suede Shoes", that was a hit song for Elvis Presley. We worked with Faron Young, and so many others.

A few days ago I answered the phone and a man asked,

"Is this Harper Garris?"

"Yes it is."

He said, "I am calling from Nashville, TN, I am a booking agent, and a friend of mine by the name of Kurt that lives up there in your area was telling me about your band, and I am calling to see if you would be interested in playing some shows for my agency."

"Oh yes," I replied.

Are you familiar with the song, "Long Tall Texan" and "If You're Gonna Play in Texas", by the band "Alabama?"

"Oh yes, our band plays those songs everywhere we play."

"Well then you must know who Murray Kellum is," he said.

"We don't know him personally, but I've sung his songs for years, even his country version of "Joy to the World".

"Sounds like your band would be just the right band to back him up, oh and Kurt told me, Harper that you had worked with Kenny Price from the "Hee Haw" show."

"Yes, I have several times, but the others in my band haven't. I will guarantee we will do a good job. I like Kenny a lot, and he puts on a good show."

"Well, I'm calling to find out if you guys are available November, fifteenth?

"Let me check my book..... yes we are," I said.

"Great, the show will be at Bosse High School, Evansville, IN in the auditorium. There will be two shows, six and nine p.m."

"Okay John, we'll see you there and I sure appreciate you calling."

We were playing in a club in Elkhart, IN, and the place was packed and the dance floor was full as it could be, we were playing Bob Seger's song "Old Time Rock and Roll". I am looking out over the dance floor and I am thinking, I am pretty proud of us, we really do a good job on this song. We came to a point in the song where everyone is supposed to put their hands above their head and clap. So I quit playing my guitar and moved to the microphone and hollered "Clap." No one ever told me that a man with dentures could not holler "clap" without their upper dentures flying out of their mouth, they do! Mine did! I do believe everyone on the dance floor was looking at me. Everybody just cracked up, not to mention the rest of the band, they laughed so hard that they could not hardly play their instruments. I looked over at Miriam and she was all bent over laughing! What's a fellow supposed to do? Keep my teeth in, I guess.

It seemed like in no time at all we are here at Bosse High school in the early afternoon, on a Saturday, unloading our equipment and getting set up on the stage, and Kenny walked in. After introductions, Kenny asked,

"Are you all set up?"

"Yes we are," I told him.

"Could we run through a couple of my songs?" he asked.

"Sure we can, any time you are ready."

"Let's do "Roly Poly", and I am ready!"

Jeff kicked it off, and he sang it along with a couple more songs and he said,

"Man, Jeff, you are smoking on that guitar, I think you know what you're doing with that thing, and this drummer here, patting Jesse on the shoulder, I sure like the way he plays them drums."

"I sure am proud of them," I told him. He invited us out to his motor home for a cold drink.

Someone knocked on the door, it was Murray Kellum, we visited for a while, we introduced ourselves to Murry, each one of us, and Murry said,

"I will play my own lead."

Kenny said, "You don't wanna do that!"

"Oh yes, I can play my own lead, I know how my songs should be played."

Kenny said, "I'm telling you Murry, you don't really wanna do that."

Murry asked me, "Are you all set up on the stage, if you are, we could go through a few songs."

"Yeah, we can do that," I said.

All of us are walking in to the Auditorium.

Murry said, "Are you guys familiar with any of my songs?"

"Yeah, a couple," I replied, "which one do you wanna do?"

He sang "Joy to the World", and "If You're Gonna Play in Texas, You Gotta Have a Fiddle in the Band".

When he sang "Texas" Jeff got his fiddle out, and played it just like "Alabama" did on their recording of the song.

When he finished singing the song, he looked around at Kenny and asked, "Why didn't you tell me about this?"

Kenny said, "H### Murry, I told you three times that you didn't really want to play your own lead guitar!"

"No, I sure as heck don't want to, in front of this kid anyhow."

Jeff had worked very hard to be an excellent guitar player, but I know he was born musically gifted. Not only could he play guitar, but he had mastered the fiddle, piano, steel guitar, banjo, and harmonica.

We had a really good show tonight. I believe everyone was very pleased. Even the booking agent, he said,

"I will be calling you soon to book your band on some future dates."

Well, we did a lot of shows for Kurt and John through the winter months and spring. We have been being so busy, but thank goodness, most of the shows were on the weekend, and at Smokercraft, where I was driving was aware of what I was involved in with the band, so if needed be, they would let me off for a couple days, when needed.

Summer is here, boat sales are very slow during the summer, so I volunteered for a layoff, and we are concentrating on our music and the bookings we have to play.

Every year, the small town of Middlebury, north east of Goshen has their town festival, and they have booked our band for their entertainment for the last four or five years, on the second weekend of August. The festival is on Saturday, and the next day, Sunday is my Daddy's family reunion, held in Great Falls, SC. Most of the people at the reunion expect us to be there to play for them, and we always do, although it means driving all night to get there. It is worth it!

We worked with John Anderson, before he had his number one song, "Swinging". We provided back-up for Murry Kellum and Charley Walker in Ft. Smith, AR, and when we are not doing shows for him, we are working shows for Kurt here in Indiana. We did a show with the Osborne Brothers, a nationally known blue grass band, in Henderson, KY. We traveled to Augusta, GA and Montgomery, AL for shows with Nat Stucky.

During the winter of 1977-1978 our band recorded an album. We titled it, "The American Travelers By Request". We were so proud of it, and we were offering it for sale everywhere we played, and they sold very good.

There is a booking agency in Zanesville, OH that books entertainment all over the country, mostly fairs, town festivals, and many other venues. One of their agents, (they had several,) called me and asked if we would play some concerts for them. I told them that we would, I was familiar with their agency.

They kept us on the road the summer of 1979. I will write a short list of the artists we provided backup for.

Heehaw stars, The Hager twins, Susan Ray, Kenny Price, Box Car Willy, several times, Sylvia, Buck Trent, Ronnie Stoneman, Peggy Sue and many, many others. We did shows for Variety Attractions from New York to Casper, WY, and Fargo, ND to Florida. What a life! We have had alot of fun, many memories. Disappointments, we had them also. What else can I say? We owe all the good times to Jeff and Jesse. Our youngest son, Jim was just not interested in playing music, he tried piano, and gave that up, and started taking lessons on the tenor sax, he got to where he was pretty good on the sax, but he still didn't want to be a member of the band, so we didn't push him. He did do some shows with us, and was always a hit with the audience.

The summer of 1979 was more of the same, working shows and driving the truck. Oh yes, we were sure busy enough.

October, 1984. We just finished playing at Hilton Inn in Garden City, Kansas, and we headed up to Casper, WY for a two week stand there.

We arrived in Casper and checked in to our motel. Miriam called home, knowing that her mother has been in the hospital in Goshen with some heart problems. She was told that they transported her Mom to Memorial hospital in South Bend IN, for open heart surgery on Tuesday. So we made the decision to go home, we checked out of the motel and called our booking agent to tell him that we were going home and we hoped he could get another band to play this club.

He said he thought he could do that and wished us good luck, and we were on our way home.

We arrived at the hospital on Tuesday afternoon and the surgery had been completed and she was in ICU, and not doing very well at all. All the family was there. Miriam and I went in to see her a couple of times, but she couldn't talk. She was so sedated. Some of the family went home. We were so tired, after making a fast trip home from Wyoming.

As it turned out, Miriam's mother did not live through the night. We were so devastated.

Halloween is coming up and we are playing three nights a week in Branson, MI. We played there last night, (Saturday night,) and I left this morning on a trip with a load of boats. I called Miriam this evening.

"Hey Sweetheart," I said, "how are you doing?"

She replied, "Not very well, you will not believe what happened!"

"Oh my, what happened?"

"Ilene called this morning and asked if it was true. I said, "Is what true?" The place where we were playing over the weekend up in Michigan burned down last night, all of our equipment was totally burned up!"

I just stood there for a few moments, man that hit me hard, not knowing what to say. Finally I replied. "Well" I said, "I guess our music career has ended."

"Yes, I think you are right," she said. "Not having insurance on that equipment, we sure cannot afford to buy all of that again. The only hope we have is, if he carried insurance on everything."

"I have his home phone number. When I return home I will contact him and see what I can find out."

When I returned from Houston, I called Dennis in Branson, MI.

"Hey Dennis, this is Harper Garris, I have been on a trip down to Texas or I would have been in contact with you sooner. What can you tell me about the fire that burned your club down last Sunday night?"

"Yes Harper, you know there's not much I can tell you about it, right now. The fire marshals are still investigating as to what started the fire, and I don't know anything else I could tell you."

"Could you tell me if you had insurance on the club, and its contents?"

"Well, I hate to tell you Harper, I did not have a dimes worth of insurance on it at all!"

"Am I to believe that all that equipment, worth approximately twenty two thousand dollars went up in smoke, and I have nothing to expect from you or your enterprise?"

"I am sure there will not be anyone to help me with this, and I sure as hell can't pay you anything, maybe you should contact your insurance company." With that, he hung up the phone.

I called my insurance company. They told me that since I was using the equipment to earn money, my household insurance would not pay me anything. He told me that I should have purchased a policy on my equipment.

We found out that Dennis was arrested for arson about a month after the fire, so I'm sure he will have to pay in some way, but not to us! That's the way life goes!

Miriam's Mother's estate was settled. With the money Miriam received from the estate, we hired a man to remove the concrete front porch and put a cement drive from the street to the garage and a sidewalk across the front yard from lot line to the other lot line, and he removed a tree that was in the front yard.

There was enough money left for materials to build a work shop.

Before Labor Day, 1987, we invited all of our relatives to a "build a shop day", and anyone else that could come and help.

We had previously had a foundation and a concrete floor put down. On Labor Day there were so many workers that I think we were in each other's way. We began at seven in the morning, at noon we stopped for a wonderful meal that the ladies had prepared, and plenty of it! At five-o-clock p.m. the building, 16x28 foot was finished, except for putting the shingles on it, and most of the people came back the next day to do that. I was so happy and thankful to have a work shop, it is something that I've always wished I had, and now I do.

I guess I will just have to concentrate on driving now, which I should have done many years ago.

I have made a lot of mistakes in the past, I know that! Bad decisions can sure cost a lot, like Miriam going with me on trips in the truck and leaving the boys with relative's years ago when they were very young. We regret that now, but I loved her, and I wanted her to be with me, and she loved me so much that she didn't want to be at home without me. I am sure that was a mistake by both of us.

Much too late we realize that a married man with children should never be a long distance truck driver, never.

A gentleman that owned a local redi-mix company called me today.

"Hello Harper," he said, "how are you?"

I recognized his voice, "I'm great, how are you? I haven't talked to you for a while."

"We are fine, and you are right, we haven't talked for some time now. Well say, you know it's that time of the year again, I need to get you lined up to play our company Christmas party. How about December 9th, are you guys available then?"

"Mack, I have some bad news to tell you, obviously you are not aware that we lost all of our equipment in a fire."

"Golly," he said, "I sure do hate to hear that. What in the world happened?"

"We were playing in a club up in Branson, MI over the Halloween weekend and on Saturday night when we finished, we left our equipment there like we usually do when we are gonna play the next weekend. And the place burned down over night, there was no insurance, and we could not afford to buy all new equipment, so we just decided to call it quits."

"Oh Harper, you guys are just too good to give it up! Is that really what you want to do?"

"I'll tell you Mack, we just really don't have any other choice!"

"Maybe you do," he said. What would it cost to get the equipment you need to set up and play?"

"Well, just a quick guess, not less than five thousand dollars, and sorry to say, we just don't have that kind of money."

"I do," he said. "What if I loaned it to you, with no rush to pay me back. You could get some equipment and play our Christmas party. What do you think about that?"

"Oh my goodness, are you really serious about that?"

"Be in my office after eight-o-clock in the morning, and I'll show you how serious I am."

"We will be there for sure, thank you!"

Here we are Saturday morning.

"Here is a check for five thousand dollars, just like I told you, now you have got some shopping to do," he said.

"Well Mack," I said, "I don't know how we could ever thank you enough. You are so kind, and we appreciate it."

He said, "How about that booking, will you play our company Christmas party?"

"Now Mack, right now you could not keep us from it," and we laughed. "We will see you then, if not before."

Of course, we could not replace the piano, steel guitar, or fiddle that burned up. Jesse had just bought a new set of drums, but we could not replace a set of equal value. We bought what we had to have to do a booking.

We played the Christmas party for Mack, that was great, a big time.

We began to play just about every weekend, but not as much as we did before, Jesse and Jim were still in school.

Jesse was into football, and I think he was kinda losing interest in playing music.

We played together until 1985. Jeff got married, and I think he is ready to give up on the family band, and do something else.

Jesse is serious with his girlfriend, and he is ready to give it up, it is pretty obvious.

The last booking we played together was Middlebury Town Festival. We have played that festival for several years, the second weekend in August.

Miriam and I announced to the boys that the band was all finished after the last festival we played. They seemed to be alright with the decision.

After all, we played together for twelve years; we have had so much fun, and it has been a long journey, but it just has to come to an end. We have so many wonderful memories from the last twelve years.

Chapter Nineteen

Shortly after our family band decided to end our musical career, a friend who was driving for a trucking company suggested that I come up there and get a job where he worked. He told me how good it was, working for that company.

I went there and talked to Denny, who is the owner of the company and after we talked for a while, he told the dispatcher to take me for a test drive. I drove down the road about five miles, and he said, turn around and take me back to the office. I don't have time to be out here riding around with a truck driver, so we went back to the yard. I went in to the office, and talked to Denny.

He asked, "After what you have seen and heard about our company, are you still interested in driving for us?"

"Yes I am," I said. "I just want to tell you one thing, and see if you still want me to drive for you. I will not pull a load that is overweight and run all over the country dodging D.O.T. scales."

"We don't expect you to, and furthermore, we don't want you to do that."

"Okay," I said, "I'm ready to go!"

I made a couple trips to Dakota City, NE and picked up a load of beef and brought it back to Goshen to a cold storage, and then he asked me,

"How about running team to California with your buddy, Dan?"

"Yeah, sure, that sounds good to me. When do we leave?"

"Saturday noon, you will have to be in Los Angeles area first thing Monday morning when they open!"

"Okay, I'll be ready."

There was a trailer load of frozen pizza setting in the yard, we hooked up to it and, Dan and I left on Saturday morning at eleven thirty, and made a fast trip to El Monte, CA.

We arrived there Monday morning at five forty five. The cold storage opened at six. We got unloaded, and left at eight thirty, and made three stops at what they call "coolers", and we call "cold storage's" and loaded eight pallets of broccoli at the first stop in Oxnard CA. We went up to Santa Maria and loaded eight pallets of carrots, and one more stop in Paso Robles and finished filling up the trailer with lettuce. Then we drove to a truck stop and weighed the truck to make sure that we weren't over loaded and we were not. We headed for Cincinnati, OH to make our delivery. We made the trip back in fifty one hours.

Dan and I made three trips together to California; we carried two loads of pizza and one load of camper trailer parts. We hauled produce back each trip.

I was in the office yesterday talking to Denny, and he asked me,

"Why don't you get your wife to team with you in the truck?"

"She has never driven a semi in her life, and I don't think she would!"

"Well, tell her to get her chauffeurs license and I will dispatch ya'll to the west coast, and I'll bet she will know how to drive a semi when you return here."

I came home and told Miriam what Denny had told me, and we talked about it. We could make twelve hundred dollars per trip to CA, and of course that sounded pretty good.

We made the decision that Miriam would go take the written test to get her chauffeurs license. She got a book and studied it for one hour and passed the test, she was so surprised, and so was I.

And then we made the biggest mistake of our life. We waited until Jim came home from school and told him our plans that Miriam was gonna start driving with me, and asked him if he would be alright with that. Jim is sixteen years old now, and I thought he would not have any problems with us being gone. We told him that we would be home every weekend, to do laundry and buy groceries. Jim has always been a kid that never got in to any trouble to speak of; he has always had responsible friends as far as we know. He is working at a body shop here in New Paris.

"Do you think that you will be okay at home, with us being gone four or five days a week?"

He said, "I'm sure I will be okay, I'm not afraid, if that is what you mean. Ya'll go ahead and do that, I'll be just fine!"

"I think we will be leaving for California in the morning, but we will be here when you leave for school."

This morning we got our clothes all packed and got some snacks to take along on the trip, and we went up to the yard and got all hooked up to the trailer, and we are on our way. Miriam said,

"Don't ask me to drive for a day or two."

"Don't worry about that," I told her, "just tell me when you are ready to get behind the steering wheel, I am just glad that you are with me."

It hasn't been very long since I talked about a married man with children being a truck driver, and how and why he should never do that, and here I am doing the very thing that I said a man should never do. Maybe worse, because Jim's Mom and Dad are leaving him at home without either one of us being at home with him.

But let me say something in our defense. Jim is the kind of child that never stayed at home anyhow, ever since he was very young, I'm talking about maybe five or six years old, he was next door or across the street playing with his friend. Oh, he would come home to eat a meal when we called him, Mom always had a hard time keeping him at home, and that's the way it has always been with him. Way too late we realized that we should have been more adamant about him being home more. And for that we are very guilty.

There is no way you can go back and have "do-overs", I am sure we will always regret not having more time with Jim, especially me.

We made it down to Joplin, MO, and we only stopped two times for a short restroom break. We will fuel up here and get supper, and then be on our way down to Tulsa, OK. This could be a long night because Miriam is not driving yet, but that's alright, I'll stop around one a.m. and get some sleep, and get going again at daybreak. Denny knows this is not going to be a rush trip, with me teaching Miriam how to drive.

We made it on out to CA and delivered our load, and loaded a full load of lettuce to deliver to Dayton, OH. We are on our way home, as we came past Flag Staff, AZ, Miriam said,

"I guess it's time for me to get behind the steering wheel, and see if I can drive this thing!"

This thing that she is talking about is about a ten year old Peterbilt cabover with a thirteen speed transmission. I pulled the truck over on a wide berm of the road and stopped, and she slid under the steering wheel. I just set here on the dog house so I could help her with the gears or anything that I can do to help her. I guess I should explain what the dog house is. On a cabover truck, the engine is actually between the driver and the passenger seats. Of course it has very thick padding so the engine is not so loud for the ones in the cab.

Miriam put the transmission in second gear, as I had showed her when I was driving, let out the clutch and accelerate, and here we go. I looked at her and she was crying, I'm sure she is very nervous.

I said, "Honey, you don't have to do this, just pull over and I will drive."

"No," she said, "I have to learn how to do this sometime, it may as well be now. I'll be alright soon, I'm gonna take my time."

"That's fine, I am not gonna rush you, but try to drive fifty five miles per hour if you can, you know the speed limit is seventy five. You are doing very well!"

Miriam drove to the New Mexico state line, I had her stop three or four times so she could start getting used to the air brakes, and changing the gears.

She handles the truck real well on the interstate, of course she needs a lot of practice, and she will get it.

We have made a lot of trips to the west coast and back, Miriam sure helps me a lot, I can sleep when she is driving, and that way we can get our rest.

We were picking up some produce almost down town, in Los Angeles. We finished loading, I pulled the truck forward, and went to the rear of the truck and closed the trailer doors. And a car pulled up pretty close to us and a guy got out and came over to the truck and asked me if I wanted to buy a cell phone. I told him no.

He said, "Man, cell phones sell for over three hundred dollars, this one is brand new, and I will sell it to you for only one hundred dollars."

"Well, I don't carry that kind of money, and besides that I would not pay that kind of money for a cell phone.

He asked me, "What would you pay?"

Miriam said, "Tell him fifty dollars! I would not pay one penny over fifty dollars."

"Ok" he said, "you just bought yourself a cell phone." I paid him and threw the box in the sleeper. It was too dark to look at it now.

The next morning as I was driving, and Miriam was in the jump seat, I said,

"Hey baby, get that cell phone and let's see what it looks like." She went to work trying to get the clear plastic wrapping off of this box, after she got it off and the paper telling all about the phone inside, she took off more paper, and found out that we had payed fifty dollars for a Los Angeles telephone directory.

She said "Darn! We got ripped!"

On another trip to California, we had seven pickups at coolers, to get our trailer loaded with produce. Most drivers don't call it produce, they call it garbage. Our last pick up was in Yuma, AZ.

After the trailer was loaded, we went to a McDonalds, where they have truck parking, to get something to eat. As we were walking from the parking lot to the restaurant, a man approached us and said,

"Do you see that International pick-up truck over there? The transmission went out. I just got word that my wife was rushed to the hospital in San Diego. I am asking for any donation that you could help me with to get my transmission repaired." Miriam opened her purse and handed him a twenty dollar bill.

He said, "Oh I just thank you so much, may God bless you two."

We ate our supper there under the big M and Miriam got behind the wheel and we are headed east on Interstate eight, and it is just getting dark. I was in the sleeper and just about to fall asleep when Miriam hollered,

"Honey, Honey, get out here, you have got to see this!" It scared me, I jumped out of the bunk as fast as I could and the headlights were shinning on an old International pick-up truck with a four wheeler in the back. It was the man that needed money so bad to get his transmission repaired back at McDonalds, and he was headed east bound. "Suckers again"! When will we learn? I'm sure he was headed out to the desert to play.

I happen to run in to a man that I knew a long time ago, he was a car salesman. Be careful, I told myself, you know how car salesmen are! I had some, I'll say, serious disagreements with him several years ago.

As we got in to a conversation, he told me that he had a van conversion business in Elkhart. I told him I had a wood working shop.

He asked, "Could you make the wood parts that we use in manufacturing our van conversions?"

I replied that I could, but I did not have any idea what to charge for each part.

"Don't worry about that," he told me, "I will have my secretary make copies of invoices that the other company was charging me for the parts he made."

"Alright" I said, "I will be over to see you and pick up the invoices and some of the parts that you want me to make."

I told Denny that I was leaving and not driving any longer, and what I was gonna do and he wished me, good luck.

I went up to see Mike at his office in Elkhart, and when I entered his office he told me,

"Hang on just a minute, Harper." He went in to another office. He came back pretty soon, holding the door open, he said to me,

"Come on in here Harper, Debbie will give you the prices we are paying for the wood parts."

She handed me a clip board and pen and said,

"Have a seat over there," pointing to a chair on the other side of her desk. She began telling me prices of the parts that I would be making for them.

We began making his parts, and after three months, there just had not been any profit at all, so I visited another shop that was doing the same kind of work that we were doing, and got information about prices he was charging, and I found out that he was only paying me half the amount that other shops were charging.

We are "ripped off again". We should have known better than to have any dealings with him. I guess we haven't learned. During that time we never made our house payment, or any of our other bills, we were almost ready for bankruptcy.

I went up to Coff Trucking and talked to Denny. He said he would be glad for Miriam and me to come back and drive for him, so now we are back on the road.

We drove for about six months or more and they got the new trucks in that they had ordered, all Kenworth's T-600, and we got one of them to drive. It is really nice, but there is no place to set a beverage cup. Of course we are still running the west coast most of the time.

Sometime we will haul a load down to Georgia to deliver, and go to a processing plant and pick up a load of dressed chickens that they ice down in the trailer and take that load to San Leandro, CA,. We have been doing that quite often. After a year of no place to set my coffee cup, I decided to make me a console. I have the wood, and the tools to make it with.

I asked Denny if I could take the tractor home after a trip, and he said sure, that will be o.k.

Well, we brought the tractor home and I went to work designing a console. I guess I had in my mind what I wanted it to look like. Of course it will be made out of solid oak wood. A portion of it slides under the dash, and there is a drink tray on the top of it where two beverages can set without falling over, and between the cup holder there is an indent for an ash tray, and another indent for items such as gum, pens or rolaids. Under the drink tray there is a drawer for small miscellaneous items. And under the drawer there is ample space to keep log books are whatever you want to put there. I stained it dark walnut, and sprayed several coats of clear lacquer on it. It really looks nice, and I mounted it in our truck, and had a place to set my coffee!

Well, as we traveled and stopped for fuel and had our door open other truck drivers would see it and ask, where did you buy that console? I would tell them, I made it. Boy, they would say, I'd love to have one of them.

After a while, I'm beginning to think that I could sell some of the consoles, if I made more of them. So I began to make some of the consoles like I had made for myself.

I took four consoles with us on a trip to California. At the Petro truck stop in Joplin, MO I went into the travel store and talked to the manager. His name is Alex.

"Alex, I make consoles that are custom made to fit under the dash of a Kenworth, and I just want to ask if you might be interested in putting them up for sell in your travel store?"

"Do you have any with you?" he asked.

"Yes I do, I will bring one in and show it to you. I will be right back."

I brought one in and set it down on the floor, and he took a good look at it and said to me,

"How many do you have with you?"

"I have three more out in the truck."

"If you want to leave them here, I will display them, but I will not pay you until I see if they will sell, and that does look like something that will sell."

We brought in the three more consoles that we brought with us and he put them on the shelf.

We continued our trip on to California and on the way back, we stopped in at the truck stop in Joplin and they had sold all four of the consoles that we had left there.

Alex told me, "Bring us some more of those. If you are driving and making them in your spare time, I can probably sell all you can make."

"Okay, I will try to bring some on my next trip down this way."

Alex told me that the truck stop there in Joplin was owned by the same company that owned the I-80 truck stop in Wolcott, IA. We began selling consoles at that truck stop, the biggest truck stop in the U.S. and they bought a lot of our consoles. They would order as many as fifty consoles at a time. I had to quit driving to try to keep up with the console orders. I was sure happy about that!

We drove for Coff for almost four years, that was a lot of trips to the west coast!

The truck drivers would take their trucks to dealerships to get them serviced, and someone in the dealership would see the console and many of them would call and order consoles. We began shipping consoles all over the country. We had to hire people to help us try to keep up with the orders that we received. One of the good things was that our youngest son, Jim worked with us for a year, we got to spend that time with him.

We were manufacturing consoles custom made for eight different makes of trucks. Life is good! We are actually doing quite well financially. We purchased a new fifteen passenger van and removed the back seats to deliver the consoles. If a customer within a thousand miles ordered twenty five consoles or more, Miriam and I could get out of the shop for a few days.

Good times do not last forever. 2001 brought a big change to our business. A lot of the truck manufacturing company's began installing cup holders in the new trucks, and more space in the cabs for the drivers to put their paper work.

We made consoles for about twelve years.

The political scene changed when Bush took office. With that happening we were out of business, just like that.

And 9/11 happened the same year. The economy seemed to hit bottom. The war began in Afghanistan and moved on to Iraq. So what are we gonna do now? Miriam went to work in a cabinet manufacturing company here in New Paris. I signed up for social security, and we were doing o.k. I'm staying home keeping house, washing dishes, mowing the lawn and all the stuff that women do. I don't like this at all.

In the spring of 2003, I decided that I was just not very good at being a house keeper, so I went about trying to find some kind of employment that I could do.

Our county "Elkhart County" is the RV capital of the U.S. I see many campers of every make, being pulled out of this county with pick-up trucks every day, delivering all over the United States, so Miriam and I talked about me doing that.

Chapter Twenty

I went to a company that was in the business of RV delivery.

They directed me to the Driver Recruiter office and I talked to Howard, I asked him if they were adding any drivers?

"Oh yes," he said, "we are always interested in taking on good drivers. Do you have any experience driving trucks?"

I said, "I have twenty seven years experience driving tractor and trailers."

"You are just the candidate we are looking for! Do you have a pick-up?"

"No, but I am gonna get one." I said. "What do you recommend for pulling these campers?"

"You will have to have a diesel, it could be a three quarter or a one ton truck, either single wheels or double wheels on the back, of course, a fifth wheel in the bed, and a heavy duty trailer hitch. You will have to go through a three day orientation class, and you will have to take a driver's test, before you will be dispatched."

"I do believe I can handle all of that," I told him.

I have a 1999 Dodge fifteen passenger van I can trade in for a pick-up truck. Tomorrow is Saturday and I will take Miriam, and we will go looking for a pick-up truck.

We stopped at the Dodge dealership and they were not very interested in selling us a vehicle. So, we went to the Ford dealership and traded our van in on a 2000 four door, one ton pickup truck. I will probably be making my first trip next week.

I have made many mistakes in my life. I could not remember all of them. My first and biggest mistake of all was quitting school, I know that now, and I have known that for many years. If I had really tried and made an effort like I should have, I probably would not have made the mistakes and bad decisions that I have. I do not want any sympathy from anyone. I want to say that parents should keep their children in school until they graduate, at any cost. They will be glad as they get older. I do not blame anybody for the mistakes that I have made. I do hope if a parent should read this book and have a child that is thinking about quitting school, do everything possible to keep them in school. I sure could have used more encouragement to stay in school.

The next worst decision I made was playing music. I wish that I had never played with a band, I wasted a lot of my life playing music. Yes, I did enjoy playing music, I loved it at the time. Now, I realize that it was a big mistake. Playing music, in ways, has caused some separation in the family, which I thought would never happen, but it did!

The next biggest mistake I made was working in a gas station with such low pay. That never would have happened if I would have had more education.

The next major mistake I made was being a truck driver, leaving our son Jim home alone, at sixteen years old. The day Miriam started driving the truck with me, that is my biggest regret.

I believe the very worst career that a married man with children can have is being a truck driver. There are some exceptions, no doubt. I always believed that with my lack of education, it would keep me from having a real good job that paid better. I believed that I was making the best money that I could make, driving a truck. That was a mistake also.

The biggest regret of all! Buying a pickup and pulling campers, but I did not know that at the time. There are thousands of pickup drivers delivering campers out of this county every week. I sure did not do something right. It was profitable for a while, fuel didn't cost as much then. I believed that I was doing okay for a couple of years.

Then the cost of repairs began to stack up. I thought that I could find another used pickup and trade mine in, of course it had over two hundred thousand miles on it. I went looking around at a dealership for another pickup and what a mistake that was. I let the salesman talk me in to buying a new 2005 Ford pickup.

The same year, the last of August, Hurricane Katrina hit the city of New Orleans. Three weeks after that, we began pulling campers to that area. Because of that we were able to see a lot of the destruction. Yes, it sure did look like a war zone! We had to be escorted in and out of the city to deliver campers for the people who were working in the city. We pulled campers for several months to the areas like, Baton Rouge, LA and Purvis, Mississippi.

I put two hundred and fifty thousand miles on this pickup by February, 2008, and seventeen injectors and more repairs than I can name, just hoping things would get better. Things never got better! I filled a credit card to the maximum, paying for repairs on the truck. I feel like I am up against the wall. I only knew one thing to do.

Get a lawyer and file bankruptcy. So I talked to a lawyer about our situation. She asked,

"What are your obligations?"

We had all of our statements written down, and I handed her the paper. I told her the ones that were in my name, but not Miriam's.

She said, "Harper, call the finance company that has your truck title and tell them to come and get the truck, and I will take care of the rest. I will be in contact with you later."

As it turned out, the bankruptcy was only in my name. It has not involved Miriam's credit at all. All of this came about because I was buying the wrong truck for the job that I was doing. I don't believe a one ton truck is strong enough to pull the campers coast to coast day in and day out, that is my opinion. As it turned out, Ford had a large lawsuit against them for the 2005 6.0 diesel, it had several problems.

The bankruptcy did relieve us from a one thousand dollar a month truck payment and a high monthly credit card payment. I do not know why a finance company would be willing to loan that amount of money to someone doing that kind of work anyhow.

They came and got the truck and we are out of a job. There are not a lot of jobs that I am able to do because I have COPD very bad. I got COPD from working in our shop, building consoles and not wearing the proper protection from the dust and the lacquer that I was spraying. I am able to do about anything for a short period of time and then I lose my ability to breathe very quickly.

Miriam got a job at Wal-Mart as a door greeter, and after a month or so I got a job there as a greeter also. This was in March of 2008. After a couple of months we realized the income we had coming from Wal-Mart and my social security was just enough to meet our monthly obligations, and there was nothing left. I sure wish that I hadn't quit school! I am sure that you have concluded long ago that I was not a money manager, and you are correct, I never could manage the money that I earned. No education.

I have a sister and brother-in-law, Howard and their son, Ron living in Enterprise, AL. Ron has suggested many times that we should sell our home here and drive our motor home down there and park it on their land and just live there. He said it would not cost us a thing to stay there. His sister, Judy and her husband, Joe live very close to them.

Another bad decision!

We talked and talked about it and decided that we would put our house, that we lived in for forty years, up for sale.

Jim, our son and his wife Kristi agreed to buy our house and have it as a rental property.

On Labor Day, 2008, Jim loaded up a box trailer, and our nephew from AL loaded up his trailer and we are on our way to Alabama. We do enjoy living here close to my relatives. We purchased a big storage building and placed it at the front end of the motor home, and we built a large deck and a roof that was as long as the motor home. We could walk from the deck right into the storage building. That gave us alot more room for many other things.

For a couple of years we drove up to Mount Juliet, TN, just out of Nashville, every month, and stayed with Jeff and his wife Jill, and daughter Sarah, for a few days. He hired Miriam to clean their house. They have a large house! It was a nice get away.

Well as you might imagine, we began really missing our children back in New Paris, although we did come up here at least once a year to visit them.

December of 2012, Jim and his family surprised us big time, walking in on Christmas Eve. We could not believe they came down for Christmas, what a surprise! We sure did enjoy seeing them. In our conversations, Miriam said, "Well, we are about ready to move back home."

We had mentioned it just between the two of us a few times.

Jim said, "Just let me know when you are ready, and I will come and get you, and move ya'll back home."

I have been working at the Winn-Dixie grocery store since November of 07 bagging groceries, and bringing carts back into the store, and it's about all I can do, but I like it and it keeps me moving. I just don't want to sit in the 'ole rocking chair yet.

In March we started making plans to move back to New Paris. We were getting pretty excited about that. We told everyone down here what our plans are, they said they wished we wouldn't leave, but that they understood that we wanted to be back in IN with our family and friends, that we miss so much.

With several phone calls and other correspondence we managed to have an apartment waiting for us when we arrived back in New Paris. We stayed a few weeks with our son Jim, and his family, until our apartment is ready.

He is so busy with his work that he is not going to be able to go to Alabama and move our belongings up here now. He is in the business of renting porta-potties, pumping septic tanks, installing septic systems, and repairing septic systems.

There is a couple who live here in New Paris who are very dear friends, that we have known for many years, Tom and Edna. Tom told us that he would take us down to Alabama and haul our belongings up here using Jim's trailer. We made a fast trip down there and loaded the trailer, and we stayed there overnight and left early the next morning, and we were back here tonight. And we are so glad to be here, and we just thank God that we are here. It is so good to be back home in Indiana again.

We have been back in Indiana now for a year. Miriam has a job cleaning offices for a big counter top manufacturing company in Goshen. I was helping her with that job for several months until the dust began to get the best of me, and I had to quit doing that. She has two jobs cleaning houses every other week and we clean our church every week. God is good!

There have been so many people tell me I should write a book about my Daddy and his wives, and all of us children. This book, as I have written it has brought back so many memories in my life. If you happen to know anyone with the name, Garris, they just might know someone in our family. We have relatives all over the country.

Miriam and I are very happy living here in New Paris, IN in our one bedroom apartment. We visit with Jesse and Jill at least once a week, Jesse works at a boat factory here in town in shipping, and loves riding his Harley Davidson.

Jesse and Jill lived in Nashville for seven years, while in Nashville, Jesse played drums with Vern Gosdin for a while. Jill is marketing manager at a big Amish complex in Middlebury, IN. They have a beautiful home in the country near New Paris. And Jim lives a mile out of town with his wife Kristi, and son, Coty. Their daughter, Kelsey lives in Nappanee with her husband, Andy. Kristi is the office manager at the Goshen Municipal Airport. As I have written about Jeff before, he is a professional guitar player. When John Michael Montgomery was recording his hit records, Jeff played guitar for him for seven years, plus many other artists he worked for, he is still working very much out of Nashville. He has flown airplanes for years, and does flight instruction. His wife, Jill, works out of her "in home office" in the medical profession. Their daughter Sarah is in her third year of college studying toward being a veterinarian.

Miriam and I celebrated our fifty third anniversary on Sept. 4th. 2013.

PS

The reunion of my father, Harper B. Garris Sr. is still held the second Sunday of August in Rock Hill, SC every year.

About the Author

Harper Garris is the last born of twenty-seven children. In his lifetime, he has been a sign painter, woodworker, musician, and storyteller. Harper and his wife of fifty-three years have three children and live in New Paris, Indiana.